This is the first full-length survey of one of the leading playwrights of the post-war generation. Through his career as playwright, film-maker and director, David Hare has been at the forefront of modern theatre and his work is frequently seen as a reflection of the contemporary political and social environment of Britain.

In this analysis, Carol Homden examines the work of David Hare, including the screenplays of *Plenty*, *Wetherby*, *Paris by Night* and *Strapless*, as well as the plays he has written for the Royal National Theatre. Through her study, Homden identifies the key themes which have dominated and influenced Hare's writing throughout his career and closes with a discussion of Hare's most recent work, the trilogy of plays *Racing Demon*, *Murmuring Judges* and *The Absence of War* and, from these, identifies a new direction for the playwright.

With an informative list of plays and other writings by David Hare the book will be of interest to students of theatre, film and British contemporary literature as well as to the theatre-goer.

The plays of David Hare

The plays of David Hare

Carol Homden

CAMBRIDGE
UNIVERSITY PRESS

Published by the Press Syndicate of the University of Cambridge
The Pitt Building, Trumpington Street, Cambridge CB2 1RP
40 West 20th Street, New York, NY10011–4211, USA
10 Stamford Road, Oakleigh, Melbourne 3166, Australia

First published 1995

Printed in Great Britain at the University Press, Cambridge

A catalogue record for this book is available from the British Library

Library of Congress cataloguing in publication data

Homden, Carol.
The plays of David Hare / Carol Homden.
p.   cm.
Includes bibliographical references and index.
ISBN 0 521 41715 5 (hardback) ISBN 0 521 42718 5 (paperback)
1. Hare. David, 1947– – Criticism and interpretation.
1. Title.
PR6058.A6788Z69 1995
822'.914 – dc20 93-42187 CIP

ISBN 0 521 41715 5 hardback
ISBN 0 521 42718 5 paperback

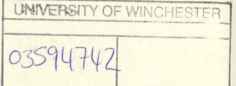
TAG

For my son, Freddy, without whom this book would have been finished sooner.

Contents

ACKNOWLEDGEMENTS

Amber Lane Press, Derbyshire; Beacon Press; Michael Billington; British Broadcasting Corporation; British Film Institute; Cambridge University Press; Casarotto Ramsay Ltd; *Drama*; Edward Arnold, London; *Elle*; English Stage Company, Eyre Methuen, London; Faber and Faber, London; The Fabian Society; *Films and Filming*; Fontana, London; Granada Publishing, Glasgow; Hamish Hamilton, London; David Hare; HarperCollins, London; Ronald Hayman; Heinemann Educational Books, London; Hugh Hebert; London Weekend Television; Macmillan, London and Basingstoke; Methuen, London; *Modern Drama*; Newspaper Publishing plc; *New York Times*; *New Yorker*; *The Observer*; Penguin, Harmondsworth; Phaiden, Oxford; *Plays and Players*; Reed International Books; Routledge, Chapman and Hall, New York; Royal National Theatre; *Stills*; *Time Out*; Times Newspapers; Weidenfeld and Nicholson, London.

Introduction: a statement of departure

David Hare's production of *King Lear* opened in the Olivier Theatre on 14 December 1986 just two weeks after the end of the run of *Pravda*, and while *The Bay at Nice* and *Wrecked Eggs* continued on the Cottesloe stage. In the autumn of 1993, Hare's trilogy on British institutions was scheduled to be performed on a single day. Such domination of the National Theatre is unparalleled in its history, and has no equivalent by a contemporary writer at the Royal Shakespeare Company; it amounts to much more than a residency of the kind Hare had at the Royal Court (1969–71) or Nottingham (1973) and assigns to him a privileged position within British theatre.

Such status is particularly rare for a dramatist of his generation writing from a 'socialist' perspective and yet, in contrast to many of his contemporaries, Hare's work stands without any comprehensive study. The omission is partly explained by Hare's own deliberately enigmatic position, but he is also a troublesome and often troubled writer who uses his work as a way of resolving internal tensions, making systematic analysis particularly difficult. Any attempt to provide such a survey of a living and still fertile writer will inevitably be superseded, but Hare will continue to raise two eternal literary and historical problems. How do you find a critical distance on a writer whose existing plays are part of an evolving and uncompleted body of work? And since those works are themselves an examination of the flux of contemporary experience, how do you find a distance on your own life and times?

The answer to the first question has traditionally lain in comparison, by looking at Hare in relation to his peer group, and it is this approach which is taken by most existing critical work. In 1968,

David Hare established Portable Theatre with Tony Bicât. For five years they toured the country with productions of their own early work and work by Howard Brenton and Snoo Wilson. Because of this, and his later role in establishing the Joint Stock Theatre Company, Hare came to be seen as a seminal figure in the alternative theatre movement, striving to widen the performance base of theatre.

In the early days after the abolition of the theatre censor, the university educated generation created shocking and overtly aggressive pieces. Portable Theatre revelled in violence, criminality, neurosis and decay, and expressed the shared view that British society in general and the West End in particular were in terminal decline in the hands of sold-out right-wing literati. Since Howard Brenton was influenced by the activities of the French Situationists and the student unrest in Paris in 1968, the Portable playwrights as a group were seen by their early chronicler, Peter Ansorge, to be concentrating an anti-establishment anger in disrupting the spectacle of contemporary life.[1] Increasingly, however, Portable Theatre (and its later subsidiary, Shoot) turned to large-scale collaborative works – *Lay By* and *England's Ireland*. These projects included not just Hare's subsequent collaborator Howard Brenton, but the writers Trevor Griffiths and David Edgar, who, having worked with companies committed to intervention in a class struggle, had a background in a different part of the alternative theatre movement.

The work of David Hare has continued to be placed alongside that of Brenton, Edgar and Griffiths – by John Bull, for example, in *New British Political Dramatists*[2] – within forward-looking chronological analysis, which posits a consistent political project: to achieve socialist change. 'At the time my sole interest was the content of a play', Hare confirmed. While working at the Royal Court Theatre, 'I thought the political and social crisis in England in 1969 so grave that I had no patience for the question of how well written a play was. I was only concerned with how urgent its subject matter was, how it related to the world outside.'[3] The chapters on *Brassneck* and *Fanshen* consider Hare's work against the European inheritance of political theatre – the documentary theatre of Erwin Piscator and the epic theatre of Bertolt Brecht.

In 1973, Portable and its subsidiary, Shoot, went bankrupt. As the fringe movement dissipated, Hare (and Brenton) stepped into the mainstream with the production of *Brassneck* at the Nottingham Playhouse. Here David Hare put aside the contemporary parody which had preoccupied him in *Slag*, *The Great Exhibition* and *Knuckle*, and turned to the past in search of an historical explanation of the present. Inspired by Angus Calder's *The People's War*,[4] Hare began, as he was to continue to do throughout the seventies, to examine the effects of a war on two fronts – the class war and the Second World War – in his history plays. Hare shared both the idea of reassessing the childhood inheritance of the war and the particular catalyst of Angus Calder's book with other writers of his generation. The answer to the second question posed above of how to find a distance on your own life and times lies in *Brassneck*. Within the flux of contemporary experience there stands a clearly identifiable moment, and it is this moment that this book takes as its starting-point.

With the final shedding of empire, Britain joined the European Economic Community in January 1973 and there was a mood of workers' militancy unseen since before the war. The primary question in an analysis of a political theatre then becomes – as it does for Catherine Itzin in *Stages in the Revolution*[5] – whether the move from fringe to main stages was a process of 'strategic penetration' by the writers or one of defection, whether the fruits of revolution are always conservative or whether Brenton and Hare are simply at ease in a bright red tie.

To address this question one must ask whether the use of the National Theatre stage for *Plenty* and *Pravda* constituted a strategic penetration, and whether turning to television in *Licking Hitler* and *Saigon: Year of the Cat* was indeed an attempt to infiltrate an alternative history. If analysis suggests that it was not, then there is an urgent need to reassess the theatrical inheritance presumed for David Hare. Is anger always political, or might Hare's railing instead be a form of revenge for a supposed class alienation – the complaint at the disinheritance of a generation really a disguised nostalgia? Certainly, Hare has been determined to avoid giving the audience or the critic easy handles with which to pigeonhole him, and all too frequently those plays or aspects of plays which failed to fit into the critic's analysis of David Hare as a political playwright have been ignored.

In fact, five years after *Brassneck*, Hare explicitly disowned the methods of the theatre of the Left, asking how there could be faith in a history which confronted the writer only with stasis and questioning the audibility of his own medium in the modern age. As the seventies ended, Hare started – in films as much as on the stage – to use women protagonists as a way of gaining a perspective from which to judge which itself raises questions about his own attitude towards them.

As a period of extended Conservatism began, Hare, wracked with doubt and with *Dreams of Leaving*, sought more literal distance on England and his own disaffection. He began to redraw his *Map of the World*. A decade after Ansorge identified the war on two fronts within Hare's work as the world war and the class war, those fronts became rather a world war and an eternal, psychological war in *Wetherby*. As Hare, in his despair, seemed to turn his attention towards questions of identity and civilisation and away from those of class and society, he felt the lure of the absurd and argued with himself about the role of art culminating in *The Bay at Nice*. As the body of work has broadened, Hare's position as a major dramatist has been consolidated. Despite this, his work of the 1980s stands almost entirely unassimilated.

By the age of 40, David Hare was pitting his own talents against those of Shakespeare and of tragedy. It was Peter Brook's production of *King Lear* in 1962 which made Hare want to enter the theatre and his production of the play in 1986 therefore stands as a statement of arrival in the theatrical establishment. The invitation to be viewed in relation not to history but to tragedy casts light across the whole body of Hare's work and lays out the line which he was to follow in *The Bay at Nice*, *The Secret Rapture*, *Paris By Night* and *Strapless*. In dealing with the relationship between history and metaphor, his work up to this point becomes intelligible as a gradual move towards classicism and back to Aristotle. Perhaps he was, in some sense, *Heading Home*. Just as Aristotle explored how epic poetry, tragedy and comedy differed from each other by differences in means, in objects and in manner, so it needs to be explored how Hare's plays of the eighties differed from those of the seventies, how investigation of betrayal, revolution, propaganda and corruption gave way to romantic love, to death, to faith and to art itself.

As the work of a contemporary writer develops, the apparent project of the intentions and interventions of youth form a dialogue with later work and maturity. This book therefore rejects a strictly linear chronological approach: a chapter-by-chapter analysis of plays and films published since 1973 is presented in overlapping strands. The thesis of a political genesis is opposed by the antithesis which has its roots as early as 1975. Consideration of *Teeth 'n' Smiles*, which comprises chapter 1, reveals not only history – the world war and the class war – but the birth of tragedy, not only political models but psychological and linguistic ones.

As the nineties began, Hare was, in his own words, still *Writing Left Handed*. Having concluded the existential/artistic debate of the previous decade, he was moving back to examination of the great estates of the English establishment and even to a version of Brecht's *Galileo*. In dissecting the current state of the Church of England, *Racing Demon* marked the beginning of a trilogy on public institutions, the second part of which committed the crime against the judiciary of *Murmuring Judges*. As the writing of this book was being concluded, the final play *The Absence of War* was premiered. Even in its opening image of the annual ceremonial tribute to the war dead at the cenotaph, the play again addressed the historical agenda set by *Brassneck* some twenty years before, but at its heart was a Labour leader whose defeat is presented as tragic. The wheel is come full circle.

1 The sixties revolution

A war of attrition?

Teeth 'n' Smiles begins with a call to destructive action. The play seems to declare itself as a piece of aggressive confrontation where it is right to smash things up and in which the audience is invoked as 'us'. The 'them' under attack is, however, not immediately clear. As at the opening of *Knuckle*, there is a deliberate refusal to identify the place for what it is. Cambridge and the May Ball of 9 June 1969 remain unnamed until after the members of a minor cult band have been lived with. For the band on the road it might as well be Canterbury, but Cambridge is to education what Canterbury is to the church and in some sense it is an oppositional subculture which is at centre stage.

With the dropped aitches, expletives and loose syntax of working-class accents, with their clear aggression to Snead, the college porter, and dislike of Anson, the fumbling medical student, who represent the university on stage, the band is apparently engaged in a class-based aggression. The length and romanticism of Anson's verbal seduction of the lead singer Maggie contrasts with the pithiness of her highly contemporary description of the act as 'for thirty minutes it is like trying to push a marshmallow into a coinbox' (p. 49). In parodying Lady Capulet's speech on Paris in *Romeo and Juliet* (Act One Scene Four), Anson belongs to the same literary world of 'high' quotation as Arthur the songwriter who, sitting alone on stage at the beginning of Act Two, quotes verse. In contrast, the band paraphrases from 'low' culture figures like the chauffeur to Keith Moon, the drummer with The Who. Throughout Scene One, an electric plug remains unconnected on the stage. From across the class divide, apparently, Arthur and Anson cannot touch it. In his lyric to *Bastards*, Arthur makes it clear that 'I come from the rulers and you come from the ruled' (p. 66).

It is not until the final scene, however, that Saraffian, the manager of the band, explicitly invokes this idea of the class war by comparing the band with those looting the dead after the bombing of the Café de Paris on 9 March 1941. He concludes the longest speech in the play by saying, 'There is a war going on. All the time. A war of attrition' (p. 84). As it was to be for Archie MacLean in *Licking Hitler*, so it is for Saraffian that the Second World War was also a class war.

In *Licking Hitler* the country house was a microcosm of that war, In *Teeth 'n' Smiles* it is a different but equally poignant setting of affluent society. The Café de Paris was a replica of the ballroom on the Titanic and, just as the Titanic was believed immune from natural disaster, so – we are invited to believe – the upper classes thought they could avoid the blitz. In the final words of the play, Maggie's song tells us that this is the time of the 'Last orders on the Titanic' (p. 91). The May Ball revellers of Cambridge are 'people dressed up and performing a complete parody of life that was over many, many years ago…'[1] As the Titanic sank, the orchestra carried on playing; as the upper deck of Cambridge burns, Maggie goes on singing. The ship might be different, but 'the music remains the same' (p. 92).

The metaphor in *Teeth 'n' Smiles* fails to convince, however, because neither the band nor Cambridge has the appropriate class solidarity or political motivation. The band talks neither of political parties nor of political aims, and the anti-Vietnam marches of the sixties, for example, are notable only by their absence. Inch does not take part in the verbal games and, unlike the other men in the band, he cannot get a blow-job because he is the roadie.

If the aim of *Teeth 'n' Smiles* were – according to Marxist analysis – to affirm the ascendant proletariat, Snead (as a porter) would need be part of it, while Arthur and Anson (as the privileged middle classes) would be excluded; instead, Snead's most frequent word – 'Sir' – embodies, with eloquent economy, the ambivalence of his position within hierarchical, male and elitist Cambridge, and Anson and Arthur are in uneasy alliance with Inch and the band.

Anson might want to get his degree first, but after that he just wants to 'groove'. He barely finishes a sentence precisely because he is aware it sounds so dreary and second-hand.

If there is a class war, Anson is one of three contradictory inter-mediaries, agreeing with Arthur that Cambridge is 'still the same shithole' (p. 58). Like Arthur and Laura, he is concerned about the time which, for the band, 'is a sophisticated detail' (p. 21). As a former student-cum-songwriter, however, it is Arthur who becomes the key figure in the complex oppositional structure of *Teeth 'n' Smiles*. Standing both inside and outside Cambridge, he is uniquely placed to comment upon its 'airless, lightless, dayless, nightless time-lock', and the 'rich complacent self-loving self-regarding self-righteous phoney half-baked politically immature neurotic evil-minded little shits' (pp. 21-2) who inhabit it. Arthur uses the language of Cambridge (a well-constructed complex metaphor) to criticise Cambridge with ironic humour. He is sitting on the paradox of the radical middle class, which must either con-demn itself or be held to be lying and which cannot (and does not) affirm a class-based revolution.

When Saraffian offers – at excessive length – his idea of the his-tory of class struggle in explanation for Maggie's act of arson and the restoration of faith in the young, it is heralded with an obvious lead-in line and dismissed as an outmoded and impotent form of comfort. Scene Eight is a coda which exists both to posit and refute the protective belief of the class war. The action of the play moves logically without this coda progressing from Maggie and Arthur's delayed explanation of their relationship to a mirror-image of the opening (Arthur alone with Snead as he had been with Inch). Like the music, 'It all comes round again' (p. 52). The revolutions Hare perceives in *Teeth 'n' Smiles* are not Marxist but Yeatsian, an exam-ple of 'The Gyres' from which Arthur quotes.

The final line of dialogue is Arthur's unanswered question, 'Why is everyone frightened?'. It has a multiple-choice answer, contained in the placards, in Arthur's song and in Maggie's song, with no political imperative. As Arthur says at the beginning, 'It's absurd' (p. 24) that the plug lies unconnected, rather than a politi-cal imperative. The word 'absurd' occurs again in *Dreams of Leaving* and becomes the keynote of *A Map of the World*, but in *Teeth 'n'*

Smiles it invites consideration of the two separate spheres of expression within the play in terms other than class.

What unites Arthur/Hare, as well as Laura and Anson, with the band is not class or political intent, but age. All the characters save Snead, Saraffian and Randolph are aged 26 or under. In September 1975 David Hare was, like Arthur, aged 26. In June 1969 Hare had been, like Maggie and the band, on the road with Portable Theatre, equally exhausted and equally substituting neurotic intensity for public meaning and audiences. Like Arthur, he was a product of the system he would condemn, educated to degree level and then dropping out. *Teeth 'n' Smiles* is, then, autobiographical, an examination of Hare's own youth. Hare was duly photographed for *Time Out* wearing Arthur's top hat.

David Hare went to Cambridge to be taught by the Marxist Raymond Williams, but claims that they spent all their time arguing and that Williams did not shape his opinions. Certainly Hare was not, as Brenton was, politicised by the events of 1968. Hare wore his CND badge at school and describes, as the 'only political experience I had', his disillusion with the Labour government of 1964.[2] It stimulated not *Teeth 'n' Smiles* but *The Great Exhibition*.

Similarly, as Howard Brenton explained, 'Part of the energy behind Portable was simply: the bastards won't do our plays, we'll do them ourselves. That was a good reason at the time, but there was nothing more behind it than that. It was against the bastards, it was boiling for a fight against the established values in the theatre.'[3] During a time of almost perpetual unease at the Royal Court in 1969–71 Hare – in contrast to socialist writers like Wesker and Bond – had only one play, *Slag*, presented on the main stage. The new generation of writers had no home.

Arthur's explicit condemnation of the university he attended expresses Hare's own much-quoted view, but it is worn brazenly on the sleeve of the first scene. The audience is not expected to discover the character of Cambridge, which is immediately juxtaposed with Wilson's contribution to the game of Pope's balls. Arthur's criticism is as 'boring' as the life expectancy of a deck chair. As he says to Saraffian at the moment he is about to criticise Saraffian's Al Capone approach, 'It's not worth saying. Nothing's worth saying. It's all so obvious' (p. 61).

If there once was a love affair between the young of the working class, in the shape of Inch, Maggie and the band, and the supposed radical middle class in the shape of Arthur, to make the sixties look like the moment of effective political revolution, it is, like Maggie's and Arthur's affair, over. As Hare says, 'If you have a period like in 1968, when you believe in a revolution and then afterwards, the objective criteria for a revolution are missing, indeed definitively absent as they were in this country, you're soured with the impossibility of change.'⁴

> ARTHUR: I can see us all. Rolling down the highway into
> middle-age. Complacency. Prurience. Sadism. Despair.
> (SARAFFIAN *gets out his hipflask*.)
> SARAFFIAN: Don't worry have some brandy.   (p. 88)

Hare has made it utterly unambiguous that 'I was very pissed off with life while I was at university, and very disillusioned about the activities of the Left. It's really only as a writer that I've begun to think myself straight, work out for myself the answers to political questions.'⁵ What stands at the very centre of *Teeth 'n' Smiles* is not a question but an assertion:

> ARTHUR: Leonardo da Vinci drew submarines. Five hundred
> years ago. They looked pretty silly. Today we are drawing
> a new man. He may look pretty silly.   (p. 52)

In *Teeth 'n' Smiles* Hare gives only an oblique picture of what the potential qualities of the new man might be: humour. Only the young make jokes. It was, however, Trevor Griffiths who, in 1975 in *Comedians*, was turning his attention to the role of humour as liberation. Arthur, like Hare's humour, does not stay to the end.

> In the morning I drove for the border
> And Spanish he stayed till the end
> But he has resources of humour
> To which I cannot pretend.   (p. 66)

Hare has explained that he collaborated with Howard Brenton on

Brassneck and on *Pravda* partly because of his sense of humour and partly 'because I know he'll be there at the end'.[6]

Sex and drugs and rock 'n' roll

The point of the youth rebellion is made concrete in Smegs' acoustic guitar number when all except Maggie join in with the chorus. With the faces illuminated in spotlights in the highly theatrical rock-gig form of the mid-seventies, out of the cavern does come a collective voice and it says 'this is my message to you':

> Don't let the bastards come near you
> They just want to prove you're sane
> To eat up your magic and change you
> So I'll help keep the bastards away.   (p. 66)

It is a message of individualism which is anti–establishment but it is not pro-socialist and it is expressed in the language of youth culture – rock 'n' roll. The background to *Teeth 'n' Smiles* is a bank of amplifiers which turns the theatre into a rock venue. The distinction between the theatre and the rock gig, the shared vocabulary of 'set' and 'play' is, from the moment of opening, being deliberately blurred, making the actor into a musician and the playwright into a songwriter.

Throughout the first scene we are waiting for the electrical plug to be mended and the 'play' in the musical sense to begin. Unlike the plug in Pinter's *The Caretaker*, written fifteen years earlier, this technology is enabling. Once the plug is mended electronic music crashes on. Suffocated in repressed niceness, a generation exploded with as much noise as possible. By putting such experience at the centre of the stage Hare is filling in the gaps, claiming the theatre for his generation, writing for the audience he will get and 'making a film of our lives' (p. 66).

Brought up in the peace and security of the late fifties and early sixties, a generation inflicted upon themselves the hardship of life on the road, of sex and drugs and rock 'n' roll, because 'The louder we play, the sooner we won't be able to hear' (p. 88). For this reason, the fact of the music in *Teeth 'n' Smiles* and the way it is structured within the text is as important as its lyrical content.

By its position in front of the stage, the audience in the theatre is made into the May Ball audience for whom the band performs. There the audience would be standing and dancing; in the theatre it remains sitting. The band is therefore 'fucking the dead' and 'the dead still outnumber the living by thirty to one' (p. 14). Hare has talked of Portable Theatre's basic contempt for the audience, when 'The days and the nights were alive with hatred directed at you' (p. 66). For Hare, Portable 'was blatantly aggressive because aggression was then (1968–71) still a useful virtue in the theatre. I'm not sure it still is.'[7]

Teeth 'n' Smiles does not, however, become the kind of assault on the audience which Trevor Griffiths was to create a decade later with his skinhead band in *Oi for England!* 'In common with other writers who look with their eyes,' complained Hare, 'I have been abused in newspapers for being hysterical, strident and obscene, when all I was doing was observing the passing scene, its stridency, its hysteria, its obscenity, and trying to put it in a historical context which the literary community seems pathologically incapable of contemplating.'[8] Hare, like Maggie, had discovered that shock wears off, just as Jim Morrison ruined the effect of taking his trousers down by repeating it every night. The supposed affront of a sexually explicit and aggressive play like *Lay By* becomes part of the expected repertoire, nothing more dangerous than stage effect or exhibitionism.

Portable Theatre in the hands of David Hare and Tony Bicât was initially a literary group, interested in artists like Kafka and Genet, trying to expand the number of available theatre venues and the range of subjects under discussion but still asking *What Happened to Blake?* It was under the influence of Howard Brenton and John Grillo that Portable developed from these origins. As a writer, David Hare was never really part of the fringe. In *Slag* he explained that 'From the start there were those who said marry, infiltrate, get in there, and a different crowd who argued – separate, the divorce is total. It's between intercourse or isolation' (*Slag* p. 22). Hare favoured intercourse. With the exception of the unpublished *What Happened to Blake?* which he wrote and directed in 1970, his other work for Portable was collaborative. The bulk of his independent work of the period, *Slag* and *The Great Exhibition*, was first performed at the Hampstead Theatre Club. *Slag* was commissioned by Michael Codron, a West End producer, and transferred not only to the Royal Court, where it did well, but to New York. It was not that Hare was soon welcomed into the establishment, but that he had spent his apprenticeship in its training-ground and was therefore in an important sense always part of it. For David Hare the teeth (and the *Knuckle*-dusters) always give way to the smiles and humour.

Teeth 'n' Smiles does not become a *Sprechstück*, such as Peter Handke's *Offending the Audience,* which abandons visual spectacle in favour of a verbal one and whose subject is the audience. Since the band is playing not on a stage watched by the theatre audience but on a stage within a stage (the equipment which Inch erects is on the band's van) watched by Arthur, it is he to whom the songs speak and whom Maggie abuses, and not the theatre audience direct. Like the turns in John Osborne's *The Entertainer*, the three musical sets are a logical part of the event being portrayed – the May Ball – and in that sense they reinforce the action of the play and ironically preserve the unities of time (one night) and place (offstage in Cambridge). The songs are not a disruption of the spectacle but an extension of the spectacle.

In *The Birth of Tragedy from the Spirit of Music* Nietzsche explored the distinction between the artistic realms of the gods Apollo and Dionysus. The Apollonian state is the civilising urge of history, society and morality of the 'plastic' arts; it is epic, whereas the Dionysiac is the intoxicating urge of music. For Nietzsche, it is the Apollonian embodiment of Dionysiac insights which comprises tragedy.

The Nietzschean model is specifically invoked by Wilson and seen within that framework, the literary quotation and metaphor of Arthur and the urge to education and religion represented by Jesus College, Cambridge, are 'Apollonian', whereas the rough poetry of the slang, the sex and drugs and rock 'n' roll are 'Dionysiac'. Peyote can barely operate unless he has a guitar in his hands. Maggie too is fine as long as she is singing or drunk. It's the bits in between she can't do. She is, in Nietzsche's terms, a Dionysiac Man feeling the pain of understanding that nothing she can do can change things or as she puts it: '... there are no great, there is no beautiful, there is only the thin filth of getting old, the thin layer of filth that gets to cover everything' (p. 49). Maggie's understanding, therefore, is not limited to the political conditions of a late capitalist society but touches on something eternal and profound.

For Nietzsche, every artist imitates either the Apollonian or the Dionysiac. In David Hare's play, the historical analyses are primary, for the May Ball is itself contained within *Teeth 'n' Smiles*. Arthur may be a *song*writer and Hare may aspire to the tragic, but at this stage in his career his work is epic. For the band, Maggie's 'pain' is mostly in the arse and Wilson denies the Nietzschean model even as it is invoked. It was to be the late 1980s before Hare returned to the idea of tragedy, but it is significant just how early in his career the concept appears around a central female figure.

Teeth 'n' Smiles is a three-cornered love story, but any expectations that Arthur will get the girl in the end are denied. Maggie refuses to be Arthur's object of adoration, the Mona Lisa of the romantic Cole Porter songs he quotes from his second line; she stands similarly opposed to the Petrarchan ideal of womanhood represented by the under-written Laura. Maggie is flamboyantly promiscuous, an alley-cat describing the loss of her virginity and taking Anson offstage to sleep with him. In 1969, the ratio of men to women at Cambridge was 15 to 1. Jesus College, like many others, was a men-only college, forcing men, like the Pope in the game of pointlessness, Pope's balls, to deny their sexual urges. *Teeth 'n' Smiles* is a deliberate offence to that polite society. Just as the band takes the Lord's name and the name of the college in vain, so it asserts a supposed sexual gratification in a world of blow-jobs and 'butterfly flicks'. Such promiscuity is not, however, a satisfying alternative.

In Scene Seven, Arthur and Maggie are alone onstage, disembodied voices in the dark, without any physical dimension to their tattered relationship. The scene is only sixty lines long: their affair and the sixties love-in has burnt out as quickly as the match they strike, leaving only an emotional vacuum in which there are no stable relationships. In *Teeth 'n' Smiles* sex occurs only offstage; it remains outside the walls of Cambridge. The sexual terms which flaunt promiscuity therefore also comprise its bragging exaggeration. In an important sense their promiscuity does not exist.

Anson's severed finger falling to the ground graphically visualises not only Laura's loss of Arthur and Arthur's loss of Maggie, but the impotence of the so-called sexual revolution, in which the traditional double standard continues to operate. No one in *Teeth 'n' Smiles* suggests that the male body should be sold to buy petrol. Simply wearing a dress is sufficient to invite proposition to Peyote in drag. Terms of abuse remain sexual: men who fuck around are still leaders of the pack and women who sleep around are tragic.

Like the women's talk of 'turkey neck and turkey gristle' in *Plenty*, Maggie's 'candy peel' language may be born out of a genuine desire by Hare adequately to represent adult women. It also gives expression to the male dislocation at the sexual liberation of women, male fears that (even if Anson does succeed) women's autonomy will prevent the marshmallow from getting into the coinbox.

In addition, in the authorship of *Teeth 'n' Smiles*, there is a division between the creative mind producing the music, the creative mind producing the words (two senses) and the interpretative artist. Maggie sits at the still point at the base of a spiral of five male creators – Hare, Tony Bicât, Nick Bicât, Arthur and Saraffian. The male Svengali (Arthur/Hare) stands in a triangle with the angel (Laura) or the whore (Maggie) and the dropping finger is, finally, an image of castration, a subject which Hare and composer Nick Bicât were to take up again some twelve years later in the opera *The Knife*.

While sex is not physically visible in *Teeth 'n' Smiles*, drugs are. Joints are handed out liberally, pills are chosen according to whether or not they match a shirt. *Teeth 'n' Smiles* begins where *Brassneck*'s final scene, which was also set in 1969, ended. Throughout Scene One Peyote, who is named after a Mexican hallucinogenic plant, sterilises his equipment and shoots up. All his subsequent acts within the play are drug-induced.

Such drugs do not so much distort reality as make it an irrelevance. Peyote may see chariots with wheels of fire coming out of the sky, but no one else does. He has very few words, most of them 'off and fuck' (p. 20). In this one could agree with Pinter that 'the more acute the experience, the less articulate its expression'.[9] Peyote's 'release' from society can only leave that society intact, reinforcing rather than challenging a taboo, just as the band has converted people to classical music. If Peyote does in some way escape society, the escape is self-defeating, choking on its own vomit like the Joplin–Hendrix rock 'n' roll suicides of 1970–1. Those mentioned by the band – Keith Moon, Jimi Hendrix, Bessie Smith, Jim Morrison – are distinguished by the fact that they are all dead. Drugs might provide an excellent alternative to society but they are a poor strategy against it.

The drugs bust comes as a curtain line to the interval, the deviant resumption of normality within the hallucination of the performance. The subsequent police questioning effectively takes place in the bar when the audience resumes its normal active role. In this way the audience (now most likely over 26 years of age on average) is made into the police, asserting normality where the concern is not the truth, but the maintenance of order. As Saraffian puts it, 'The point is, who gets to go to jail' (pp. 64–5).

If Peyote can still be put on a shelf and need not be lived with, however, Maggie cannot. She has been through a range of drugs and has chosen alcohol. Alcohol is the socially accepted form of escape and revelry, consumed by the theatre audience in the bar, but Maggie drinks precisely to avoid happiness. She is not addicted, but deliberately dominates the band by making them service her needs. Even though she is on stage for only about forty-five minutes out of three hours, the others talk about her all the time. Whereas no one asks why Peyote takes drugs, they do ask why Maggie drinks, explaining that drinkers 'want to be invaded so there's an excuse. So there's a bit intact' (p. 69).

In his examination of the work of Sylvia Plath, Alvarez gives a similar explanation for the 'manic defence' of extremism. Just as Sylvia Plath accepts the violence of the concentration camps, saying 'I think I may well be a Jew',[10] so Maggie accepts the multiple roles of the individual with 'I was a Viking, I was a Jew...' (p. 69). By admitting all the worst excesses of the Holocaust into her art, Sylvia Plath created an ironic space in which morality might breathe. The same could be said of Portable Theatre and of Maggie.

Where Sylvia Plath was confronting a post-Freudian pain, Maggie's is of a different order; it is rather the guilt of affluence, the fact that, as Hare puts it in *The Great Exhibition*, 'We are rich, we are white, we are middle-class, we are English. We are the single most over-privileged group of people in the world.' As Patrick tells Curly in *Knuckle*, 'Life is pain. Pure and simple. Pain. Around. Below. All pain. But we have a choice. Either to protest noisily – to scream against the pain, to rattle and rail – or else – to submerge that pain, to channel it … (*Pause*). Preferably in someone else's direction' (*Knuckle,* p. 46).

In Maggie's song she makes it clear that she is not a sacrifice; she is a martyr burning herself down with the marquee, an act which generates the only moment of affection between singer and band. Cambridge may stand unscathed, but Maggie's suffering is heroic: she denies the power of the establishment to decide her fate by her own act of choice. After *Knuckle* and after the failures of the post-war Left, no excuses remain. The source of meaningful action in Hare's work is not collective action but the individual statement, even if it results in Maggie's imprisonment or Susan Traherne's madness in *Plenty* or Isobel Glass's death in *The Secret Rapture*.

By failing to prevent Maggie's wrongful imprisonment, it is Hare – as much as Arthur and Saraffian – who looks like the Svengali laying to rest a creation who was in danger of getting out of hand. Just as, by exploiting the spectacle of rock and illusory indulgence of youth rebellion, the entertainments industry of the sixties and seventies deflected the anger and impatience of the young and found a new source of profit so *Teeth 'n' Smiles* and David Hare gave the Royal Court its biggest hit for some time by turning confrontation and rebellion into entertainment.

It is not those on the upper deck who are having their 'Last Orders on the Titanic'. The ship which is sinking as the curtain falls is not Cambridge, but the band and the generation it represents. Hare is revealed, as Saraffian complained, to be one of those people who 'crap on about Hollywood in the Thirties' (p. 73). Not content with quoting from songs by the millionaire son of America, Cole Porter, Arthur/Hare uses his piano solo to emulate the style. This is not the nostalgia for the dead decade of the sixties;

this is nostalgia for a time of certainty and elegance before Hare was born, with Hare clearly asking:

> ARTHUR: What matter? Out of the cavern comes a voice
> And all it knows is that one word: rejoice.   (p. 57)

In direct reply to the question 'Why's everyone frightened?', Arthur's song is a soliloquy which reveals that he is there not for politics or for ideology but for love. The question points beyond the failure of the class war and the aggression of the sixties rebellion to a greater disjuncture, where good and bad are intertwined and reversed. In a belated modernist landscape, 'The world is spinning round decidedly too much' and 'We must hang on or lose our sense of drama' (p. 89). Just what that sense of drama should be if it is to be more than the romantic Hollywood musical of Cole Porter was to occupy Hare throughout the eighties. It is unresolved by *Teeth 'n' Smiles,* but marks the beginning of an argument with himself which Hare was explicitly to continue in *A Map of the World*.

In *Teeth 'n' Smiles* everything appears to be documentarily accurate; it appears to be an epic event, a history play where the political urge takes precedence and Hare digs around in the time that he was born in search of roots and explanations. It is authenticated, however, not by documents but by memory. It is this primacy of individual experience over research or ideology which links all of his plays after *Plenty* in 1978. In addition, the projections in the final moments of *Teeth 'n' Smiles* might bring the characters up to date – as they were, far more successfully, to achieve for *Licking Hitler* – but in *Teeth 'n' Smiles* they tell us nothing. The theatre audience might not see Peyote's death but they already knew it would occur. The projections are but a faint-hearted attempt to give the fictional characters the status of real people, to make the perspective gained simply through age look like objectivity and to make personal experience look like history. History has not behaved how it should, and Hare was already feeling that the disaster might be more profound and the fear more deeply based than a political solution could answer.

Playing the language game

Game metaphors occur throughout Hare's work. In *Brassneck* political consensus is reached on the golf course; in *Licking Hitler* the tactics of black propaganda are played out on the billiards table. The frequency of the games in *Teeth 'n' Smiles* uniquely fore-grounds the issue within the play. The games which Nash, Smegs, Wilson, Randolph and Arthur play become increasingly non-verbal, starting with 'boring' information, moving through the telephone directory game, where you have to keep quiet for as long as possible, and progressing to the ball-in-the-hole and the conga. What is important about these games for Hare is that they are actively *played*. If language is deteriorating and ultimately absurd, then it does still alleviate the boredom of life on the road and deaden the pain of our eternal situation, as it did for Gogo and Didi in Beckett's *Waiting for Godot*.

In the *Philosophical Investigations*, Wittgenstein identifies a num-ber of 'language-games', such as giving orders and obeying them, reporting an event, play-acting, making up a story, questioning and translating. These games are played according to public rules of use which make possible the distinction, according to public criteria, between correct and incorrect playing of the game. In the first scene of any play, the playwright is playing a naming game. Within the first sixteen lines of *Teeth 'n' Smiles*, Inch, Arthur, Maggie and Laura are named. This process is not explicit, not obviously directed at the audience, as it is in *Fanshen*. The characters already know each other and the audience is apparently being trained into a pre-existing game, just as the audience is later trained into the language of the drugs culture, when Anson describes what Peyote is doing from his position as medical student. In Scene One, Laura reports the event of someone putting sugar in the petrol tank and gives it in explanation for their late arrival. We recognise this as the report of an event according to the accepted criteria established by usage – the past tense is used, it is told as true, spoken in prose and so on. And this reporting is also a story being related by the actress and by the author within the game of theatre-going in English society, the rules of which we already know.

When we learn a language, we are trained into something more, what Wittgenstein calls a 'form of life'. We do not agree to the conventions of language but in a form of life, a community of reaction. The language-game of English is the frame of reference for all distinctions, including that between the normal and the political or revolutionary; what constitutes rebellion and the language for it are defined and created by the prevailing system. Left-wing theatre is defined as 'political' because it aims for a change in the rules which would render it normal. Hare uses Wittgenstein's favourite analogy of the game of chess to make the same point.

> ANSON: I'm hoping to drop out, you know. When I get my
>   degree. I just want to groove.
> ARTHUR: Course you do. But it's not so easy is it? I mean,
>   the rules are so complicated, it's like three-dimensional
>   chess.   (p. 59)

In *On Certainty*, Wittgenstein asserts that doubt about one or other of those rules can come only after belief. Reappropriation and subversion can come only after training into the language game and is therefore parasitic upon it. Cambridge contains the band and its slang, which can come only after normal meaning. The band may find it appropriate to say 'like fuckin' the dead', but the term 'necrophilia' could have been, indeed is, used (p. 33). Similarly, Peyote is able to converse with the medical student and use medical and not slang words for the drugs.

This realisation grants a third perspective on Hare's answer to the final question of the play, 'Why are you frightened?'. The reason is precisely that Maggie, Arthur, Saraffian and the band are all 'alive, well, living in England' (p. 91). Although the new man needs a new vocabulary, there cannot – in an absolute sense – be a revolution. When Arthur says 'Nothing is worth saying' he is like the 'totallys' who complain 'The whole system's totally corrupt an's gotta be totally replaced by a totally new system' (p. 58); he is making a statement which must be false. As Václav Havel demonstrated in *The Memorandum*, you cannot replace the language-game in its entirety because any new language would be understood only by its creator. Any plank can be removed from the boat of communication and it will still remain afloat; if you remove all of them, you have no boat. It is an evolutionary and not a revolutionary view of change in which, as Maggie made explicit, the real revolution must be inside.

Inherited from previous situations, language is a permanently inadequate descriptive instrument but it is constantly being changed for particular purposes by groups to meet differing ends. If one cannot doubt everything, nonetheless anything can be doubted. Far from indicating a degeneration of language, then, slang demonstrates its health. A 'bit o' wobble on the vox' (p. 33) is needed only in relation to electronic musical equipment. It is irrelevant to an older generation which does not play electronic instruments and is, therefore, perceived as a deterioration by them. The dialogue of *Teeth 'n' Smiles* is bursting with the new vocabulary and abbreviations required by drug-users to describe the range of substances on offer and the outlawed experiences they provide, and by their generation to render it inaccessible to the outside (adult) world. So Arthur redefines the fine imposed on him by the college for having a woman on the premises as 'a brothel charge' (p. 22) and Peyote refers to Snead as 'waiter' (p. 17).

Every revolution creates new words and only some of them stick; not all new words are a revolution. Slang, the rebellion words of one generation, either become the normal usage of the next or are forgotten. How dated 'groove' was to sound to the generation of 'suss'.

> ARTHUR: They invent a few rules that don't mean anything
> so that you can ruin your health trying to change them.
> Then overnight they redraft them because they didn't
> really matter in the first place. One day it's a revolution
> to say fuck on the bus. Next day it's the only way to get
> a ticket. That's how the system works. An obstacle
> course. Unimportant. Well, perhaps.
> NASH: The word Cicero literally means chick-pea.
> (pp. 22-3)

In a model of containment, the fruits of revolution are always conservative. Order, politeness, decency and control can be re-read as class, rules, repression and oppression, but the two parties are playing different language-games. Nothing is fundamentally changed by it. By the end of *Teeth 'n' Smiles*, the question 'What are you on?' has its usual allocation and receives the reply 'Motor-sickle' (p. 85). Only in *Fanshen* does the language of revolution achieve a community of use.

Hare records the contemporary language of 1969 but also puts in an historical context by contrasting it with Saraffian's musical dialect of the fifties. Punk had another dialect, the designer eighties yet another. *Collins English Dictionary* (1980) notes the slang use of 'groove'; it is institutionalised and, in employing it in the theatre, Hare hastens that assimilation. It is the same way that the language-game of the theatre is rejuvenated from its fringes by Portable, by Joint Stock.

Hare's self-conscious quotation strategy makes the text aware of its own part in the game of literature but the quotation, isolated from its original context, can be given a new meaning. Irony, parody, juxtaposition and metaphor can rupture normality and only Snead and Anson, those within the prevailing game, do not employ them. They are Hare's weapons of happiness. For Hare, then, like Arthur, the survival strategy is not humour but art itself and it is the artist who is the mediating point, the linchpin at the heart of multiple overlapping oppositions of *Teeth 'n' Smiles* and in the overlapping strands of Hare's body of work. Out of the cavern comes the poet's voice. After 1978, Hare does not invoke class analysis in his work; the model of containment has become dominant over that of opposition. In Wittgensteinian terms, he is playing a different language-game.

2 Stepping into the past

An alternative history

'Reading Angus Calder's *The People's War* changed all my thinking as a writer', wrote Hare. 'An account of the Second World War through the eyes of ordinary people, it attempts a complete alternative history to the phoney and corrupting history I was taught at school. Howard Brenton and I attempted in *Brassneck* to write what I have no doubt Calder would still write far better than we, an imagined subsequent volume 'The People's Peace', as seen, in our case, through the lives of the petty bourgeoisie, builders, solicitors, brewers, politicians, the Masonic gang who carve up provincial England.'[1]

When the projected photograph of Churchill on VE day 1945 opens *Brassneck*, the time of the action at the beginning of the play – the end of the Second World War – is established before a word has been spoken. Within a few moments of his entrance, the apparently old and senile Alfred Bagley is offering the van driver money for his load and begins his descent into Stanton. Named as the transaction is completed, Bagley is defined by it; he is the personification of the rejuvenation of post-war British capitalism. As the elders of the town fluster after the Labour landslide election victory, it is Bagley who is the lower-middle-class intermediary in the class war with Bassett and Edmunds; it is Bagley who becomes the compromise candidate for Master of the Lodge. Through him the audience is initiated into the secret pseudo-religious mysteries of the English establishment and the way the rules of the game of post-war politics were drawn.

Brassneck, as all of Hare's 'history plays', thus portrays instances of what Hare perceives as class struggle; but writing the alternative history of the people's peace does not mean putting the people on the stage. This is, at least in part, a product of his own background. 'There are', as Hare acknowledged, 'a lot of left-wing tenets which are unavailable to me…'[2] and this fact is an important leverage on his work. *Chicken Soup with Barley* chronicled a similar span in years, from 1936 to 1956, but Arnold Wesker writes from the point of view of a working-class Jewish family and although he showed the welfare state and restructured capitalism as instrumental in the loss of radicalism, he did not invoke them in explanation.

Where, through Ronnie, Wesker asks, 'What happened to all the comrades, Sarah? I even blush when I use that word. Comrade! Why do I blush? Why do I feel ashamed to use words like democracy and freedom and brotherhood? They don't have any meaning any more',[3] Hare has an answer in the grotesque characters of *Brassneck* and the stockbroker belt of *Knuckle*:

> MRS DUNNING: I wonder why all the words my generation believed in words like honour and loyalty are now just a joke.
> CURLY: I guess it's because of some of the characters they've knocked around with.   (*Knuckle*, p. 12)

It is people like Bagley and Patrick in *Knuckle* who understand that the red flag flying over the Town Hall will not mean nationalisation and are determined to exploit the opportunities of the mixed economy.

With eighty-one lines to Bagley's sixty-eight in Scene Two, Avon had controlled the gentleman's-club language of the Tory bigwigs and the Masonic Lodge. By Scene Seven, the slum houses Avon had secured for Bagley have become the site of his undoing and Avon has only forty-one lines to Bagley's eighty-five. Bagley's 'brassneck' – explained by the authors in their preface as a northern term meaning 'cheek' or 'nerve' – is one of 'new-fangledness. New approaches, new ways of looking at things. New ways of organising public contracts' (p. 42). These new ways use bribery and corruption and are utterly devoid of compassion or morality.

Alfred Bagley celebrates and consolidates his victory at the wedding of his grandniece, Lucy, which comprises Scene Eight. In the absence of the bridegroom and his family, it becomes a perverse incestuous marriage between them, and the screening of the Coronation on the same day creates an explicit parallel between local and state power. Unlike John Arden's *The Workhouse Donkey*, with which *Brassneck* was often compared, Brenton and Hare are interested in the regional power nexus only as an image of national corruption.

In 1945, Browne and Edmunds were faking their part in the heroic officer tradition of Clive and his father. In order not to be marginalised, they had a spot of lunch with them, they infiltrated and, as the second longest speech in the play (although only twenty-seven lines) acknowledges, the chances for change were squandered:

> HARRY: We 'ad a chance in 1945. Finest government this
> country ever 'ad. But not good enough. Not quite good
> enough by half. By the end, in rags. What am I now? I
> know. Don't answer that, 'Arry Edmunds. 'Ow can we
> ever forgive ourselves? I can't forgive myself. Labour
> party, the party we all love.   (p. 85)

Hare's aim as a playwright is not to further the revolution, but to explain a profound disillusion at its failure. His work from this point is informed by his 'passionately felt belief that the legacy of 1945 has been totally betrayed and there is a generation that has been tainted with hypocrisy'.[4] Although *Knuckle* was not produced until 1974, it was completed before *Brassneck*. Although it evoked the atmosphere of the time by its pastiche of the thriller, like *Slag* and *The Great Exhibition* it did not invoke history as an explanation of the present. It is this strategy which marks *Brassneck* as a turning-point in Hare's work.

A documentary theatre?

In their preface to *Brassneck* the authors say: 'Projected scenery was used throughout. This solved many of the play's staging problems, and gave the documentary sequences between the scenes their proper weight.' In this comment the authors deliberately foreground the documentary material as the basis for their coming narrative.

'Documentary drama presents and re-enacts records from history. Unlike traditional drama, it is not founded upon freely imagined plot. Historically, documentary drama is still in its infancy, dating from Erwin Piscator's production of *In Spite of Everything* (*Trotz Alledem*) in 1925.'[5] As Alfred Bagley hands over his empire to his nephew, *Brassneck* apparently presents and re-enacts the history of the rise (to ownership of the largest architectural practice in Europe) and fall (to bankruptcy in 1972) of John Poulson, thinly disguised in the character of Roderick Bagley.

It is Tom Browne who carries the brunt of the extended parallel. Act One's independent communist becomes chairman of Stanton's housing committee and the town's youngest mayor. By Act Two he is Bagley's public relations consultant and Labour campaign manager in a career which parallels exactly that of T. (Thomas) Dan Smith, who became Chairman of Newcastle City Council and its housing committee, and extracted £155,000 in consultancy fees from Poulson companies.

The analogy makes undeniable one of the play's principal charges – that the upper echelons of the Labour Party were implicated in the most serious of contemporary corruption cases. One of Smith's companies handled Labour Party publicity for three general elections. As the Bagley family discusses the fraud at the beginning of Act Three Scene One, the slogan 'Let's Go with Labour', used for the election campaign of 1973, is over the stage. Written as it was before the Poulson affair was concluded, *Brassneck* was to prove prophetic. In 1974 John Poulson was sentenced to seven years imprisonment. Just as Roderick goes off to prison as the token prosecution, so the handcuffs did not extend to parliament or to Reginald Maudling, the then Home Secretary in the Heath government mentioned during the Poulson investigations, and soon to become, like Raymond Finch, a 'Tory ex-minister'.

If it was largely correct that the truth was to be found in the Poulson trial, *Brassneck* – like *Pravda* after it – does not name those it accuses. Although this was undoubtedly a protection against a suit for libel, not all the characters in the play have analogies in the Poulson affair and not all those instrumental in the Poulson affair appear in the play. *Brassneck* is not, then, a confrontation with pure historical veracity, the showing of unfiltered reality in the manner of Piscator's 'documentary' theatre. Piscator used a montage of authentic documents to replace the traditional elements of plot and character as the basis of his theatre. By removing the distinction between theatre and the world, he wanted to involve the audience as in a political meeting.

Hare recognises that 'Writers have traditionally had this informative function, pointing to the iniquities of the system, or the corruption of public men',[6] but the role is attributable to *England's Ireland*[7] – where allegory and eyewitness accounts were used to tell the public what was happening in Ireland – rather than *Brassneck*. The newspapers of the early 1970s were full of stories about Poulson, and the American Watergate scandal was exposed by investigative reporting. Since the 1920s, the informing function of documentary theatre has been usurped by newspapers and TV news.

In so far as it is still used in the theatre, the documentary method relates most often to oppression in other countries, as in Ronald Harwood's *The Deliberate Death of a Polish Priest* or Norman Fenton and Jon Blair's *The Biko Inquest*. As Hare perceived it, 'The traditional function of the radical artist – "Look at these Borgias; look at this bureaucracy" – has been undermined. We have looked. We have seen. We have known. And we have not changed. A pervasive cynicism paralyses public life.'[8]

As Hare was to explore in *Licking Hitler*, the content of any document – the informative function in which the finger is pointed – cannot but be a propaganda allowing the audience simply to adjust its perceptive category from 'play' to 'left-wing play', leaving the categories themselves unchallenged. If a play is not to be merely another message in the blizzard, another form of propaganda corrupting the audience towards an end, then it must be conscious of its own status as document. In using actual documents in its staging *Brassneck* reveals a guilty awareness of the public system of presentations (of which the stage is now a lesser one) which creates the public memory.

Documents themselves are not a guarantee of truth and *Brassneck* is theatre *with* documents and not the theatre *of* or *by* documents. Since it is unable to portray all the events of history, the stage is necessarily selective and therefore generalises from the particular. Since each scene is necessarily time-bound, it is the documentation which moves the time forward across the years 1945-73 within an episodic structure. It is this absence of the unity of time which distinguished epic poetry from tragic poetry for Aristotle and the presentation of a single action as opposed to a single period which distinguished epic from ordinary history.

The photographs and the historical parallel demand an articulation between the external reality of the history of Britain and the internal reality of the play, generalising the fictional action as a statement about the nation. Historical accuracy in reference lends credibility to the action, but if the placing of authentic, pre-existing and accepted photographs within this work of fiction authenticates it, the fiction equally dislocates the documents from their assumed truth value precisely to expose the naivety of documentary.

Bagley's wedding speech, which is by far the longest in the play, is the central point of *Brassneck*, despite the three-act structure. Beginning with the wedding-day clichés he soon shuffles the wrong pack and comes up with the joker – his own biography. He is not the big bad boss of socialist realism, nor a Victorian melodrama villain like Butterthwaite in John Arden's *The Workhouse Donkey*. Bagley is a specifically twentieth-century phenomenon, the product of the trenches. When man ate man, morality became inverted, language – like Bagley's own – fragmented, and traditional certainties dissolved into nothing:

> BAGLEY: ... But... but... but... but... (*He wags his finger.*)
> Cr. Cr. Cr. Cr... I've got a beady eye. Cr... Cr... Cr...
> Cr... goes the crow on't gate... Dirty old crow.
> Believing nothing... thinking nothing, but with a beady
> eye for... (*He suddenly shoots his hand out and points at*
> AVON.) T'WORM.   (pp. 55-6)

The worm, James Avon, has already been gobbled up and leaving is the only course open to him. In Act Two he has only seventeen lines. 'I'm sorry, I fell' (p. 60) he mutters to complete an extended allusion to *King Lear*, which began with Sidney's naming of Alfred Bagley as the fool's 'Nuncle' (p. 43), and continued with 'Poor Tom' (p. 66) Browne seeking revenge on his previous disinheritance alongside Brother Edmund(s). Alfred Bagley, however, is not a Lear; his nihilistic forerunner is to be found rather in Ted Hughes' *Crow*, a collection of allegorical poems first published in 1972.

When Bagley cuts the cake and reveals the sign of the Masons, BOAZ, he is, in the terms of the Masonic oath, 'branded as a wilfully perjured individual, devoid of all moral worth and totally unfit...' (pp. 21-2). He does not die for his revelation but commits the revelation as he dies. What is supposed to be a punishment worse than death is powerless over him and as Lucy cries 'I wanna divorce' (p. 59), the wedding becomes a funeral, the final rite of passage enabling the successful transference of authority and money from old king to new queen. If he had not died, Alfred Bagley might have become an anti-hero like Richard III, turning disgust to admiration by his very control of the stage. With 384 lines all in Act One – more lines than anyone else can muster in the whole play – he in any case unbalances the play and makes anything which follows an anti-climax.

When Sidney, an utterly pragmatic spiv, takes over, the family is no longer a warm overcoat but a monster which lurks in the Lower Depths of a night-club strip den, a *Dear Octopus* with eight sucker-ridden tentacles. The club of which they are all members is a Dionysiac misrule of drink, drugs and sexual and moral degeneracy. He not only quite literally has the girls but owns the brothel, a tightly streamlined international crime syndicate dealing in Chinese heroin, the ideal commodity in the purest form of the market economy.

The role of moral critic is only half-heartedly taken up by the other member of the Avon family, Clive, in his exposure of Finch, but it is prompted not by moral disapproval, but by revenge for his sexual humiliation by Lucy. It does absolutely nothing to harm the Bagleys, who defuse the assessment by acknowledging its truth. When Bagley marries to become "Mr Lucy" by Act Three, even his name is consumed by the black widow. When morality is inverted women offer no alternative, only further evidence of the depth of the betrayal. Vanessa's repressed decency is parodied throughout and Lucy is defined through her sexual availability in multiple marriage, incest, divorce and sexual humiliation. Despite her blonde hair and blue eyes, she is the inverse of the Shirley Temple angel, of the angel in Stanton Town Hall and the angel over the investiture. If there is no ideal, if moral critics in their own time are powerless and humiliated, if the official opposition is compromised by corruption, then how is a valid perspective to be found? The problem in the late twentieth century is not one of gaining information but of finding a position from which to judge.

English Borgias

Following straight on from the decision on the golf course to elect Alfred Bagley as an interim Masonic leader, Act One Scene Five finds the Vatican cardinals choosing and investing a new pope. The explanation of the scene lies in its final word, 'Borja'. It is that single word which makes explicit for the audience the other extended reference between the families of the Borgias and the Bagleys on which Act One of *Brassneck* is based.

Alf(red)onso de Borja (1378-1458) became Pope Callistus III in 1444. He was, like Alfred Bagley, chosen for his great age and as a mediator (between the Orsini and Colonna families in Italy). Just as Bagley used his 'impending' death to best advantage, so Alfonso de Borja failed to meet the anticipated early death. His nephew Rod(erick)rigo Borgia (1431-1503), who himself became Pope Alexander VI in 1492 by means of bribery, was the beneficiary of his nepotism. He was accidentally poisoned by his son Cesare (Sidney), one of four children born to his favourite mistress Van(nessa)ozza Catanei. Her daughter Luc(y)rezia had three husbands, each acquired – like Lucy's first husband Dennis – to further the dynastic claims of the family.

This heavily schematic parallel by names (which omits only Martin) sustains an implicit link between events of the past on which the judgement of 'corruption' is firmly fixed and the dealings of today, which are so close that the kind of critical distance necessary for such a judgement is denied to us. Hare had done the same thing in embryo in *Slag*, where one of the few remaining unseen pupils at Brackenhurst is referred to as Lucrecia Bourgeois.

For David Hare, 'Judgement is at the heart of the theatre.'[9] The purpose of the investiture scene is to make such a distance possible and such a judgement inevitable by dragging the audience from one consensus judgement to another controversial and therefore highly political one. The same process takes place as Sidney wears Franky-boy clothes (Scene Seven), and throws his flick knife into the joint of ham (Act Two) so connecting the Bagleys to the Mafia. Like Michael Corleone in Francis Ford Coppola's movie of 1972, he is training as the next *Godfather*.

Reading the play within the context of Brenton's work, *Brassneck* has been seen as a disruption of the spectacle of public life as it is reported in the media. It is, however, the very relativity of the stage itself which allows the propaganda – in this case the myth of change in post-war Britain – to be revealed as propaganda. When the characters react to documented events, their reality takes on the same status of truth as the documents. At the same time it puts them into a context where they can be revealed as a construct rather than as impartial and passive describers of a given external reality. *Brassneck* cannot disrupt the spectacle, it must also preserve it, but by exposing the mysteries and privileges of Freemasonry as the masque of big business, it is challenged to fulfil its own prophecy and to die.

In making the historical parallel explicit, the play avoids the fact that to write about a distant period may leave the perceived relevance unguaranteed. As Hare explained in 1978, 'When I first wrote, I wrote in the present day, I believed in a purely contemporary drama; so as I headed backwards, I worried I was copping out, avoiding the real difficulties of the day.'[10] The pomp and ceremony attendant on the Vatican is minimalised so that it should not become celebratory, like costume drama. By merging the scene into Stanton railway station, the implicit grandeur and the self-dramatising tendencies of the Masons are undermined.

Although it ties the origins of mercantile capitalism to its twentieth-century development, the Vatican analogy is a substitute for the argument of the play and not a generalisation from it. The effect remains reminiscent of the shock tactics of *Lay By*. Since such a scale – twenty-two actors in twenty-nine parts – had been unavailable within the Victorian confines of the Royal Court and the commercial constraints of the West End, and the Portable solution of touring large-scale shows had led to bankruptcy, Hare and Brenton positively revelled in the spectacular facilities available to them at the Nottingham Playhouse.

In *Brassneck* the forced parallel across time which comprises the investiture scene – the shortest scene in the play – appears only in embryo. It does not recur in any of Hare's subsequent plays but was taken up instead by Howard Brenton in *The Romans in Britain*, to force a parallel between the Roman invasion of Britain and the British military presence in Ireland, and by Caryl Churchill in *Top Girls*, where women from different periods and countries sit together around the same dinner table demonstrating the similarities in the position of women in all their societies. In each case the contemporary demand for change stands defused by the fact that the historical parallel shows that nothing has changed with time.

Unable to effect the highly theatrical analogy, the television version of *Brassneck* cut it altogether. To preserve a chronological disruption and some distance on the irresistible rise of Alfred Bagley, a flash-forward to the end of the play was instead included. This technique was to appear again in *Plenty* and in *Heading Home* to ensure – in contrast to the thriller or crime movie, where the question is who did it – that the uppermost question in the mind of the audience is not what happens but how and why it happens:

> It took me time to realize that the reason was, if you write about now, just today and nothing else, then you seem to be confronting only stasis; but if you begin to describe the movement of history, if you write plays that cover passages of time, then you begin to find a sense of movement, of social change, if you like; and the facile hopelessness that comes from confronting the day and only the day, the room and only the room, begins to disappear and in its place the writer can offer a record of movement and change.[11]

If that change is not demonstrated by jarring together two disparate bits of history, it can be achieved precisely by moving progressively across time, and Hare continues to use the technique in *Licking Hitler*, *Plenty*, *Dreams of Leaving* and *Heading Home*.

In *Brassneck*, there are no radicals and the end of capitalism is announced by the capitalists themselves, who still control the stage. It is precisely the problem of reaction and opposition which Hare was to confront continuously from this crucial turning-point. Repeated every night in the theatre, the play itself becomes an ironic celebration of that decadence, and if the final line of *Brassneck* had used the word 'end' instead of the 'last days' in its description and naming of capitalism, the play could have revelled in its own irony still further.

When Ted Hughes' *Crow alights*, 'He blinked. Nothing faded. / He stared at the evidence. / Nothing escaped him. (Nothing could escape)'.[12] In *King Lear*, too, 'Nothing will come of nothing' (I.i.92) and 'nothing can be made out of nothing' (I.iv.135). So too the positive Nothing can escape from the Great Britain Ltd (pp. 93-4). Howard Brenton confirmed that:

> A really great outburst of nihilism like *Fruit* or the last act
> of *Lay By* is one of the most beautiful and positive things
> you can see on stage like the scene with the dead in
> Genet's *The Screens*. Nihilism is the end of everything –
> the closing down of all possibilities … But an audience
> survives all these assaults and horrors – it survives. And the
> fact of survival, no matter how we degenerate, is surely
> important in itself.[13]

The boil may not be pricked but it may still burst. As in Jacobean tragedy, having destroyed everyone else evil may consume itself; having addicted and killed everyone in its greedy market, the ultimate product may finally destroy its manufacturers. As Martin declares that 'there are contradictions inherent in a capitalist system which in the end will destroy it' (p. 95), the play declares itself where it need not have done, and the words drop unconvincingly from Martin's mouth. In a Genet-styled ritual, the stage stripper begins in the mayor's robes and goes on to expose the Masonic apron, the bowler hat and the rubber tube of drug addiction (p. 101) lurking underneath, and Hare and Brenton are indulging what in Marcusean terms could be called a 'consciousness of crisis' (*Krisenbewusstein*). It is in anticipation of this that 'The floor slowly gives way beneath them, and they descend as the lights fade and they are swallowed up' (p. 102). Documentary film and theatre may be required to adhere to the letter of reality but imaginative drama is under no such constraints. It can reach forward into possible visions of the future.

A statement of faith

In the 'Authors' Note' to *Brassneck*, Brenton and Hare claimed that 'every scene, every word was jointly worked: there is nothing which is more one of us than the other'. The collaboration between Hare and Brenton was not an expression of a belief in collective writing but, according to Brenton, the product of insecurity. 'We wanted a show about corruption in England, in a town like Nottingham, but neither of us felt that independently we were wise enough to write it, so we decided to write it together.'[14] Having written it together, many critics and analysts continued to bracket their subsequent work together, and the writing of *Pravda* for the same reasons in 1985 only reinforced the tendency.

If *Brassneck* is 'indivisible', it is not because the contribution of the two writers cannot be seen. Howard Brenton had examined the reciprocity between crime and the law in *Revenge* and *Christie in Love*. Hare had expressed disillusion with the Labour Party and the amoral charm of capitalism in *The Great Exhibition* and *Knuckle* respectively. In *The Romans in Britain*, for example, Brenton's imagistic language of sexual degeneracy runs, in the same way as in *Brassneck*, as a cumulative assertion of political and moral corruption; in Hare's work, in contrast, metaphor is clearly limited to an individual speech, as a subtle contextualising pointer to the moral impetus of the piece.

For these reasons – coupled with the observation that Hare's previous independent plays had been distinctly scaled-down visions of decaying institutions, requiring a small cast – *Brassneck* has been accommodated within the body of Howard Brenton's work. As a result perhaps David Hare was often taken to share political ideals well to the left of the Labour Party. In fact, even in the early seventies, Hare confirmed that 'Howard's really a revolutionary in a way that I'm not.'[15] Hare had made this explicit in his first play, *How Brophy Made Good*:

> BROPHY: ... The need was for change.
> SMILES: For revolution?
> BROPHY: No, for change.   (*Brophy*, p. 106)

Brassneck is not a political imperative but, as Hare confirms, a statement of belief: 'To write a play at all you have to work extremely hard on what you believe about the subject – and the writing process is finding out the truth or otherwise of what you believe by testing it on stage.'[16] Hare explained that in *Brassneck* 'Howard and I stopped short at exactly the point where we began to diverge politically in our approach to the subject. *Brassneck* is as far as Howard and I can go in agreement. The play ends with the simple statement that these are "the last days of capitalism". On how exactly the system will be transformed, how the future would shape, we couldn't agree.'[17] It has a distinct tone of voice and if *Brassneck* is 'indivisible', it is because it is an irrelevance to pore over such divisions within a work for which – in contrast to *Deeds*[18] – both writers claim total responsibility.

As he said of the Royal Court, so might Hare have said of *Brassneck*, 'I could see what everyone was against, because I was usually against it too – the hysterical torture of Shakespeare's texts at the RSC, or the absurd degrading comedies we had to endure in the West End – but when it came to defining what we were for, well, it was harder. It was almost a faith.'[19] In this, he echoes the later Piscator who began to reformulate his ideas in terms of *Bekenntnistheater*, a confessional theatre making a statement of faith. For Piscator that faith would be a *Bekenntnis zum Politischen*, a statement of faith in politics. For at least one of the writers of *Brassneck*, 'It is hard to believe in the historical inevitability of something which has so frequently not happened, or rather, often been nearest to happening in places and circumstances furthest away from those predicted by the man who first suggested it.'[20] Hare's faith is not in politics but in the theatre itself, because 'Words can only be tested by being spoken. Ideas can only be worked in real situations. That is why the theatre is the best court society has.'[21]

3 A turning over

Showing a revolution

Fanshen may well be without precedent in the history of British theatre. A dramatisation of the chronicle history by William Hinton of land reform in the Chinese village of Long Bow in 1947, it puts onto the stage a descriptive model of the process of a successful revolution. In introducing themselves, each of the people tells of external, verifiable facts and each states his or her position in economic rather than personal terms. The subsistence existence of a pre-industrial village is precisely quantified in simple objects, each of which has a vital practical significance to the peasants. On stage, they become emblematic: it is a quilt which carries the weight of the first redistribution after fanshen, a tangible improvement in one person's life implying the improvement in everyone's lives.

The uncluttered simplicity of the language built upon those basic objects and on the natural environment echoes the imagistic style of Chinese poetry. Hare's paring away of usual shades of literary encumbrance in his own work and English drama as a whole is a function of the fact that these people have neither the luxury nor the moral preoccupations of the west. It is a language where our senses of 'good and bad don't come into it' (p. 50).

Since the title is the only Chinese word in the play and is repeated constantly throughout, it carries the more resonant significance. Literally it means 'to turn the body or to turn over' (p. 15) and to understand that word is to understand the revolution. Immediately before the houselights dim for the opening of the play

proper, the definition is given. Neither the audience nor the peasants understand what the implementation of that word means: in
the course of the play, they undergo a parallel education about the
meaning of revolution, the turning over from feudalism to communism. The fanshen is not the result of a single change but a continuous process of definition and redefinition. Although the
audience is invited to believe what they will see as 'true', there is
no presumption that the turning over will be a success.

By asking Basic Questions, the peasants study their present situation and learn a new vocabulary of rights and accusation under
the guidance of Secretary Liu. Happening on opposite sides of the
stage, the dialectic itself is made concrete. The simultaneity makes
it more difficult for the audience to follow, so increasing their
understanding of how difficult it was for the peasants to find the
answers. 'I feel that the debate itself is what is interesting', says
Hare. 'For me, therefore, there is a lucky coincidence between the
nature of the Chinese revolution and the nature of what works in
the theatre ….'.[1]

Fanshen does not hero-worship the revolutionary and neither
does it hero-worship the revolution itself. Understand this and
everything is changed. Having been crudely politicised, the peasants seize the wealth of the landlords, but their first attempt at
redistribution in accordance with the level of suffering and activity
in effecting the fanshen – visualised by the scales on stage – fails
because the peach tree is not heavy with fruit. Wang Yu-Lai and
Cheng Ku'an therefore decide to seize goods from the middle
peasants, running the risk of alienating them. The answer to this,
they consider, is 'strong leadership', the continuation of a self-per-
petuating cycle of revolution and cynical decay. The energy has
dissipated, with the 'scenes' becoming shorter to a single page.
'The history of China is a history of bloody and violent rebellion.
But always the blood runs down the gutter and nothing is changed.
How are we to make sure this time, in this tight circle, the over-
turning holds? The difference is, this time, we think' (p. 21).

Juxtaposed with such apathy and abuse of both the language and
the fanshen in Long Bow is the description of the village, seen
from a distance by the approaching work team. The swallows of

spring come with new hope, new terminology and new direction beyond eye-for-an-eye redistribution and decayed leadership. Following the attack on Chang Ch'uer, the work team suspends the village leaders and takes over the affairs of the village. It will re-examine the whole village's fanshen in the new language of comrades, brother and sister, of commandism, hedonism and opportunism. Their more sophisticated vocabulary finds expression in a long confident speech about the Draft Agrarian Law, which will formalise the spontaneous uprising.

The new redistribution is based on need and a rigorous process of classification according to Self-Report, Public Appraisal. The poorest hold the knife in their hands and they are determined, unreliable, and biased, as demonstrated by the classification of Huan-Ch'ao, blacksmith. The complaints at the poor quality of his work are regardless of his economic position. It is the only moment in the play to foreground value words and the only moment of humour and it demonstrates both the complexity of human motivation and the difference between theory and praxis.

The central point of the play comes at the moment the work team realises (end of Section Six) that 'The place is rotten. We must start again ' (p. 46). Rather than breaking on this downbeat for the interval, however, the means of starting again – the Draft Agrarian Law – is given exposition before the humour of the implementation of its classification creates an upturn, and Little Li sounds a note of optimism for the audience to take into the bar:

> LITTLE LI: I was at college, many years ago. People used to say China is poor, it's poor because it lacks fertilizer, it lacks machinery, it lacks insecticides, it lacks medical care. I used to say no, China is poor because it is unjust.
> (*Pause. Then he smiles.*)
> HOU: We must prove it comrade.
> LITTLE LI: Yes.
> (*The house lights come up.*)   (p. 53)

That whole pattern of progress, error and renewed optimism is to be repeated. After the second redistribution according to the banner of absolute equality, the second Leucheng conference gives its equal and opposite exposition of failure of the Draft Agrarian Law and the work teams implementing it.

Section Eight, the Gate, defines the meaning of Little Li's justice in terms of the accountability of the leadership to the led, of purification, of self-criticism and public accusation. The demand of equal and opposite suffering for Chen K'uan is rejected as itself the product of feudalism. His suspension from office will be followed by another chance to pass the Gate, the object being improvement and not retribution. At the Leucheng conference, therefore, the Long Bow delegation is held up as an example of Left extremism for being uncritical in the face of the accusations of the people. The criticism produces a crisis in the leadership of the work party which is explored through their own self-criticism in the most effectively dramatic section in the play.

The four fully individual members of the work team demonstrate their essentially human character to show that self-criticism affords no platform to heroism. Neither should it allow a place for despair; both are the luxury of the individual character. As Bill Gaskill made clear, 'The centre of our work on *Fanshen* does not lie in character at all',[2] although – as Max Stafford-Clark interjected – 'we do often arrive with "character" as an end result ... The scene is therefore "characterised" as a result of having decided what it is we want to say with it.'[3]

Each scene therefore is in Brecht's term 'gestic', because it expresses a simple action which can be translated into a single statement. In *Fanshen*, such a simple action can be identified for each of the twelve sections and they are sometimes made explicit by the slogans. In their playing, the actors are 'quoting' the gestus. With a cast of nine and some thirty roles each performer, of necessity, plays more than one role. The actors are therefore also quoting 'character' rather than empathising with it. Audience confusion is prevented with a simple change in costume, such as a headband. One might say that the people have identity but not character.

Since no single individual has control over the flow of information, it is narrated by Man-Hsi, Cheng-K'uan, Yu-Lai, T'ien-Ming and Shien Ching-Ho. Anything irrelevant to the political point of the scene – the spitting and the dirt for example – is removed. The stripping and torturing of the landlord Ching-Ho is

presented as a silent tableau. This might result in an idealisation of
the people, but it also releases the theatrical questioning from the
grime of the gutter.

An epic theatre?

As Brecht's historical method was a reaction against the bourgeois
German theatre as he found it in the 1920s, so what Hare and
Brenton had in common was a dislike of a rhetorical, over-pro-
duced, lavish, empty and conventional theatre. Hare had already
dabbled in the West End, however, and, where Brenton has continued to write in tandem for major subsidised and fringe theatres,
he has stayed resolutely on the main stages. As Brecht said in 1948,
'Let us treat the theatre as a place of entertainment ... But let us
enquire what kind of entertainment we regard as acceptable.'[4]
    Bill Gaskill, who served his apprenticeship at the Royal Court
and, as its artistic director, pioneered the work of Edward Bond in
defiance of the censor, has been heralded as our leading Brechtian.
He may well have viewed the new company as an ensemble group
similar to the Berliner Ensemble. The establishment of Joint Stock,
however, was a response not to the inertia of the main theatrical
institutions, but to the aesthetic limitations of the supposed alterna-
tives.
    It was the peculiarity of Joint Stock that the productions were
evolved in workshop by both the actors and the writer, working
usually on documentary material in the form of an existing book.
As a reflection of the search for equality amongst the Chinese
peasants, company members were classified according to income,
actors and directors swapped roles, and everyone took part in self-
criticism. The aim was to gain a greater understanding of the
process of the communist revolution but, in the course of it, the
company became a collective.
    This evolution of the company Hare had helped to found is not
central to a study of his plays. In adapting Hinton's massive work of
some 600 pages, Hare was ultimately autonomous, as he makes
clear in his introduction to *Fanshen*. 'If the play had been a failure
at its first appearance that would be much more apparent, but success concretes things over in a way that makes it almost impossible

to retrieve them.'[5] The details of the workshop process have been substantially discussed, often in preference to consideration of the text itself, yet, in common with other writers who subsequently worked with Joint Stock, the play Hare wrote for them was quite distinct from the rest of his work. It is by intent that *Fanshen* was to be Hare's only adaptation until the early 1990s, when he wrote the screenplay of Josephine Hart's novel *Damage*[6] and a version of Brecht's *The Life of Galileo*,[7] and that it marked the end of his involvement both in substantial collaboration and in touring productions.

The concentration of the peculiarities of the *Fanshen* experiment may also have distorted the history of Joint Stock. Just as Rob Ritchie says of Joint Stock, so might one say of Hare: 'After *Fanshen* it might be thought a revolutionary perspective was adopted. Far from it. The politics were largely determined by the accidents of the research',[8] and Hare insists that throughout all of his work, 'It's the subject matter that dictates everything'[9] and not some overall strategy of his own. It is for this reason that Hare's films are certainly part of a continuum with his stage plays. Commitment to represent accurately people's suffering was a 'human' impulse and not a revolutionary one, as Hare explained: 'Although the subject matter of the play was political, the instincts of the company were in essence moral. We were not revolutionaries.'[10]

It remains true, however, that the facts shown in *Fanshen* are not those normally portrayed in European culture, but Hare took on the role of an alternative historian by default. He informed the audience of something otherwise ignored, but he did so as a function of (at others' request) adapting Hinton's book written precisely to that purpose. The work does in part, therefore, have a didactic effect, but it is at one remove, since it is not the history of the audience which is being retrieved. When *Fanshen* was published as part of a collection (albeit for marketing convenience) it was classified not as one of *The History Plays* but as one of *The Asian Plays*.

The institution of history and of the stage admits of these alternative readings: informed by the Marxist tradition, committed to the research categories of class, mode of production and hegemony, they are subsumed under the heading, 'Labour history'. It is not a revolutionary act sufficient to rupture the dominant perspective of 'normal' history; nor was it accessible to a working-class audience. The television version of *Fanshen* went out as part of the arts programme *Second House* on BBC2 on Saturday 18 October 1975 at 8.40pm after a 20-minute talking-head introduction by presenter Melvyn Bragg.

If, as Hare considers, 'A play is not actors, a play is not a text; a play is what happens between the stage and the audience',[11] then one must look at the nature of the audience a play and a writer received. Brecht wrote in the context of a strongly politicised culture where the choice between communism and fascism was a real and urgent one. Even if Hare had not felt distanced from such a movement by his class, *Fanshen* could not plug into any working-class militancy. The year 1975, in which Mrs Thatcher was elected leader of the Conservative Party, saw an oil crisis and a failed miners' strike and Britain had no positive and vibrant popular culture to which the production could contribute.

John McGrath might have aimed at and even succeeded in finding such an audience and such a culture, but he has succeeded largely in Scotland. David Hare, Portable Theatre and Joint Stock never intended to reach a working-class audience. In 1972, Hare said of Portable, 'We have a very bad record with working class audiences – we've hardly played to any. Our weapon has always been a middle-class, middle-brow weapon really.'[12] It was, like the Brechtian theatre 'a theatre designed to arouse indignation in the audience, dissatisfaction, a realization of contradictions – it is a theatre supremely fitted for parody, caricature, and denunciation, therefore essentially a negative theatre'.[13]

> A play is a performance. So if the play is to be a weapon in the class struggle, then that weapon is not going to be the things you are saying; it is the interaction of what you are saying and what the audience is thinking. The play is in the air.[14]

What was in the air was political disillusionment. In 1970, *Slag* had examined the sterility of political idealism, while, two years later, *The Great Exhibition* dissected the decline of the Left in jaundiced professional socialism. In addition, Hare had directed, for a National Theatre tour, Trevor Griffiths' *The Party* – a play which examines precisely the blind alley into which the post-68 generation had driven itself. In his introduction to *Fanshen*, Hare summarises the problem:

> In 1948 George Orwell wrote: 'When you are on a sinking ship, your thoughts will be about sinking ships.' ... Writers have been trapped in negatives, forced back into sniping and objection, or into lurid colours of their private imaginations. At some stage they will have to offer positive models for change, or their function will decay as irrevocably as the society they seek to describe.

The problem for these writers is to find a positive model for change. In *Brassneck*, Hare had examined how the apparent socialist revolution in Britain had merely hastened society along the old grooves. In order to find his model, Hare had to look not only to the past, but to a different continent.

If *Fanshen* had a political intention it was not to stimulate action outside the theatre but to resuscitate or generate a belief that change is sometimes possible. The play ends – after the work team has returned and begun again – with only an ambiguous call to action for the audience to take home. This is especially true of an audience and a culture with no revolutionary tradition.

> JOANNE: Why are the workers silent, Ann? Why does the revolution land with such a sigh? Twenty-five years the war is over, and everyone is trying to get the workers to respond. And they won't. Where are the working women? Lulled by romantic love and getting home to cook the dinner. (*Slag*, p. 75)

Fanshen is, therefore, as the introduction makes clear, a play for Europe, for the west: 'For *Fanshen* seeks to explain to an audience who have no real experience of change what exactly that change might involve and how it can in practice be effected.'

If *Fanshen* established Joint Stock's identity, after a decade its method seemed no more than one of the 'ripples on the surface of the broad yellow river' (p. 83) and its democracy merely a minor irritant to directorial intention. There had been no major shift in British theatre practice towards the democratic workshop approach, but the level of discussion surrounding the production methods on *Fanshen*, its screening on television and its repeated revival throughout the late seventies doubtless have contributed to the continued assimilation of Hare within a European tradition of political theatre. In 1988 Hare made his own view quite clear: 'the dialectical method by which we worked only works on dialectical material and companies come to grief when they try to be co-operatives with bourgeois subject matter'.[15]

Brecht might stand as the great mentor behind the 'tradition' of post-war drama marked 'Political' just as Beckett is placed at the head of a theoretical school of the 'Absurd', but he was neither Hare's nor Brenton's guiding light. The Berliner Ensemble first visited in 1956 – when Bill Gaskill saw and was undoubtedly influenced by them – and again in 1965, both before either Hare or Brenton were involved in theatre. Their influences were profoundly Anglo-Saxon. From Robert Bolt's *A Man for all Seasons* to Arden's *Serjeant Musgrave's Dance*, Britain's first wave of post-war anti-establishment playwrights had evolved a form of open staging for plays with public themes. Brenton cites the 7:84 production of Arden's play as an important one for him and spoke highly of Bond. As an undergraduate, Hare directed *Oh, What a Lovely War!*

If the pages of *Drama Review* were preoccupied with Brecht, the same is not true of the pages of *Theatre Quarterly* a decade later, where Snoo Wilson talks about 'Beckettian epic theatre' and David Edgar of the changing nature of theatrical ammunition. In throwing his Petrol Bombs through the Proscenium Arch, Brenton also throws them at Brecht. Although, almost twenty years later, Hare like Brenton also adapted *Galileo*, in his early career he chose instead the literary self-consciousness of Pirandello and *The Rules of the Game*. Against a setting of elegant doors and in the confines of the Almeida Theatre, Hare's version of *Galileo* became an intimate discussion on the responsibilities of knowledge, which was full of contemporary resonances but lacked Brecht's own 'alienation' techniques and historical specificity.

> The A-effect was achieved in the German theatre not only by the actor, but by the music (choruses, songs) and the setting (placards, films etc). It was principally designed to historicise the incidents portrayed and to reveal man as a function of the environment rather than a universal and eternal human constant.[16]

The titles in *Mother Courage and Her Children* inform the audience of events to come in order to free them from the suspense of plot and to liberate thought about what is being shown. In *Arturo Ui*, they are used to draw the parallel between the Chicago gangsters shown on stage and the real historical rise to power of Hitler. There the titles contextualise and generalise the action in the same way as *Brassneck*.

Far from disrupting the flow of the play, however, the captions in *Brassneck* ensure its continuity, enabling the audience in shorthand to understand where and when the scene is located. For Hare, 'Brecht, in deliberately breaking things up, seems to me not to be working in the best interest of epic.'[17] The photographs in *Brassneck* were both a substitution for elaborate stage settings, for naturalism, which is in any case unnecessary since – like all of David Hare's plays – *Brassneck* deals with a time within living memory of at least half of the population. If it was an epic model, however, as Brenton himself explained, 'the search for something other than what Brecht was doing goes on endlessly amongst the writers of my generation'.[18]

Alienation makes the natural or familiar seem remarkable. The details of revolution in a Chinese village are in any case alien to us. As Hare makes clear in his introduction to *The Asian Plays*, 'A European audience is asked to examine a process of change which is very different from anything which they might anticipate. But I try to retain every situation with which they might identify.' Man with a capital M rears his head and *Fanshen* is therefore, as Hare acknowledges, 'a classical play about revolution', interested in the very universals Brecht condemned.

The combination of almost ritualistic stylisation and slogan placards was evolved in the eclectic absorbant atmosphere of a work-shop. Just as *Fanshen* evokes the 'Agitprop' techniques of the Russian revolutionary theatre without becoming either agitation or propaganda, so it assumes Brecht without becoming Brechtian. In this way the politics of the revolution are declared, but the play itself does not become one-dimensional. Just as *The Great Exhibition* does not become exhibitionist because it uses the idea of exhibitionism as a metaphor for political disillusion, so *Fanshen* remains descriptive and not prescriptive. Hare is self-consciously evoking the naivety of political theatre techniques, and the dynam-ics of what is being repesented should not be mistaken for the dynamics of the representation.

In 1978, Hare clarified his opposition to the Marxist playwright who thinks that the play itself is part of the class struggle, and declared his allegiance, saying, 'To me this approach is rubbish, it insults the audience's intelligence; more important is it insults their experience; most important it is also a fundamental misunderstand-ing of what a play is.'[19] In this way, he tacitly rejects the declara-tions he made in *Brassneck* and in *Teeth 'n' Smiles*.

As Hare has said, the audience is not in the theatre to find out what someone on stage thinks or even what the writer thinks, 'they're there to find out what they think'. Hare therefore tried 'completely to obliterate myself' so that preconceptions about the writer should not intervene between the audience and their con-frontation with the play, and in 'Coming Out of a Different Trap', he made it clear that in this, *Fanshen* was part of a continuum from *Knuckle* .

> As you can't control people's reactions to your plays, your duty is also not to reduce people's reactions, not to give them easy handles with which they can pigeon-hole you, and come to comfortable terms with what you're saying.[20]

Brechtian theatre techniques are just another easy handle. Naturalism as Brecht found it has shifted its ground to become the dominant medium for cinema and television rather than the stage. The fact that the critics of *Fanshen* and *Brassneck* could bracket Hare with Brecht, and that the play is now marketed on his name, demonstrates that the latter has become as familiar as any other theatrical form. Brecht's technique has been dehistoricised and become a form of open staging; its English version of *A Man for All Seasons* is a school play in *Wetherby*. Near the end of his life, Brecht decided to stop using the term 'epic theatre' and to refer instead to 'dialectical theatre'.

For Hare the audience is to be assumed intelligent and, if their expectations are to be denied, one must be resourceful. If they enter the theatre expecting from *Fanshen* a simple one-dimensional message, their expectation is subverted by a complex open question; if they enter expecting from the writer of *Knuckle* a witty piece of social manners, they are confronted by the undeniable and challenging experience of alternative historiography where such manners do not apply.

Brecht fought very hard with the weapons of his time and that is still his challenge. Brenton and Hare were developing what Brenton termed 'An epic style that has nothing to do with Brecht.'[21] As Brenton makes clear they were simply after plays on public themes: 'I don't like the label "political play"', he declared. 'A better word for "political" is public.'[22] In the case of David Hare, a better word for 'political' is moral. 'My plays argue that the main reform needed is moral; at present people know they are damaging themselves by their behaviour, and need to change.'[23]

A classical play about revolution

Until the premiere of Joint Stock's *Fanshen*, William Hinton had ignored the adaptation of his book. Afterwards he confronted Hare with a list of 110 required changes. The result was a compromised and legally binding text of *Fanshen* and a permanent dialectic not only within the material of the revolution itself, but between its two authors.

Where Hinton had tried to be exhaustive of a particular moment in history, *Fanshen* makes a universal statement. The dual contradiction of putting history on the stage is that it cannot be epic and it cannot be past. There is therefore a tension within *Fanshen* between the Hinton play – an epic documentary about the specific historical phenomenon in this village, with its attendant evocation of the epic theatre tradition – and the Hare play, which is a well-made play in two acts, concerned with what happens in any village and the way any change takes place. Despite the naming in sections and numbers, *Fanshen* builds towards the longest section (Section Ten) and it follows the simple baddies-get-their-come-upance-in-the-end story of Wen-te and Yu-Lai. The play was a personal response to the book, and 'It never seemed to me a propagandist play but about two classical questions. How do the people get to limit the leaders; how do leaders get scrutinised by the led.'[24]

It seemed to Hare also a universal question of language, which was to become central to his work in *Teeth 'n' Smiles* and *Licking Hitler*. It is through metaphor that the Party persuades the people of the need for and possibility of fanshen. Metaphor is parasitic on ordinary language and stands in a critical relation to it. That metaphor remains in the mouths of the Party leaders until the final moment at which the turning over is clinched.

The debt of Hare's play to Hinton's book focuses not in the detail of the selection but in its truth claims. Inherited from Hinton is the object of seeking to present what happened to real people in the real world. The external existence of the characters and events is unquestioned, and this commits the play to an empirical belief in verifiable facts in the world. In the preface Yu-Lai announces, 'This is the book *Fanshen* by William Hinton' with the publisher and current price given. The events in the village of Long Bow are taken as objective facts of history and the book by Hinton, which filtered those facts, is not only acknowledged as source material, but taken as an accurate record. *Fanshen* makes use of the form of self-criticism adopted by the Chinese peasants in their struggle, but is not itself self-critical. In his introductory directions to producing companies, Hare writes:

> On stage people are defined by what they can and cannot do and say, as much as by what they can. Look through the text. See what is missing in their experience. Then see what is assumed. Hinton himself points to one simple example: nobody in the book ever questions the value of the revolution, they only question its direction.

Look at the play. See what is missing in Hare's experience. Then see what is assumed. Hare does not question the truth value of the book on which the play is based and which provided a shared basis for collaboration. So *Lay By* began with a newspaper article; *Brassneck* had its structure in Poulson and the Borgias; *Pravda* used Rupert Murdoch's takeover of *The Times*; and *The Absence of War* traced the defeat of the Labour Party in the 1992 general election.

If, then, the documentary mode attempts to conceal or simply does conceal its own 'lie' by failing to foreground this relativity, then it does so because it is accepted as the established mode for the presentation of 'truth'. Documentary can be nothing other than propaganda, an unselfconscious presentation towards a declared end. The facts it presents may indeed be correct, but they are not out there passively to be received. Facts only become facts when they are collated and ordered according to some purpose, whether by the historian like Hinton for a book or the playwright like Hare for a play. Brecht certainly understood this when he wrote:

> The chronicle play Mother Courage and her Children –
> with the term chronicle corresponding roughly to that of
> 'history' in Elizabethan drama – does not of course
> represent any kind of attempt to persuade anybody of
> anything by setting forth bare facts. Facts can very seldom
> be taught without their clothes on and, as you rightly say,
> they are hardly seductive. It is, however, necessary that
> chronicles should include a factual element, should be
> realistic.[25]

Like Brecht before them, Hare and Brenton do not consider themselves to be innovative. Brenton numbers himself among the the 'new Jacobeans'; in 1972 he undertook a version of *Measure for Measure* and has confirmed the importance of Shakespeare's use of multiple styles to his generation. Both he and Hare would seem to agree with Peter Brook that 'Our need in the post-Brecht theatre is to find a way forwards, back to Shakespeare.'[26]

In a close examination of, say, *Richard II*, as in *Brassneck* and *Fanshen*, one can find 'alienation' techniques such as soliloquy, gestus, the juxtaposition of scenes and absence of naturalistic illusion.

These were, however, the product of the 'natural' conditions of the pre-naturalistic stage of the time, just as for Hare and Brenton they were the product of the 'natural' conditions of life on the touring circuit, where literary values cannot survive long. Brecht's great contribution was to assimilate these techniques into a Marxist reading of theatre, but use of these techniques does not necessarily make a play into a Marxist reading.

If the documentary mode is a writer's mode and not the guarantor of unfiltered objectivity, then Hinton's *Fanshen* is naively taken to be a sacred text as an act of deliberate optimism in the year that *Teeth 'n' Smiles* was showing just how another revolution – that of the sixties generation – had failed. To this extent, then, Hare's own criticism of the theatrical Left applied to him and to *Fanshen* when he said, 'I felt it was utopian to go on creating left wing fantasies on stage. I found a creeping historicism wanting to set plays thousands of years ago in funny costumes as if they were saying they can't deal with the problems of today.'[27] One could say the same of setting plays thousands of miles away as if they were saying they can't deal with the problems of home.

The stage, however, necessarily 'exposes' the relativity of history (and relativity *per se* if you wish to see it) – it overcomes the definitional disjuncture between the categories 'history' and 'fiction', 'true' and 'false', making the status of each relative to the position of the observer. Despite the inclusion of slogans and the espousal of Hinton and China's optimism, the houselights which mark the end of a performance of *Fanshen* do not conclude a straight progressive line, but rather a cyclical repetition of the first scene. It is a play of and for the west and its critical thrust – as ever in Hare's work from this moment – lies not in its slogans but in the unanswered question, which deviates from the answered questions in *Fanshen*: 'What do you think about this?' (p. 84).

In placing the question within the context of an adaptation, however, Hare agreed that 'I'm in a morally doubtful position.'[28] He did not subsequently engage on an adaptation of Hinton's follow-up book *Shenfan,* and his play is in any case his own. The declaration within the text of *Fanshen* as adaptation is proleptic, then, a dishonest strategy, a way of evading responsibility so that any criticism levelled at it can be offset with the corollary, 'It's an adaptation.' Without Hare's interjection, there is still no obvious parallel to be made between the feudal society of China undergoing land reform in *Fanshen* and the complex capitalist post-industrial society in which Hare and his audiences live. As Hare said of explicit political theatre in his controversial condemnation of it in 1978, 'to flaunt your sincerity, to assert and re-assert a simple scaffolding of belief in order not to face the real and unpredictable dangers of a genuinely live performance is all a way of not being judged'.[29] As a piece of declared alternative historiography, *Fanshen* − on television and on stage − is 'safe' in its distance from us not only in time but in geography and culture, an anthropological curiosity and not a political imperative.

4   The people's war and peace

Picking up the dual inheritance of *Brassneck* and Angus Calder's *The People's War, Licking Hitler* and *Plenty* were written together as companion pieces for showing on television and at the National Theatre respectively in 1978. Coinciding with Hare's clear articulation of his aims as a writer in his lecture at King's College Cambridge, and the sustained dispossession of the tactics of the theatrical Left which it contained, it is at this point that Hare's history plays reach maturity. What both plays share, and share with works by several of Hare's contemporaries, is the use not only of history to find a perspective on the present but of women protagonists, both of which were set to continue in later work. Just as Hare's use of history can be seen as an evasion and the disguise of a deep nostalgia, so – although a major contribution to the British stage – his presentation of women is deeply problematic.

Licking Hitler: a war on two fronts

When it was first screened on BBC1 on 10 January 1978 *Licking Hitler* met with a level of acclaim previously unknown to Hare in Britain, and won for him the BAFTA award for Best Single Play of 1978. It is still regarded by many as his finest work. In an often praised introductory sequence, Hare introduces the main characters, the context of the war and the country house setting and conveys a complex set of signals about what is to come. A convoy of military vehicles jars its way past a classical sculpture; in the hall an elderly chauffeur and maid carry luggage out of the house while the camera tracks back down a corridor, through the servants' quarters and into the gun room near the back door. There Archie MacLean is standing in shirt sleeves calmly addressing the audience as 'loyal Germans'. His rhetoric becomes increasingly violent and the cumulative metaphor of the human sewer that is Germany culminates by establishing a vital connection between sexual deviation and political power.

The language and its content are heavily at odds with the setting and the accent, yet this abrasive Scot is engaged in something official, and even has a secretary. As MacLean turns to look out of the window, he sees a young girl, Anna Seaton, struggling with heavy suitcases in a deserted lane. She is contrasted immediately with the strong servicemen easily carrying suitcases into the house (shot six), and as Archie is describing the portrait of Goebbels, Anna's is the 'extraordinary face' (p. 15) we see. From the title and the disruptive nature of the visual information received comes the early warning that words are not necessarily to be trusted, and that the process of 'licking Hitler' is not to be one of 'arselicking'.

Dressed throughout in prim up-to-the-neck clothes, Anna is soon revealed as very sheltered, sexually unaware, practically incompetent and economically ignorant. Confronted with this relative of the Second Sea Lord, Archie sends her to make the tea. It is in that female territory of the kitchen (and in one scene in Eileen's bedroom) that Anna's friendship with the secretary, Eileen, blossoms. Each of the different levels in *Licking Hitler* has its own location within the country house. The social niceties of servants and piano-playing occur in the dining room and the drawing room, where the old order carries on, despite the inconveniences of the war. There, the besuited Fennel explains to the new arrivals and to the audience that 'This is a research unit within the Political Warfare Executive' (p. 18).

The unit exists to disseminate counter-propaganda. If propaganda is to be effective, however, mere contradiction is not sufficient, since 'You fight a war, you expect propaganda, you expect your enemy to tell you lies' (p. 21). More subtle deceit is required and a British counter-propaganda broadcast will be made to seem an apparently private conversation between two loyal German officers. As Archie sits framed by the window (shot ten) next to the portrait of Goebbels, the parallel is drawn and, in the longest speech of the play, Langley makes clear the self-conscious muck-raking of their work: 'And if this involves throwing a great trail of aniseed across Europe, if it means covering the whole continent in obloquy and filth ... then that is what we shall do' (p. 48).

To this end, the emotive repetition and the assonance of Archie's tirade (p. 30) will be used to send millions to their deaths on the Russian front and, in order to weaken civilian morale inside Germany, attacks will become ever more personal until, finally, the actual/plausible exploitation of privilege by the Burgomaster of Cologne is constructed through a speculative/implausible leather fetishism.

The factual base for such campaigns was *Black Boomerang*, an account by Sefton Delmer of the black propaganda units which he directed. Hare, however, has no intention of creating a documentary reconstruction. In his introduction to *The History Plays,* he explained that 'Although I was thrilled by Angus Calder's proof in *The People's War* that it was the war itself which educated the working class towards the great Labour victory of 1945, I must also, if I am honest, admit that the urge to write about it came as much from a romantic feeling for the period: for its violence, its secrecy and, above all, its sexuality.'

Hare's war-time thriller of the fictional German soldier whose call-sign is 'Otto Abend Eins' is played out in close-up in a converted billiards room. Earlier Archie had stood surrounded by decaying sports equipment. 'The game is. [*sic*] This is a radio station' (p. 20). The game metaphor, which was evident in *Brassneck*, has become central to Hare's point and the country house a deeply suggestive metaphor. As Archie says, 'this house is the war' (p. 46); it is a microcosm of the war effort and of British society.

If Minton, the owner of the house, is the old aristocracy – decayed, unable to speak and deaf to the changes in society – Will Langley, a half-blue in fencing hoping for Olympic honours, and a commanding officer, is part of a new social elite. In contrast, Archie is a working-class lad who has fought his way up as a journalist and hates the environment he finds himself in. He is a Scot and, for Hare, the Scots were fighting not only the north–south divide, but the class war.

Archie is the 'savage' tolerated for the duration, just as the women are admitted to the male preserve only temporarily. As Anna looks uncomfortable sipping her beer out of a pint mug, she in some sense shares Archie's isolation, and Archie's look at Anna cements the special relationship between them. They both speak German and Anna is, then, a mediator – the upper-class woman. After her departure, the final killing of Otto is enacted in German without translation (although its meaning is clear).

These detailed and satisfyingly suggestive, overlapping metaphors of the house, the Second World War and the class war, achieved in this economical pattern of visual juxtaposition, scene paralleling and allusion without schematising the individuals who comprise it, account for the success of *Licking Hitler*. They do not, however, account for its point.

On the first night a drunken Archie bursts into Anna's room, declaring 'I'll smash a bloody bottle *in* yer if yer bloody come near me' (p. 21, my italics). Similarly, lit only by the half light of the romantic moon, Anna's bedroom resembles that of the wireless room. The two are linked together as sanctioned invasions and clandestine excitement, and at the very heart of the narrative Archie rapes her. There is no intimacy between them. She looks ravished, still calls him Mr MacLean, and confesses to Eileen, 'I don't know what he thinks about anything. We've never had a conversation. We just have a thing' (p. 44).

Archie is both exerting the conventional power of men over women and – like Jimmy Porter in his ambiguous relationship with Alison in *Look Back in Anger* – is taking a hostage from the class war. Just as Alison decides to stay with Jimmy, however, it is Anna's realisation that 'I don't know anything' (p. 33) which leads her deliberately to leave the door to her bedroom (and implicitly her legs) open. Anna takes a conscious decision to acquire sexual knowledge to complete her growth from girl to woman. The rape itself takes place between shots and the camera is not a voyeur.

Just as in grief Eileen could no longer bear to perpetuate the means of her brother's death, the awakening in Anna is more than sexual: for the first time she refuses to obey Archie, she finds a perspective from which to begin to question the validity of their work. As Hare says, 'I write love stories. Most of my plays are that. Over and over again I have written about romantic love because it never goes away. And the view of the world it provides, the dislocation it offers, is the most intense experience that many people know on earth.'[1] It is through a woman's first experience of love that Hare has found a distance on the war-time thriller he has written.

In a pattern which is to occur repeatedly throughout Hare's work from this point, Anna has become the (female) preserver of the 'radical' values of truth and decency against the (male) manipulators. As well as serving to move the action forwards and capturing her early isolation, the two montage sequences to the melancholy Chopin 'Waltz in A Minor' (prompted by 'Somebody talk to me' (p. 27) and the pain of her bruises (p. 39)) grant her a unique position within the narrative.

Because a man affected by emotion, by contemplation, by humanity is an unbalanced man, and because he cannot work if he thinks, Archie tells a lie. The cumulative distortion and perversion required for his job are translated into his personal life, public and private worlds merge; truth is no longer of any consequence. The screen is blank and an off-screen voice informs the audience that 'Five months later in July 1942, Otto Abend Eins made his final broadcast' (p. 49).

Licking Hitler differs from conventional war films not only in being scaled down in a single location but in bringing the characters up to date. In the fast-forwards coda at the end Archie is seen to betray his origins in poverty on Clydeside by producing exploitation feature films. The class he hated is still firmly in control, with John Fennel seen resuming a career in politics and Will Langley becoming a world-famous thriller writer. The audience can speculate that Archie might be John Schlesinger in disguise, that Fennel is Crossman and Langley is Ian Fleming, but Hare deliberately avoids giving enough information to allow these sources fully to be deciphered.

The voice-over serves to generalise the metaphoric events of one propaganda unit to show that its wartime deceit has become the norm of the post-war professions of education, politics and the media. The (re)presentation of the past becomes explicitly a way of understanding the present. In making this explicit, however, Hare seems to slip into the same failure that Archie had earlier identified for propaganda, by preaching where he should allow people to overhear, but the ending of *Licking Hitler,* where the penultimate lines go to Anna Seaton, is far more ambiguous than it might at first appear.

Shown in stills, Anna's fragmented 'future' of divorce, promiscuity and rural retreat is visually consistent with the montage sequences. Rejecting her upbringing, her class and its professions of advertising and politics, she is isolated still within that 'honest life'. The process of that post-war dissent stands in embryo waiting to be born in the story of Susan Traherne and *Plenty.*

In her final lines, Anna has apparently achieved the same status as the documentary-style authorial voice-over, commenting from a position of knowledge on the distant (historical and political) events. But, despite her privileged position, Anna remains part of the fiction, part of the love story which Hare controls and, like Archie, trapped in myths about her own past. We see what she cannot see and she does not have the last word.

The voice-over by its very nature makes a truth claim not for the characters but for the voice itself. That voice is David Hare's own. The lies perpetrated by the wartime wireless station have already been distinguished from the BBC's 'literal attitude to the truth' and thus from the writer's own medium. That distinction is vital for Hare for, as Archie says, it is 'from that trust our influence will grow' (p. 21).

Hare ensures that trust – as Trevor Griffiths was also to do in *Country* – by writing a traditional country house drama containing both a love story and a thriller. A scene-by-scene analysis of the printed text of *Licking Hitler* reveals that – despite the use of film – *Licking Hitler* has a conventional three-act structure with epilogue hidden within its seventy-six shots. The first act (fifteen sides) comprises six scenes (of which the first broadcast of straight propaganda is the longest) and concludes with a black-out after the first loneliness montage sequence. The second of twelve sides ends with a black-out after the second social montage sequence. The third act (ten sides) is fifteen sides with the epilogue (with Anna's dismissal the longest at some three sides), punctuated with a blank screen and followed by a final montage of shots of the deserted house. The black-outs and blank screens are curtains falling between the three acts and the central and pivotal point in this symmetrical structure is the violent seduction of Anna between shots forty and forty-one (p. 34). It is a single play, but one which expresses oppositions not normally found on television.

If the thriller within *Licking Hitler* finds a resolution with the death of Otto Abend Eins, the love story does not. Archie's failure to reply to Anna's letter turns the question of Hess into the question of Archie, an inversion which, like the theatrical parody Hare had effected in *Slag*, *The Great Exhibition* and *Knuckle*, is dependent on the very health of the formal language to tolerate such break-downs. The plays 'are intended as puzzles – the solution of which is up to the audience'.[2]

In its ambiguity *Licking Hitler* is differentiated from Ian McEwan's *The Imitation Game*, which was directed by Richard Eyre and screened as a *Play for Today* on BBC1 on 24 April 1980, in which middle-class girl Cathy Raine goes to work as a wireless operator at Bletchley signal station. Where Hare puts class as the primary category in the relationship between Archie and Anna, McEwan sets about deciphering another of society's codes – patri-archy. Anna Seaton is a vulnerable sheltered child of nineteen. Although the same age, Cathy Raine is from the outset a defiant teenager critical of male domination of women and of the false morality of war which those traditional roles enshrine. To Hare, such articulacy was simply unconvincing, because 'I value research over ideology.'[3]

The Imitation Game deliberately reappropriated history as her-story, a project undertaken for feminist women and sympathetic men. In contrast *Licking Hitler* was criticised by feminists for the fact that a woman chooses to go on making and making love to a man who has originally taken her by rape. Hare's response – that Anna is the 'conscience of the play'[4] – is inadequate for the simple reason that the feminist point is not that Anna's seduction parallels the intellectual discovery of the harsh realities of life, but that her 'education' should be 'wi' a broken bottle'. They object to the fact that Hare has chosen to make Anna learn by the physical pain of the rape, has chosen to make her learning process sado-masochis-tic.

The insufficiency of Hare's disclaimer becomes increasingly evident as one examines the body of his work. What was already clear was that if Hare was making a reappropriation of the war then it was not specifically for women. 'I try to show the English their history', he wrote. 'I write tribal pieces, trying to show how people behaved on this island, off this continental shelf, in this century. How this Empire vanished, how these ideals died.'[5] Those who lived through the war could judge the authenticity of the people's post-war plays, which started with *Brassneck*, next to their own experience. The point is precisely that – however at home they might feel with that time as writers – Hare and his contemporaries had not lived through the war. Their experience was rather the Suez crisis of 1956, the fizzling out of sixties idealism and the failure of trade union militancy in the early 1970s. It was to explain their perceived disinheritance and betrayal that they went back to the moment in which the clear ideological divisions of the 1930s became clouded by annihilation and propaganda.

What distinguishes *Brassneck*, *Licking Hitler* and *Plenty* from the rest of the post-war plays derived from Calder, and indeed from *Knuckle*, is their very scope. Hare was surveying the whole of post-war Britain, explicitly determined to use that past to explain his/our present. David Hare set himself the task of being that chronicler and to reinstate a belief in change for the generations for whom, after Jimmy Porter, there seemed not only no good causes left, but no possibility of good causes. Christopher Hampton made the point in his version of George Steiner's *The Portage to San Christobal of A.H.* that 'the reason your generation's so dim and cautious is that we used up all the risks. We drank so deep of history, there's very little left in the bottle.'[6]

What was left in the bottle was a mythical version of the war perpetrated in television drama serials such as *A Family at War* and *Secret Army*, and comedies such as *Dad's Army,* which every person who lived through these years knows, at least in part, to be false. In order to intervene directly at the point of their consumption it was to television that *Country*, *The Imitation Game* and *Licking Hitler* turned.

The ways in which the television construction of history bolsters a specifically bourgeois ideological need is covered in Colin McArthur's succinct monograph *Television and History*, but the title of *A Family at War* sums up the construction of the past and present of British society on offer in the drama serial. It is a history where external events are peripheral to the individuals and their key social formation of The Family.

The audience for such programmes is large (up to 20 million) and it comprises a much higher proportion of 'working-class' viewers than most theatres could ever hope for. For the majority of the people drama means television drama and it is to address this audience that Trevor Griffiths has, since 1976, virtually abandoned theatre, preferring to attack what he sees as capitalism's strongest point with a 'strategic penetration' – injecting socialist content into the flow of viewing and into the familiar dramatic experience of mass-populist forms. In this process, writing about the past becomes a way of avoiding or minimising censorship. Griffiths' plays are, like Hare's, well made and mount to a dramatic climax.

Such an injection of an alternative does nothing to counter the individualistic appropriation of history as the story of great men; it simply alters the men. In addition, *A Family at War* was a long-running serial and not a single play. The audience for, say, *Play for Today* was neither so large (at a maximum of around 8 million) nor as diverse as the serial/series audience, a fact which compromises Griffiths' intention and which may have contributed to his decision to write the serial about a Labour MP, Bill Brand.

The activities of the black propaganda units are little known, and to that extent *Licking Hitler* and *The Imitation Game* have a revelatory function, but Hare explicitly denies that he has a penetrative strategy or indeed any plan. Where Griffiths sees an ideological (state) apparatus defended tooth and nail because of its great power of hegemony, Hare sees a petrified medium run by journalists who have made an unhealthy pact with government in the attempt to preserve public broadcasting. Hare objects not to political censorship but to bargaining 'two buggers for a shit' as he did over *Brassneck*.

As a result, he was determined to protect *Licking Hitler* from the institutional pressures of the ghetto of good taste and waited a year to direct it himself at BBC Birmingham. He wanted film for its wit and flexibility and he wanted to confront the BBC moguls with a *fait accompli*. To that extent, then, Hare did effect a strategic pene-

tration. For Griffiths the point is political; for Hare it is artistic ego-
ism.

That ego might be flattered by a large audience, but Hare's
choice of the medium of television for *Licking Hitler* was motivated
not so much by the desire to reach a mass audience (which is in any
case at a great distance from the writer and not confronted as a mass
but individually at the fireside), or to raise consciousness (which he
considers already achieved), but by the demands of the setting, the
demands of the art. In *Licking Hitler*, the medium is the message, but
'because the message of the film is to say distrust everything you
hear; whatever you hear, somebody has manufactured in order to
peddle some particular point of view; then, if this is true, whose
point of view is this film peddling and who's making it?'[7] A concern
with the writer's medium itself comes to the heart of Hare's work.

Certainly, it relies on the convention of the middle-class establishment male voice-over to convey truth, but does not fill that
convention with an 'alternative' message. It rather provides the
critical distance on events needed for judgement and simultaneously asks us to offer such judgement, but without directing that
judgement to a specific end. The writer is offering himself up as a
moral voice in an age which finds doubt more appropriate, not as a
purveyor of a different 'truth', but, as Hare was to explore in *A
Map of the World*, as an exposer of lies. The process in which Hare
perceives himself to be engaged is, therefore, not one of penetration of an alternative message, but one of mischief.

Since the screening of *Country* in 1981, there have been far
fewer programmes about the war. The more recent popular comedy series about that time, *'Allo 'Allo*, is a parody of the genre's
former self (*Secret Army*) and when *World at War* was last repeated it
was to the much smaller Channel 4 audience. Whether *Licking
Hitler* and the other single plays contributed to the process or were
'allowed' their say in some kind of Marcusean 'repressive tolerance', as Griffiths believes and Hare had intimated in *How Brophy
Made Good*, is irrelevant, since the result is the same. If penetration
is to remain strategic and not be relabelled as absorption, if the
writers are not to become middle-aged and/or reactionary, they
must constantly find new subversions and/or new places to put
them.

Country was intended as the first in a series of dramas which was never made. The better to reach his working-class target audience, Trevor Griffiths returned to the drama serial with his adaptation of D. H. Lawrence's *Sons and Lovers* and, in *The Last Place on Earth*, took on television history at its strongest point – the prime-time serial about a great historical individual. Meanwhile, Alan Bleasdale, whose *Boys from the Blackstuff* used video to create in Yosser Hughes a new anti-hero for the eighties, attempted an alternative look at the Edwardian certainties of *Upstairs Downstairs* and the First World War in *The Monocled Mutineer*, and the series stood at the centre of the increasing number of rows between the BBC and the government as Mrs Thatcher's second term came to an end. Despite being asked to write a series about the sixties, Hare has not taken up the offer.

As Fennel says of the unit in *Licking Hitler,* so might we say of Hare's work: 'I'm afraid you will know very little about the success or failure of your work. You are throwing stones into a pond which is a very long way away. And there will be almost no ripples … Perhaps even when the war is over you will not know what good you did' (p. 18). And, like Archie, Hare seems less interested in measuring the final score at the end of the game than in playing it.

Plenty: a life in dissent

His first original play for the National Theatre, *Plenty* picks up where *Licking Hitler* left off: it begins Hare's exploration of the nature and implications of reaction and opposition and establishes as the key figure a woman who serves as a reflection of a disjuncture in the society of which she is part. 'The clearest way I can describe *Plenty* is as a play about the cost of spending your whole life in dissent.'[8]

Plenty has two beginnings, which are in different ways mysterious. In Scene One we have no doubt where we are, as one of the two women on stage says, 'The wet. The cold. The flu. The food. The loveless English.' A man lies naked on the floor of a house which has been stripped bare. The play is beginning at an end.

There has been violence; there is not only rejected but latent sexuality. More questions are added with the second opening when we see a British undercover agent make a parachute drop into occupied France to be greeted by a young English Resistance agent. The unifying element is clear by Scene Three: it is a woman, and the opening scenes are deliberately disjointed snatches from her life.

The dates are given in the programme of *Plenty* and onstage in a sophisticated pattern of carefully chosen period detail. After the flash forwards, the play works in straight chronological order from 1943 to 1962, from Susan's experiences behind enemy lines in France to her withdrawal into that past following the end of her marriage with Brock. The role of that flash forward is – as it was in the television version of *Brassneck* – to replace the suspense of what happens in favour of the analysis of how and why it happens.

In the war, Susan camouflaged her feelings for survival; after the war they are trapped beneath the uncracking veneer of English politeness, a deep-rooted inability to face life as it truly is, an hypocrisy. In France, she told such glittering lies; afterwards – as Brock is asked to decide whether to tell Tony's wife about his affair with Susan – 'It makes no difference. Lie or don't lie. It's a matter of indifference' (p. 26); it's a way of getting Susan into bed. Where the lies of France concealed a greater truth and purpose (that of defeating Hitler), 'where's the fun of lying for a living?' (p. 44).

When Susan first meets Brock in the British Embassy in Brussels, they seem to share an impatience and irreverent black humour about the post-war reconstruction and about his superior, Darwin. In the four years which intervene between Scenes Three and Four, however, Brock asserts that if Sir Leonard is a joke, 'He's a joke between us. He is not a joke to the entire world' (p. 35). If he is a joke, it is to be shared with him. It is with Alice, however, that Susan now shares her sense of humour.

It is in Scene Four, the longest in the play, that it becomes clear that these women are forging a bohemian lifestyle of jazz culture and of active, unrepressed sexuality. The line 'You excite me' (p. 66) has been taken to suggest that Susan and Alice were having a lesbian relationship; there is no evidence of this anywhere else in the play.

Like Maggie in *Teeth 'n' Smiles* and Caroline in *Dreams of Leaving*, Susan chooses to sleep with men she does not know, as she did in the war; Alice talks casually of venereal disease and unwanted pregnancy and is the forerunner of the 1960s hippies – love and let love and float through life living off others and off your head. The encounters with Lazar and Mick take place outdoors – outside the convention of marriage, outside the middle-class confines of wife or mistress. As Susan and Mick go off together at the end of Scene Five, the point is reinforced by the repetition of the earlier exchange with Lazar about the beauty of the mackerel sky (p. 43). Susan's liaisons with Brock are firmly within those confines where she can only gaze longingly out at it.

As Alice says, 'I had an idea that lust ... that lust was very good. And could be made simple. And cheering. And light. Perhaps I was simply out of my time' (p. 76). They are indeed both out of their time, speaking the language of the seventies. Hare therefore opens himself up to the same criticism that he levelled at Ian McEwan and *The Imitation Game*. When the writer admits as much himself, saying 'it was a great deal of instinct and not a lot of research',[9] one begins to suspect that history is a diversionary smokescreen cast by Hare to authenticate his imaginary creations.

They talk like adult women – about Brock's penis, about the clitoris – in a way few male writers present and in a way that the aspiring Brock finds uncomfortable. He speaks the stilted language of a 'bit of a tight corner' and 'one hell of a spot', and cannot bring himself to use the word 'prick'. His English is still that of public school gentility, the *coup de grâce* of Leonard Darwin and Sir Andrew Charleson, of a profession which – if it no longer has a blooded belief in the imperial values – accommodates pragmatic ambition of making money and career from the remains of Empire.

When Mick complains that 'you people are cruel' and 'dangerous' (p. 48), he means a gender and not a class. Within *Plenty* female idealism is anti-establishment only because it is anti-male. If Susan were able to have a baby by herself, she would. It is only as second best that, as the fireworks are about to go off for the Festival of Britain in 1951, which is one of Hare's own earliest memories, she chooses working-class Mick for the job of conception. In the following scene, however, the efforts of Mick and Susan to conceive are shown to have failed – Susan's independence of men and of their establishment has failed. Although the dramatis personae lists her as Susan Traherne, she is never called by her maiden name. With that infertility, however, something else has failed, the 'united' victorious Britain, which was celebrated in the Festival of Britain.

Where the Second World War was honourable, Suez was dishonourable. The rhetoric which had controlled the British Empire collapses under its own weight; Darwin's sexist affronts to Madame Wong are no longer disguised as gentility, his racism no longer disguised as paternalism. That language again is out of tune with the genteel environment, but it is a particular form of language which has fallen apart. Susan has fractured the etiquette with an imagistic language of parachutists descending from the cold night sky and expletives are used only when Brock finally explodes at her. He is expressing not a permanent state of non-communication, but the breakdown in a marriage and a career (p. 56).

It is the plenty of the title, in the form of an opulent dinner party on the eve of the Suez crisis, which stands at the heart of the play. 'Everything is up for grabs. At last. We will see some changes. Thank the Lord' (p. 57). It is at this point, supporting Susan's hope for change, that the interval comes and the funeral which opens Scene Eight (after the interval) is not only for Leonard Darwin but for his (old) age of the Empire, turning the feast into a wake. Hare, like Susan, welcomes the death rattle of the ruling classes, the exposure of the sham, and of the days of plenty which Brock believed in.

Susan's position is that of Hare himself, a moral critic sitting on the contradiction of being part of that which you wish to criticise. For Hare, the National Theatre 'always seemed to me the best place for new writers, both because of the scale on which you could write, and because of the audience you could reach'.[10] That audience is highly educated, affluent and influential.

In 1978 there were few major roles in contemporary plays for women; even fewer at the National Theatre. Susan's complex and ambivalent character is calculated to slip through audience expectation, to 'avoid giving them easy handles with which they can pigeon-hole you, and come to comfortable terms with what you are saying'.[11] As Susan says to Brock, 'I should have come here this evening and sat with my legs apart, pretended to be a scarlet woman, then at least you would have been able to place me' (p. 26). Instead, they get a calculated shock with Alice talking of 'Turkey neck and turkey gristle' while holding Brock's penis between her fingers in the first scene. 'From then on', says Hare, 'the audience should see that it's a way of looking at things which is almost upended.'[12] David Hare is not interested in women in and for themselves, but uses them to provide a moral distance on events over which they have no power.

Each historical moment in Susan's life is expressed through her 'relationship' with a man – it was an exciting affair with Lazar in 1943; an empty affair with Tony in 1947; a sordid affair with Mick in 1951; a hollow marriage with Darwin in 1956 and a confrontation with Charleson in 1962. And it is because of their attitude to and relationships with the men, rather than for any articulated perceptions, that Susan and Alice carry the oppositional thrust of the play. Hare has schematised his female characters to make his historical point. Women are, for Hare, a way to contextualise his own pain; they are surrogate men, as he almost confesses when he says, 'I find women's attitudes after the neuroses and hang-ups of male society a tremendous relief.'[13]

With the passing of Empire, however, 'there is little to believe in. Behaviour is all' (p. 72). Dissent is not allowed and those who make too much noise are silenced. By the time of Suez, Susan has already been hospitalised. Even Alice refers to Susan's outburst as 'psychiatric cabaret'. And the literal centre of the play (rather than the placing of the interval) comes at the end of Scene Seven when Mick asserts 'She is actually mad' (p. 48). The tendency to read Susan as mad cannot be dismissed, for the remaining scenes of the play crumble from the central point in parallel with Susan's failing grip on reality and Brock's failing career.

Hare has elsewhere acknowledged that 'I do believe that people do go clinically mad if what they believe bears no relation to how they live.'[14] So Susan has partially internalised her frustration as illness early in the play and Mick's statement, far from being denied, is even supported by Brock in what feels like the last word on Susan in Scene Ten as he threatens to have her committed.

It is Susan's memory which has articulated the constant parallel between the events in France in 1943-4 (twelve sides of text) and the betrayal of 'peace and plenty' up to 1962 (seventeen sides). It is this memory which makes the betrayal of the promise 'there will be days and days like this' (p. 86) completely authentic and, in one sense at least, unfalsifiable. When they meet in the same half light of that first drop in France some twenty years earlier, Lazar – rising from the dead like his namesake, Lazarus – appears to confirm Susan's desperate belief that there's 'Somebody else who's been living like me' (p. 83).

As he begins to explain how he has given in 'Always. All along the line. Suburb. Wife. Hell' (p. 83), Susan slips away – unkissed – not into a memory but a drug-induced hallucination of a French hillside. With the literal blowing apart of the stage set which is any fictional character's reality, she completely lets go of the present in a vision of what might have been, literally loses her mind.

Because of this, Susan does not provide a firm focus for evaluation of that betrayed vision. Her idealism is in one sense unfocused and in another simply that of a (mad) woman inside the male establishment of England. The survivors are not the women. Alice (like Anna in *Licking Hitler*) implicitly admits the failure of her own position by turning instead to helping the young victims of her free love philosophy – unmarried mothers of whom Dorcas is the inadequate representative within the play. It is the Charlesons, like Patrick in *Knuckle* and Langley in *Licking Hitler*, who survive and with them the English political game remains as an end in itself.

Hare's evident nostalgia for a time when change seemed possible masks an ambivalence to the (male) certainties of the England Susan challenges and the National Theatre England in which he now finds himself. Through Brock he throws the idea like gauntlet to the audience: 'Which is the braver? To live as I do? Or never, ever to face life like you?' (p. 78). Twenty-two years after Suez and *Look Back in Anger*, twenty-seven years after the Festival of Britain, railing at such events was its own kind of theatrical cliché – the belatedly Angry and somewhat self-indulgent Young Man. Hare is sitting on the poles of contemporary drama from the epic/political, in which people are pawns of great forces, and the ahistorical/absurd, where the individual is all there is. Sitting, like

Susan, on the paradox of luxuried discontent, criticising from within, Hare is saying with her 'I'd like to change everything but I don't know how' (p. 31), and ending up with the same intuitive response that 'England can't always be like this' (p. 41).

> We are living through a great, groaning, yawling festival of change – but because this is England it is not always seen on the streets. In my view it is seen in the extraordinary intensity of peoples' personal despair, and it is to that despair that as a historical writer I choose to address myself time and time again: in *Teeth 'n' Smiles*, in *Knuckle*, in *Plenty*.[15]

To address himself to it, he uses individuals as the focus for the action; he confronts the objective crisis of the system through the subjective responses of individuals within it:

> We are drawing close, I think, to what I hope a playwright can do. He can put people's sufferings in a historical context; and by doing that, he can help to explain their pain. But what I mean by history will not be the mechanized absolving force theorists would like it to be; it will be those strange uneasy factors that make a place here and nowhere else, make a time now and no other time.[16]

In that juxtaposition lies the potential for a reappropriation of that past for the writer or for the reader and a potentially challenging effect. The truth for Hare is not, like Piscator's, to be told in the experiences of the masses on the world stage of history, nor by replacing plot and character with the presentation of factual material; the truth for him is to be found precisely in 'a few individualized characters acting out their private destinies'.[17]

In placing emphasis on the pain of the individual and not the historical context, Hare is in danger of subsuming history within the personal, subsuming change within despair and of having a comforting and ultimately reassuring apolitical effect. This became clearer when, in 1983, Fred Schepisi and RKO took up the film option of *Plenty* and Hare himself wrote the screenplay. Hare describes the play as 'a film script for the stage'[18] and contextualised it within film culture alongside Fassbinder's *The Marriage of Maria Braun*. Despite pushing the proscenium Lyttleton Theatre to its limits, the stylistic result of the jolting time-switches and the flash-back of *Plenty* was still to leave the action with an annoying habit of occurring between scenes.

The result of the transfer to film, however, was the removal of the opening scene and with it the historical and disruptive frame-work, leaving a simple chronological movie that tipped the balance against the fruitful contradiction of the stage version. This shift in emphasis was consolidated by the inclusion of a gratuitous location section during Brock's diplomatic mission in Jordan, where Susan is shown literally out of her mind and controlled by drugs. It was clinched by shifts in emphasis within scenes. Where, in the play, Susan is in control of the opening drop in wartime France, think-ing of arranging a bicycle, being asked the French for a 'mackerel sky', telling Lazar not to look at her so that he could not identify her if caught, in the film all these lines go to Lazar.

The lines of the original scenes were substantially unaltered as Tracey Ullman rescued Alice from the sixties groove for eighties pragmatism; Sting romanticised the working-class Mick, and Sir John Gielgud as Darwin and Ian McKellen as Sir Andrew delivered the loaded innuendo to such perfection that the scenes in the Foreign Office became the most memorable part of the film, pro-ducing a purely comic rather than an incisive effect. Where Kate Nelligan had worked all Hare's central women of the seventies from an assumption of strength rather than neurosis, Meryl Streep has built her reputation, in films such as *The French Lieutenant's Woman,* on women whose romanticism and/or politics have led to their destruction. Susan became a martyr to that mythology while Charles Dance rectified the balance against Brock. Oozing histori-cal setting, including a jazz club unseen in the play, revelling in the coronation rather than the more specific Festival of Britain, and showing the sexual encounters with Lazar and Mick amidst a swirl of romantic music, *Plenty* became Hollywood product. The absorption was completed by Andrew Osmond's pulp novel which fleshed out a post-war life for Lazar and filled in all gaps with mushy individualistic, ahistorical, romanticised descriptions.

Hare's is a self-conscious subversion of the myth of post-war change and, with Susan, he is insisting 'Don't creep around the furniture – look at me and make a judgement' (p. 26). If the audience looks and judges Susan mad, then Hare's upending is not complete; it is either less strategic or less penetrating than he anticipated. If, in 1978, putting a woman in that position was sufficient for the play to be controversial by 1982, when *Plenty* went to Broadway, it had become the fashionable thing for male playwrights in mainstream theatre to do; by 1985, when *Pravda* went on at the National and the film version of *Plenty* was released, it was an ineffective cliché. As Hare has identified, something happened between the two productions which led him to redress the balance between the cost of Susan's dissent and that of Brock's assimilation. Looking retrospectively, one can see the turn of the tide in the election of the conservative governments of Margaret Thatcher and Ronald Reagan, which made fighting less attractive than accommodation.

If *Plenty* had ever been a controversial political play within its English theatre context, it is not clear that Hare put up much of a fight to preserve its politics. Hare even prefigured the result in *A Map of the World* as he prepared the screenplay in 1983, when Victor Mehta comments on the adaptation of his novel to the screen: 'A moral story has been reduced to the status of a romance, transformed to a vulgar medium and traduced. Very well. It is what one expects. One looks to the cinema for money, not for enlightenment. And to be fair, the money has arrived' (*Map*, p. 75).

5 Sense of an ending

Saigon: Year of the Cat was the product of two periods of Hare's own life as an expatriate. He was in Vietnam in 1973 on an aborted commission for the BBC and, in America in 1979, during a self-imposed exile after the writing of *Plenty,* he found a country re-appraising the inheritance of the Vietnam war through films such as *The Deer Hunter* and *Apocalypse Now.* They were not, he believed, true to the Vietnam he had known.

   Saigon was one of the most expensive television films to date and its making was prolonged and difficult. After failing to interest an American network, it was finally screened on Thames Television on 29 November 1983, some four years after the script was completed. This delay explains its thematic similarities (a war, a love affair, a betrayal) to *Plenty* and *Licking Hitler,* while its moment of screening reinforces its position as a hinge between the history plays and Hare's drawing of a new *Map of the World*, when he put aside questions of class for those of nationality, and historical in favour of geographical distance.

Casablanca?

The opening of *Saigon* is a sustained pastiche of the seminal wartime melodrama, *Casablanca.* Just as the credits had rolled over a map of Africa to music swirling with Arab rhythms before merging into the French national anthem and the globe had turned as a voice-over followed the trail of wartime refugees across Europe, so, amidst swirling smoke, *Saigon* has the title superimposed on the oriental dragon and the drum rhythm echoing of the American

75

Civil War films, the camera zooms in on 'the old French city, Saigon'. It is 1974, the Vietnam war is continuing and only a small contingent of Americans remain in the capital.

In *Saigon,* as in *Casablanca*, the war is to have barely any existence outside of the main expatriate protagonists; at the opening, it is not even the city which is seen but bedclothes; not a Vietnamese face or an American soldier, but that of a white woman. Stephen Frears' camera pans through an elegantly colonial living room and over the siesta bed to the accompaniment of the piano tinkling an echo of 'Love is the Sweetest Thing'. It reaches the face of Judi Dench as her melancholic and very genteel English voice begins.

Following her siesta, Barbara walks through the bustling streets and beneath a banner advertising *Love Story*. The camera is on her throughout, with the Vietnamese street vendors simply wallpaper. The style of these early shots – the camera roving over her apartment and her body like the eyes of an admirer – is adopted to establish Barbara as a desirable agent, silkily sexy with passion seething beneath the calm, controlled suburban exterior. That, at almost 50, she is a romantic heroine desirable to younger men is reinforced by her colleague Donald's furtive attempts to ask her out and his emotional confession at the end of part one before leaving for Hong Kong.

Barbara's world of the apartment, the bank and the Cercle Sportif, which comprises the whole of the twenty-eight shots of the first section, are those of the old colonial city with an atmosphere of exotic half-light and slatted blinds, wafting fans and persistent crickets. Standing outside the door of the Cercle Sportif while Frank gives the prostitutes money, as she has asked, Barbara's face fills the screen. Behind her, entering the frame in a pool of cigarette smoke, is her Rick – Bob Chesneau. He offers her a ride home in his car and in a carefully constructed set of parallels, there is jasmine, beauty, romance and sexual attraction against an exotic location. The kiss is delayed but, when it comes amongst its crescendo of strings, it substitutes for sexual intercourse with just the kind of tasteful decency Hare had claimed to despise. When we next see them, they are in bed together.

With consummate economy, the audience glimpses in the Cercle Sportif the extremes of prostitution and affluence caused by the war and the American presence. The colonial certainty is undermined by the restless movement of the camera, which pans rapidly along the bar exactly as it has just panned over the tellers in the bank. The effect is a feeling of vague unease, a feeling that something or someone is alien. The technique comes to fruition at the New Year party at Ockham's house when the bars of the bank are echoed by the railings to his house: the camera runs along the outside like the eyes of excluded Vietnamese catching a glimpse of forbidden territory.

It is for this fluidity (and after his own attempts with *Licking Hitler* and *Dreams of Leaving*) that Hare entrusted *Saigon* to director Stephen Frears. In *Bloody Kids*, Frears had used the restless camera to indicate an unverbalised and existential alienation from life in the concrete jungle. As Hare says, 'Because I'd written a script which I felt was morally subtle – its meaning is not declaimed, at no point are there long speeches of denunciation about the American behaviour in Vietnam – I wanted a film maker who can make you feel things by the way he moves the camera, the way he directs the actors.'[1]

What one then has to consider is whether Frears' camera and the feelings it generates in the audience enhance or deny the meaning (or intended meaning) of Hare's *Saigon*. In the first section, for example, there is an irritating tendency to disrupt the textual references by picking up on an irrelevant detail of the setting, such as a fan. The pacing too is misjudged, giving very little time to see what Bob is doing in his filing cabinets, but presenting a long drawn-out shot of the airport as President Thieu is smuggled out. As Hare agrees, 'I didn't really think that Stephen's attempt to make it into a pastiche of *Casablanca* was terribly helpful. I thought that he should have trusted that it had a tone of its own. In my view it did.'[2]

Hare's script is subtly subverting the genre it has invoked with an English (rather than American) and female (rather than the inevitable male) voice for the detective-styled voice-over. The nature of the romantic lead is itself disrupted by having a younger man involved with an older woman, and the asking of political questions in a scene set for seduction. As they lie in post-coital embrace, Bob initiates Barbara and the audience into the more brutal ways of the Americans who torture prisoners, revealing the unromantic side of Saigon but – unlike Anna Seaton in *Licking Hitler* – Barbara does not learn from sex but from a lover.

There is a political thriller bursting to get out, but meanwhile the facts get pushed out of the way. When the gas dump explodes, it merely causes a brief interruption in their passionate sleep, the flames providing atmospheric flickering on the faces of lovers. True to Hare's memory of the city, this 'dreamy quality' is indeed 'rather delicious' and in her letter to her mother Barbara has already normalised the heightened atmosphere. As she licks the envelope with slats of light falling across her face and pronounces that 'The Year of the Tiger will soon be the Year of the Cat', that cat is Barbara.

Through her voice-over Barbara is given prominence in the narrative. As Bob leaves for work in the embassy at the beginning of section two, the camera follows him and takes us into the big white building, the city within a city, which is indeed as white as the employees who are grabbed from the seething crowd of Vietnamese. Barbara appears in only one scene in that section, by which time the affair is on the rocks and the nine lives are running out.

Apocalypse Now?

As Bob enters the embassy, he enters a world of hi-tech equipment and harsh unflattering strip-lighting, in marked contrast to the table and desk lamps of Barbara's apartment and the bank. The maps, flags and briefing meetings trace the progression of a war; the tapes and filing cabinets speak of secret agents and conspiracy, but the camera has left the 1940s entirely behind. Wandering over the bed-clothes to land as the first still image on a discontented face echoed *Apocalypse Now* as much as *Casablanca*. With the strings replaced by punchy up-beat brass, the Bogart-styled hero has entered an eighties action thriller to tell the story of an apocalypse – the American withdrawal from Vietnam in 1975.

Chesneau is a literal intelligence inside the monolithic stupidity of the Americans. He has a Vietnamese agent who tells him that

the final attack, the Blood Scent, is coming. Chesneau is the nag-
ging voice constantly trying to persuade his boss, Ockham, to
begin the evacuation and to save the dependent community of
Vietnamese helpers and informants from the communists.
Surrounded by his pictures of Presidents Johnson, Nixon and
Ford, and the American flag, however, the Ambassador, the spirit
of Washington, is motivated entirely by political and diplomatic
considerations. As played by E. G. Marshall, the Ambassador is a
crumpled and pathetic old man who stumbles through the last days
in Saigon just as he stumbles along the deserted corridors up to the
helicopters, with an expression of beleaguered incomprehension.
He acts out of mistaken idealism rather than malice, and while the
embassy is attacked by a fighter plane and his staff fall to the
ground, he stands like an open target.

That attack is the pivotal centre of *Saigon*, a shocking incursion
into American complacency and into the established style of the
film. The first section has eight discernible scenes: Barbara and the
bank; an evening of bridge at the Cercle Sportif; Barbara and
Chesneau at her apartment; the desperation of Phu disarmed by
Haliwell; Barbara and Chesneau at her apartment; the party at
Ockham's house; the gas dump episode; and the bank when
Donald leaves. Each of these has a marked beginning as, for example, when the lock on the barred door to the inner sanctum of the
bank clicks and Barbara – sitting in her apartment – looks up suddenly because she has heard someone at the door.

The theatrical structure has continued through to Bob's
drunken arrival at the apartment when Barbara explains that the
Indian summer, and with it their relationship, is over. After their
argument, the scene structure dissolves into a quick succession of
shots and the melodrama irrevocably becomes the action movie,
despite the fact that it was Hare's intention to show not only the
fact that the Americans had lost the war but the cost of the manner
of their loss – the betrayal of thousands of Vietnamese left behind.

To claim to see the last days of Saigon through Asian eyes might
not, as Hare agrees, in any case have been unachievable. What is
transparently absurd is to claim that *Saigon* achieves it. Hare's hope
that Quoc and the plight of the local employees at the end provides
the film with its kick is a forlorn one. Quoc has no life outside the

bank and only a very small presence in the film. Similarly, the audience has no more relationship with the employees waiting silently and hopelessly at their designated pick-up point than it does with the crowd mobbing the embassy in their desperation to escape. If *Saigon* does not shift the war onto the ground of the Vietnamese themselves, but is writing an 'alternative' history in the footsteps of *Brassneck*, *Licking Hitler* and *Plenty*, it is not for the Vietnamese, who will never see it, or of them. In its attempts to lay blame for the plight of the faceless, the great betrayal of their accomplices by the Americans, *Saigon* must be a play for a western audience and specifically an American audience.

Having fought in Vietnam himself, Frederic Forrest was just such an American and he literally and demonstrably made changes to the script. This is not simply a matter of Americanising. When Forrest delivers his final line – 'God forgive us' (p. 77), the words 'God forgive me' are added. It carries an almost melodramatic resonance which implies that, being a good American, God might do just that. Forrest saw his character not in terms of a political deconstruction but a personal tragedy, and, as he explained in his introduction to *The Asian Plays*, Hare was 'trapped in evidence of the problem I had set out to illustrate. My leading man did not truly believe that the Americans had lost a war.'

The clearest example of the distortion is in shot eighty-one when, far from carrying papers in his hands, he has a machine gun thrown nonchalantly over his shoulder. He is a Sylvester Stallone-styled macho hero marked out from the comic helmet-wearing Judd and – far from commenting on the construction of such a reading – he might have stepped straight out of his earlier role in *Apocalypse Now*. Such a change could not be effected without the complicity of the director, who confirmed, 'I'm not really interested, as David is, in all the diplomatic machinations. I'm primarily concerned with the love story.'[3]

If David Hare had intended *Saigon: Year of the Cat* as a straight love story then he would not have removed the leading lady from more than half the film. If he had intended a straight anti-American reconstruction of the last days in Vietnam, then he would not have included Barbara Dean at all. It is the relationship between them and the different styles which is the creative conflict of the film. For David Hare, it is 'juxtaposition that is interesting'[4] and the relationship between Barbara and Bob articulates the worlds of the Vietnamese 'economy' managed by British expatriates with the American 'intelligence'. In these ways he sought to create an image of international complicity in occupation and exploitation.

Unlike *Plenty*, this articulation operates from personal confluence to political schema. The American intervention in Vietnam follows the pattern of the affair – attraction and excitement (twenty-two pages), apologies and misunderstanding (seventeen pages), recrimination and escape (fourteen pages). The site of the lovers' meeting – the Cercle Sportif – is the site of American military conspiracy. One of the weaknesses of *Saigon* is, however, that whereas on stage the individual in the enclosed environment has to be (indeed always is) a microcosm for society at large, on the big screen there is no 'automatic' inductive generalisation, the link needs to be explicit. This is particularly true since Barbara and Bob are not typical, but atypical. Hare's point is that the expatriate community in Saigon was not facing reality but having a love affair. That unreality is created in the visual fabric of the first part but, in order to criticise it, Hare must assert that his two central characters are facing it.

If Barbara is a filter, a way of getting inside the big white building, she is also its critic, granted by the voice-over a privileged position in the narrative. The tone is set from her first sexually charged *Brief Encounter* with Chesneau, where the sexual promise is cut abruptly short by her question about whether the South will be able to hold on (p. 20). Barbara jokes with him about the allocation of Ford Pintos, but expresses more cutting, if intuitive, doubts at Ockham's (un)white Christmas party.

Fiedler's pretence that everything is fine is immediately undermined by the explosion of the gas dump in the following shot, but Barbara's comments are tentative and her nervousness comes as one speaking from outside to those who are inside. Her position is not that of Cathy in Ian McEwan's *The Imitation Game*, where the writer disguises his own lack of knowledge about the work of the code breakers as her exclusion from the male power structure. Barbara is in the managerial level of the bank, and there are also senior women inside the American embassy. Hare has deliberately chosen to leave Barbara outside it. She is – like Rebecca in *Pravda* – not central to the action, but offering a perspective on it; she does not, like Susan in *Plenty* – a schizophrenic icon – filter history through herself, but stands outside it. Because she is left, like an ageing sex object or a wife, lingering on the outskirts of political power, she is less implicated in their betrayals.

'Every time I saw you,' says Chesneau, 'you made me feel guilty. I couldn't take that after a while' (p. 66). The fact is, however, that he feels guilty even without Barbara, and it is not because of his relationship with Barbara that he holds his position inside the embassy as a defender of humanity; she merely makes it harder for him. Although Chesneau begins the evacuation by getting papers for Barbara's friends and work-mates (and by implication for others), he is from the first distanced from the worst abuses of the CIA.

Bob and Barbara utter no words of love so Bob does not experience the same disjuncture as Anna Seaton in *Licking Hitler*. What marks Chesneau out from his colleagues is that he is the only one who is seen to listen to the Vietnamese, to an agent, Nhieu, to have solid evidence that the end is coming, which he gains before Barbara, in her tearful recrimination, states the fact.

'I never quite knew what my role was',[5] says Barbara as she and Bob start to go out together and indeed the voice-over is highly problematic. The first melancholic summary of her situation establishes her sexuality, secrecy and sultry boredom. When she says, in a perfect curtain line at the end of the first part, 'Donald did leave with comparative dignity. Compared with the rest of us, I mean' (p. 33), she speaks with the benefit of hindsight from an undefined vantage-point after the end of the film. The general becomes specific, the present is already the past and the events of 1975 are unrelated to the present day.

By the beginning of the second section Barbara is providing the link, massaging us into the embassy where the camera (and with it the audience) will see what Barbara (and Hare) could not. The information she provides, however, is duplicated in the briefing and, by her very distance from the centre of political and military power, she is not omniscient. The informal briefing of the South Vietnamese by the Americans in the Cercle Sportif takes place while Barbara is out of the room so that – even in part one – the audience has knowledge not only from outside her field of vision but also from outside her field of experience. Phu's desperation is intended to justify Barbara's own empirical knowledge that the end is coming; that this justification is inadequate to the task is one of the major flaws of the film.

Barbara's function is to allow the audience to share the vague feeling that the end was coming and to know in advance that it was to be ignoble. As ever in Hare's work, the question is not what happens, but how it happens and the audience is safe in the knowledge of the outcome – that the Americans leave and neither Barbara nor Chesneau will be left behind. The British – in the form of Haliwell and Barbara – need to get out of Saigon as much as they (the CIA and the military Americans) do, and yet 'we' are not so implicated in their mess of Vietnam. This 'we' encapsulates the confusion of *Saigon*. The British both are and are not a sub-set of America. There is not in *Saigon* – as there was in *Plenty* and had been in Hare's other earlier history plays – any structure of opposition; there is rather a structure of containment. As Barbara enters the embassy for her escape, she and her love story are absorbed by the action movie.

The Year of Living Dangerously?

'This feeling of living somewhere which you know is doomed is one which a lot of us who lived in England during the sixties and seventies felt, that it can't go on like this and yet seeing no way of being able to change it or to protest against the end. But I wouldn't stretch the analogy too far, it's a mood that the film is trying to catch and it's a mood in which people will not face reality.'[6] By 1983, in the midst of the Designer Society of the eighties, and as Mrs Thatcher began her second term with the money markets buoyant, the moment had no sense of an ending. The Left had suffered its worse defeat in thirty years for telling the electorate otherwise. Standing as a representative of colonialism in general and England in particular, Barbara prefigures some of the concerns of *Map of the World,* but in *Saigon* that colonialism is exempt from any criticism.

By 1983, Hare was in any case no longer speaking where there was silence. Anthony Grey's novel *Saigon*, was published in 1982; *Vietnam*, a full-scale twelve-hour history series produced by Martin Smith for Channel Four, began on 11 April 1983. In his play *The Last Day* broadcast on BBC1 on 30 March 1983, John Pilger focused on a journalist to expose the importance of representation in the first media war and, in November of that year, Martin Sheen played *Kennedy*, struggling with the problem of going into the Vietnam War in a three-part drama serial.

Following *Apocalypse Now*, America was well able to talk about Vietnam and probably more than a little bored with doing so. If the message of *Saigon* had ever been to tell the public – British or American – just how the Americans lost the war, then it was defused to systematic 'self-censorship'. The last days and hours of evacuation from the embassy in 1975 were ones of desperate violence, yet when the embassy comes under attack and staff run for cover, all we see is a few documents blown off desks. Throughout the sequence, the camera remains resolutely staring along a corridor, as if averting its eyes from the outside world. The strength of this scene lies in the restraint with which it reflects the state of splendid isolation which the occupying community inhabits. But the weakness is that this can be seen simply as a failure of nerve. The only shots are fired into the air; the grenades of tear-gas go off harmlessly in lifts, no one mobbing the embassy gets crushed.

Although the first third of the film remains almost unchanged from the printed script, the more 'political' sections which follow it are reduced from thirty-nine to twenty-six shots and forty-nine to thirty-five shots respectively, irrevocably to loosen the mood from the moral. The ambassador no longer complains about the cutting down of his favourite tree or the ash from the furnaces destroying confidential records dropping on the swimming pool; the $2 million rescued from that furnace no longer rain down on the Vietnamese left waiting for helicopters which will never come. It is the sure sign of a guilty conscience that Hare's first published version of *Saigon* was reprinted in *The Asian Plays* and – in contrast to *Pravda* – an accurate new edition, reflecting what was actually screened, has not been released.

Hare is, in fact, trapped within the phenomenon he attempted to expose in *Plenty* – the peculiarly British inability to say what he means or to acknowledge clearly that his primary aim is neither education nor subversion. Barbara's last real line in the film makes the point that specific questions of ideology are bound up with universal questions about language, the relationships between people (the betrayal of Barbara by Bob) with those between the individual and the world (the betrayal of Vietnam by the Americans).

> BARBARA: It's so strange. Everywhere you go you hear
> people saying, 'Oh I loved this country.' That's what
> they say. They usually say it just as they're leaving. 'Oh I
> loved this country so much . . .' I realized it in the bank
> one evening. I tried to say something affectionate to
> Quoc. That's what you're left with. Gestures of affection.
> Which you then find out mean nothing at all. (lines as
> spoken, p. 66)

Hare might not explore that conjunction here but it is evident that his gestures to politics mean nothing at all. Having exhausted Britain's war and its mood, Hare, very much the Englishman abroad, simply colonised another. *Decent Interval*, a critical account of the evacuation by Frank Snapp, an ex-CIA agent stationed in Saigon in 1975, was significant only in authenticating his own feelings. If *Saigon* has a sense of an ending, then, it is the ending of any sense of socialist realism in Hare's work. 'I have travelled there, but temperamentally I am so opposed to the idea that research will of itself validate a work of the imagination that I move about more to set me thinking, than with any idea that wisdom can be acquired by documentary means.'[7]

By 1983, Hare – like Victor Mehta in *A Map of the World* – has clearly established a hierarchy of categories, with research valued above ideology but imagination valued above both. Its touchstone is the individual and not the collective. Tip the balance just slightly and the potentially political becomes utterly personal. Like the film version of *Plenty*, and in marked contrast to *Wetherby*, *Saigon* was marketed on its star(s); as if to reinforce the point, the printed script carries a photograph of Judi Dench's face against the pillow. *Saigon* was assimilated into the genre of TV epic and, as Judd says in an oblique form of self-consciousness, 'Whether you're right or wrong, it's not very effective. You're not going to make anyone want to change their mind ... It's self-indulgent. And it doesn't have the effect you require' (p. 51).

6   The foundry of lies

Pravda opened at the National Theatre on 2 May 1985 on the eve of the Wapping dispute which signalled the beginning of the end of Fleet Street. Written for the newly established Hare/Eyre performance group within the National Theatre company, *Pravda* was the first partnership collaboration between Hare and Brenton for twelve years, and in one sense a companion piece to *Brassneck*. If 1973 in Nottingham had seen, in echoing the Poulson affair, the dissection of how the perceived socialist expectations of the British people after the war went down the middle in compromise capitalism and calculating corruption, *Pravda* effected a comparable dissection of how, in the face of even more voracious capitalism and the failure of opposition in the 1980s, it all went to the Right. Unashamedly funny, *Pravda* set out to use comedy in the theatre not only to effect a reader's revenge but as a democratic force; in fact, what was both Hare's and Brenton's most popular play to date expressed a deep ambivalence to what they would oppose.

Lambert Le Roux and the new Right

At the beginning of *Pravda* an ambitious young journalist, Andrew May, is working in quiet obscurity in the provinces on an old-fashioned Beaverbrook-type family-owned newspaper, where the office is full of old typewriters and gothic lettering and the political view is inherently conservative. When the paper is sold to generate short-term capital and the new proprietor purges the old regime, Andrew May gains swift promotion to the post of editor. From there his is a rapid rise – to editorship of 'The Victory', a prestige

Times-like national daily, and marriage to his former proprietor's daughter. Sacked for deciding to print a leaked document, however, his fall is equally spectacular. After failure at running his own independent paper, 'The Usurper', Andrew accepts a job editing 'The Tide', a tabloid *Sun*-like gutter-rag, from its streamlined computer-screened offices. With sixteen pages of text at 'The Bystander', twenty-two at 'The Victory' and five at 'The Tide', newspaper newsrooms provide the primary locations for *Pravda* and, with vendors shouting the headlines, the play becomes a kind of Living Newspaper, telling the story of the recent history of the British press.

Where *Brassneck* was inspired by John Poulson, the action of *Pravda* has its origin in the sale of Times Newspapers in 1981 to the Australian tycoon, Rupert Murdoch. In the highly partisan account of ousted editor Harold Evans' *Good Times, Bad Times*[1] there are details of the guarantees for editorial independence received by the trustees of *The Times* (Evans, pp. 489–90, *Pravda*, p. 51); of mass firings of journalists and the advertising department (*Pravda*, p. 56) which followed Murdoch's accession (Evans, p. 232); of Evans' wedding soon after taking up his position as editor (Evans, p. 349, *Pravda*, p. 56); and the award as Editor of the Year shortly before his dismissal (Evans, p. 330, *Pravda*, p. 62); of Murdoch's political leanings (Evans, p. 350, *Pravda*, p. 56) and of the absorption of *The Times* by News International, which also publishes the *Sun* (Evans, pp. 435–40, *Pravda*, p. 113).

Like *Brassneck*, however, *Pravda* does not name the individuals on which characters are modelled. Libel is the little beauty which Le Roux uses finally to bankrupt his opponents, but naming is not always required for libel actions to be successful. One reason for *Pravda's* undoubted success on the media-oriented South Bank was precisely the fun audiences could take in matching up the real events to the stage caricatures, by which Andrew May 'is' Harold Evans and Elliot Fruit-Norton, the ousted editor of 'The Victory', 'is' William Rees-Mogg.

Foregrounded in the narrative by his direct address monologue, Le Roux's opening speech is the longest in the play. He wears the uniform of business but by far the most noticeable thing about him – as played by Anthony Hopkins – was the clipped South African accent. Since Rupert Murdoch is not South African, it stands as final evidence that the play is not a documentary. In the public mind in 1985, the South African accent carried with it the charges of state violence, oppression of the majority, racism and self-seeking capitalism of the apartheid regime. In this way, Brenton and Hare effected the same smearing of Le Roux as they had, using the Borgias, of Alfred Bagley in *Brassneck*. The accent alone is sufficient to condemn him, but the name – the roux is the basic white sauce in cookery – reinforces the point. So that there should be no doubt, he is connected both to the arch-villain, Hitler, and to Richard III.

As Shakespeare used animalistic imagery to describe Richard, so Le Roux places himself in relation to the 'Jackal, giraffe, hyena, lion' (p. 27). His is, then, not the opportunistic survivalism of Alfred Bagley's crow but the aggression of a predator. Their minds full of such metaphors, following Antony Sher's definitive portrayal of Richard III as an arachnoid bug on crutches, many reviewers expanded on the intended comparison. Hare and Brenton were this time literally appropriating the Shakespearian history play to opposite ends. If *Richard III* was late Tudor propaganda, David Hare confirmed that 'We're trying to teach people to decode newspapers because we think there's a great deal of news management and that what passes for news isn't.'[2]

In so doing they are not concerned with the dynamics of practical newspaper work. *Pravda* does not, as Arnold Wesker's *The Journalists* did, accurately recreate the atmosphere of the newsroom. There is a single journalistic incident – the ruthless editing of a story on a police attack on women protesters at Greenham Common – and it stands at the very centre of the play. For the rest, the writers are interested in power and its abuse. Fleet Street is a metaphor and, even in his surname, Le Roux controls that privileged discourse.

Le Roux's vocabulary, his talk of 'choice', of 'good and bad', of the 'family' paper, is the language of the new Right, the Thatcherite conservatism of the eighties in which a leaked document is not seen as an issue of public safety or the right-to-know, but a question of criminality. Only with the word 'veldt' at the end of Le Roux's opening address comes the realisation that he is talking not about

England but about South Africa and that 'you', the audience, as much as Rebecca and the old England she has described, are contained in and by him. Just as the chosen perspective of newspapers is in danger of seeming 'natural', so Le Roux, talking of a system 'inherited from Mother Nature herself' (p. 27), is naturalising an ideology, convincing his audience that – as Mrs Thatcher in her first term was fond of saying – 'There Is No Alternative'.

This is not to say that Le Roux is a British-styled Tory. To him South Africa is 'civilisation' and Britain is a 'third world country' (p. 82). He is unhindered by the mannered decency of the British class system whose rules he bends to his own end. Just as he hires the Irving Club, so Le Roux buys the English establishment in the form of the House of Lords (Lord Silk) and the Church (the Bishop of Putney). Through the English cricket captain (Payne) he already has the national sport; through Michael Quince he has the compliance of the Commons, while Princess Jill is the royal icing on the cake. Le Roux charms the trustees of 'The Victory', and implicitly of England, with a combination of evasion of his apartheid past, by rubbishing the opposition and with profuse guarantees for editorial freedom of 'The Victory'.

In providing Le Roux's character reference, Andrew tells us the exact value of those guarantees – that they are 'not worth the paper they're written on' (Evans, p. 490) – and Le Roux's language of persuasion and conciliation, the heavy mask of irony, gives way to dictatorial behaviour and abrasive iconoclasm as soon as he has control. The use of expletives by Lambert Le Roux and Eaton Sylvester indicate, as it did in *Plenty*, the cracking of the veneer of civilised manners but also an incursion by two invaders from the colonies extracting revenge on the mother country.

Le Roux's is a voracious international capitalism whose web contains not only Britain but the rest of the world, through the Olympics, specifically the economic shrewdness of West Germany (the Exhibitionshalle), the tactlessness of Australia (Eaton Sylvester) and the militaristic discipline of Japanese Toyinka. He can buy the nationality of any country in the world and has no allegiance to any. The quality of the lives Le Roux's businesses affect is unheard, the quality of the formula product (p. 76), an irrelevance. Le Roux is not just out for number one; he is 'totally without morality' (p.

97). He does not merely fulfil *Knuckle*'s prophecy that 'there will no longer be any need for public life to be decked out in morality',[3] but destroys the very possibility of moral distinction. 'There is only one criterion in life, Michael. To succeed' (p. 33).

Like the *Jew of Malta*, Le Roux is a Machiavellian chameleon who trusts no one, not even his lubricating business, and who is sacked in the last moments of the play. Le Roux is revealed – and this revelation is the principal function of Eaton Sylvester – as an aggressive paranoiac, a capitalist obsessed with the threat of communism practising the art of Toyinka in his Weybridge home and, like Ken Yakashito, waging a war of his own making.

The dispossessed

When Andrew is sacked for his reluctant decision to print the leaked document he joins the 'dispossessed', the ex-employees who have, like Elliot Fruit-Norton, the former editor of 'The Victory', 'gone to the dogs'. For Fruit-Norton, an out-of-date traditionalist and elitist spouting Latin at a press conference, Le Roux represents the Spartan Barbarians to his Greek-English civilisation. He is an old-style Tory of *Plenty* holding on to 'Qualities of discrimination, balance and probity' (p. 55).

Fruit-Norton is joined by Quince, an appearances politician, for whom the press is not only the preserver of civilised values but a way of keeping in the public eye. Upon losing his column Quince is – like James Callaghan, who supported the Rees-Mogg attempt to buy *The Times* or Norman St John Stevas, whom Murdoch considered for a column in *The Times* – 'disinherited' and 'spurned by Downing Street' (pp. 92-3). He is, as Lambert describes with his pithy deflating one-liners, 'the urinal into which the British establishment leaks' (p. 102).

The tantrums of Fruit-Norton, Quince and Andrew May begin when they bid for 'The Usurper' with the dream of their own paper. To preserve editorial freedom, however, they will resort to cheque-book journalism by buying unverified accusations against Lambert Le Roux. To achieve a paper that is decent and honest, they will fill its pages with murderous sensationalism. Inflicting opposite and equal personal pain, however, does not preserve moral value, it destroys it. The Usurpers are united in fighting against Lambert Le Roux, but, as Sylvester says, and Le Roux agrees, to win you have to know what you're fighting for. The Usurpers are become valueless; they are all weak because they do not know what they believe. Like the content of 'The Usurper' – which has no office and therefore remains significantly unseen – what they believe comes second to the gaining of revenge.

The Usurpers underestimate the enemy, but their tools of newspaper and remaindered books are in any case blunt. The 'Leicester Bystander' was rubbish sold as a business decision to buy a stake in a racehorse. Sir Stamford lied to his employees and gave no regard to consultation. Hamish betrayed Harry, the incompetent editor, with Le Roux (p. 25). The old family way was already dead or as senile as Dame Elsa and in the race for control of Fleet Street and England, Fruit-Norton and Michael Quince's Green Fields Toryism has as much chance of winning as a tin of Pal.

Le Roux is unaffected, merely wondering why they bother. Outside power is madness: Fruit-Norton the fruit cake is 'clinically insane' (p. 85) and without his column, Quince too is 'a loon, a flat-earther' (p. 97). Le Roux does not need government as much as government needs him. Unlike the government, Le Roux cannot lose his seat at the next election; newspapers are not an access to power, they are power. Unlike the state-owned newspaper in Russia from which the play takes its title, 'English newspapers aren't government propaganda sheets', says Brenton. 'The question is, why do so many of them choose to behave as if they are?'[4] In *Pravda*, all papers support lying whether they are owned by Lambert Le Roux or not, the Press Council is a toothless tiger and all the journalists are cowardly. It is the journalists of Fleet Street and not the proprietor(s) who stand accused of complicity with political distortion by self-censorship in the single word, 'Pravda'.

When Le Roux challenges them with 'Editorial freedom. You never used it when you had it. It is fast gone. Why should you deserve freedom any more?' (p. 108), the answer is that they do not and it is literally bankrupted. For this reason, Brenton and Hare would certainly disagree with Tom Stoppard and his assertion in *Night and Day* that newspapers provide information and that information is light. Hare shares, rather, Oscar Wilde's scepticism about the fourth estate: it has eaten up the other three. For Hare and Brenton, it would make no difference if there were so-called 'freedom of information' when journalists operate self-censorship and Leander Scroop already knows about the contents of the document leaked to Rebecca, but chooses to say nothing.

For Hare and Brenton, the press offers no solution and it would have confused the picture of journalistic cowardice they were drawing with such relish to have included a hard-working genuine journalist. They did no research inside the industry and if one of the complaints against the press is that it distorts the truth about the world (and about the theatre), then one of the complaints about *Pravda* is that it distorts the truth about the press. As Stephen Andrews asks in *A Map of the World*, 'And why do writers insist on their right to distort reality? You demand it in order to make better jokes' (*Map*, p. 65).

In the opening scene of *Pravda*, a woman tries to get the 'Leicester Bystander' to print a correction to a story mistakenly associating her with a cocaine dealer. *Pravda* is her revenge, inflicting equal and opposite distortion on its subjects. If *Pravda* is a reader's revenge, however, it is also a writer's revenge. Howard Brenton had suffered the worst excesses of tabloid journalism over the private prosecution of *The Romans in Britain*, while David Hare is cast into depression by bad notices. It may be that ultimately you have to know what you are fighting for, but in the meantime the writers can have some fun. How long that fun and the play's relevance lasts is of no interest to them, because, 'In a very real sense, this finger is for all of you' (p. 63).

It is one of the great weaknesses of the play that, as a result of this obsession, it lacks a dialectic. Despite the continuity of names, Andrew May is not a disillusioned Stephen Andrews of the future; he was always, as his surname indicates, a vacillator. He rather echoes William Cofax in *Dreams of Leaving*, and would preserve people's trust in newspapers even if it meant lying to do it. From the beginning Andrew fears seduction by more than Rebecca and begins with an apology. He goes on to place his trust in a man whose guiding principle is mistrust and, as editor of 'The Victory', colludes with the Downing Street line on economic coverage.

LE ROUX: ... To everyone I pose a question. I am the
  question.
ANDREW: And what is the answer?
LE ROUX: People like you.   (p. 107)

Unlike Stephen, 'may or may not' Andrew is part of the very phenomenon he condemns and by the time of their confrontation in
Scene Nine, Lambert Le Roux has already gobbled him up, leaving
Andrew clinging to language without meaning and asking 'What's
the alternative?' (p. 112).

The alternative or the new Left

From the opening scene, Rebecca has few illusions about the profession of journalism or about England. It is she who names the
Fleet Street world for what it is, who sees Lambert Le Roux for
what he is and who initiates Andrew into the Irving. If Le Roux
refers to Rebecca as the 'left-wing wife' (p. 75), she is nonetheless
left wing only by virtue of being critical of the right-wing proprietor. She is not shown to be connected to any political party or
vehicle of dissent as Gilly was in Brenton's *The Genius* and as
Amanda and her Greenham friends were in David Edgar's
Maydays. Indeed, the Greenham extra-legal action is rubbished by
the papers' manipulation of it. If 'we need institutions. We must
have the means and the courage to buy the means' (p. 99), it is not
clear what those institutions/means are. The trade unions, as represented by the aptly named 'Breaker' Bond, are squared, there is
no worker solidarity.

Rebecca's position, like that of Hare and Brenton themselves, is
contradictory. She is not so much the investigative journalist discovering leaked documents, as the upper-class girl with friends in
high places and – as her source discovered – trust in her is mis-
placed. Rebecca remains 'A Child's Guide to the World' (p. 40),
and her book might also be 'remaindered in Foyles' (p. 85).

Rebecca might stand outside of Le Roux, but she is still inside
the old England and does not have any new language to counter
his charm. In the first edition Rebecca explicitly stated that the

rural idyll, the green fields option was a lie, but in the second edition, she is nostalgic for the old world, saying, 'Home. Back in
England again. A strange, still life. Everything misty. The low
green English countryside unchanged. In the village church always
fresh flowers on the altar. On the village green late in the season,
the wicket taking the spin. The last party of summer' (p. 9).

The same might be said of Brenton and Hare. They might stand
outside Le Roux, but they are still inside the old England and do
not have any new language with which to counter him.

> FRUIT-NORTON: I am not questioning, I am stating.
>   Lambert Le Roux is not a proper person.
> LE ROUX (*quietly*): And what alternative would you suggest?
>   (LE ROUX *smiles at* SYLVESTER, *then at* REBECCA.)
>   (p. 46)

If they cannot write optimistically about the future, cannot draw a
positive alternative where none exists on the political landscape,
neither can they offer the kind of rejuvenation which Brenton
achieved in *Romans in Britain*, where he not only examined the
cyclical creation and decay of myths but generated a new one with
bursting colloquial poetry. 'The way to fight him is with ideas',
Rebecca had said in the first edition of the play; cutting the line
does not disguise the fact that the writers did not have any. All they
could offer was that familiar voice from the seventies – the woman.

If, by virtue of being a woman, Rebecca is supposed to break the
rules not only of the male bastion of the old English establishment
of the gentleman's club but of the new Right, then the fact that the
government which presided over this change was led by Britain's
first woman prime minister makes the writers seem at best naive
and at worst reactionary. Pinpointing a moral is, in any case, not
enough in itself; you have to be sure that someone hears it. Just as
the word 'Pravda' is unheard (p. 62), so Andrew May does not hear
his wife. If Rebecca remains sane, unlike Susan in *Plenty* or
Caroline in *Dreams of Leaving*, she still leaves 'The Victory' once it
will not expose a lie and leaves Andrew after he has told the same
lie three times. 'I walked away. I got out. I did the job and stopped.
I stopped writing for papers. I stopped reading papers. It helps.

Why can't you do the same?' (p. 91). Hare and Brenton can't do the same because they don't know where she goes and, even if, as Bill demonstrates, the option is always open, leaving is, in any case, an evasion. 'You should hit a man in the face if you want his face to disappear' (p. 108).

Democratic laughter?

In 1978, David Hare made quite clear that, for him, the 'theatre is the exact opposite art to journalism'[5] because, rather than offering half-baked opinions in the guise of entertainment, it enables and demands judgement. Where, at the end of *Brassneck* – albeit ironically – the last days of capitalism were announced and the Bagleys were consumed as an act of positive nihilism, a judgement on them created by the visual morality of the stage itself, *Pravda* ends with Le Roux's welcome to the foundry of lies. It is not that Hare's earlier works showed a positive alternative or a vibrant Left, but that now there is no opposition at all.

It is precisely because the phenomenon they sought to expose was so strong that Brenton and Hare decided to use laughter as a way of poking holes in it. A sense of humour is the only quality Le Roux admires. By making the audience laugh at Lambert Le Roux, the writers hope, they might disarm him, and they declared in the subtitle that *Pravda* would be a 'Fleet Street comedy'.

Like Brecht before them, Hare and Brenton set out to write 'epic comedy – part The Front Page, part Arturo Ui'[6] but they stole their jokes. Even the rewriting of the Greenham story was not imaginary but taken from Henry Porter's *Lies, Damned Lies and Some Exclusives*.[7] And in giving many of the best and funniest lines to Le Roux and by failing to show just how the rise is/was resistible, he (Murdoch), like Ui (Hitler) before him, inevitably becomes the hero. If he becomes the hero, the audience may not be laughing at him but with him, the playwrights may not be protesting but celebrating. It was the central problem faced also by Shakespeare in *Richard III*: how to condemn while showing the momentum and charisma of power.

In *Brassneck*, this problem was avoided when Alfred Bagley was killed off at the end of the first act. In *Pravda*, however, as Hare confessed, the writers positively feast on Lambert Le Roux's villainy and he dominates the stage even into the final moments of the play. If the writers were not, as Hare was in *Knuckle*, 'trying to show capitalism in all its romance and excitement and wit',[8] that is nonetheless what they end up doing, and not only do they give a major platform to what they would oppose, but they further naturalise that phenomenon. 'As we got into it, *Pravda* began not to be about Fleet Street, but about the nature of evil. "Evil" is a difficult subject for a paid-up atheist.'[9] Le Roux stopped being the embodiment of bare-toothed capitalism and became instead an eternal universal force against which there is no recourse and for which there is no responsibility. The removal of the line from the second edition does not prevent Le Roux from seeming, finally, 'That monster, that Satan.'

In *Pravda*, 'The kind of comedy we tried to write is one, we hope, of democratic laughter. The audience are invited to dissociate themselves from the tiny clique of the ruling class paraded across the stage.'[10] What is paraded on the stage, however, is a catalogue of failure. Actively appropriating tragedy for himself, Le Roux leaves his opponents with only a comedy of errors. As Rebecca warns Andrew, so we might warn Hare and Brenton, 'if you spend your whole life fighting him, the sad thing is you become just like him' (p. 99). In demonstrating the skill with which ruthlessness, energy and brute wit contrive to make all opposition look pathetic, self-seeking and absurd, the writers can only, as Hare confesses, contribute to the process by which Le Roux's views become not only plausible but attractive.

> I'm interested in how to write about the eighties. What's noticeable so far about the most popular plays of this decade is that they borrow their vitality from immoral characters. The audience gets its kick from just how fast the handcart's going to hell. One of my favourite recent plays is *Aunt Dan and Lemon*, in which the two leading characters are neo-fascists. You only have to think of the real estate men in *Glengarry Glen Ross*, or the dealers in *Serious Money*, or, for that matter of Lambert Le Roux in *Pravda* to see that modern plays have

seemed, perhaps unintentionally, to end up celebrating malign energy. Or at least they hitch a ride from their villains. Look at *Les Liaisons Dangereuses*.[11]

If allowing Lambert Le Roux to become a hero might have been unintentional, it might equally express an ambivalence towards the character: since Le Roux is the means of their revenge against the journalists they despise, Hare and Brenton must, at least in part, approve of him. If Le Roux is taking a revenge against a country which had dismissed him for not belonging to the intellectual first division, then, again, they must in part at least approve of him.

It was Julian Mitchell's *Another Country* which explored how the establishment creates its defectors along with its spies, but – through the prominence of the revenge motif in *Pravda* – David Hare is revealed as a case in point. Like Lambert Le Roux and like Victor Mehta in *A Map of the World*, David Hare was an 'immigrant' to middle-class England, a scholarship boy to public school. 'I speak posh nowadays because my accent was ridiculed at Lancing', Hare explained. 'You learn subterfuge in England.'[12] A classical education fits Fruit-Norton for his revenge as much as for editing or dog-track management; so too it equipped Hare to create success out of his apparent attacks. If this motivation has remained disguised, it still informs his writing.

If it is Hare's sense of exclusion which has given him a satirical distance on the English establishment, the fact is that in changing his accent he revealed the strength of his desire to belong. It has scarred him with a deeply based tension between belonging and exclusion, nostalgia and disdain for, as Hare explored in *A Map of the World*, 'immigrants have the highest expectation of the society they come to. They are deeply disappointed if the society lets them down.'[13] Hare's apparent railing was, then, not directed at the lack of change in English society but at a class which let him down. What had seemed like a political anger is now visible as a form of bitter regret, and since the tide has turned and the move right in British politics makes the liberals look like the left, Hare is nostalgic for what in 1973 he had criticised as betrayal – the middle ground.

When Le Roux says 'Welcome to the foundry of lies' (p. 113), then, we have been there for more than two hours. This is not simply a matter of the truism that everything on stage is a lie, but that in turning their comic guns on the journalists at all, Brenton and Hare were positively indulging Lambert Le Roux and 'if theatre is judgement, it is also failure'.[14] What happened to all those words my generation used to believe in? They became *Pravda*.

The foundry of lies

In its title, taken from the Russian newspaper, the play is announced as 'Pravda'. The fact that the play will reveal an uncomfortable truth is brandished in advance. If this confession appeared to relieve the writers of responsibility for distortion, it did nothing to rescue a political effect for the play. Forearmed, the audience could prepare itself for a piece of left-wing propaganda and simply dismiss Hare and Brenton's outburst as precisely the kind of finger-wagging they wished to avoid.

In the same way, the subtitle 'a Fleet Street comedy' announces the play as a comedy and, far from having their expectations challenged, the audience is duly rewarded. When the dogs on wheels are taken gratuitously across the stage, the audience laughs – but this is not disruption, this is the preservation of the spectacle itself. The newspaper-vendors who punctuate the play do not interrupt the action to point morals in the play as the songs do, for example, in Caryl Churchill's *Serious Money*. Indeed, the vendors guarantee involvement by moving the action forward (for example, p. 79) covering the artificiality of the stage as the scene changes are effected.

'What reaction are you after in printing that sort of stuff? Are people concerned? Are they running in the streets, screaming my name? And are they burning my papers?' (p. 103). No, they are reading them, and just as Murdoch's newspapers continue to dominate the market, so *Pravda* was the hit of the season, running for more than a year with two cast changes. *Pravda* may be about a political phenomenon but became a conceited comedy for the theatre-going elite. As M'Bengue warned Victor Mehta in *A Map of the World*, 'Jokes are a product of security. If one is secure, one may laugh at others. Even – this is the really telling thing – one may laugh at oneself' (*Map*, p. 41). The writers confused satire with comedy and their sense of humour failed them as surely as it failed Andrew May.

In collaborating on *Pravda*, Hare and Brenton had done what Hare warned should never be done; they had 'come out of the same trap twice' and far from challenging the blandness of the product at the National Theatre, Hare, an associate director there, was responsible for it. The play is about itself and the problems of reaction as much as Fleet Street or Le Roux/Murdoch.

> LE ROUX: ... Moral feelings? They pass. A second. What are they? Little chemical drops in the brain. A vague feeling of unease, like indigestion. A physical mood. Too much dinner. 'Oh I have a feeling', then in the morning it's gone. People adjust. The unthinkable yesterday becomes the way of things. New moral attitudes. New indigestion. It all passes. Pass and move on. (p. 42)

Where will Hare and Brenton move on to? They will almost certainly not collaborate again. Seeing himself as the 'red theatre under the theatre's bed', Howard Brenton continued 'Slogging the Road to Utopia',[15] culminating in a season at the Royal Court and a Labour MP's experiences in *Greenland*.

For David Hare, however, 'the coming to power of Mrs Thatcher scattered a lot of writers. We'd been arguing for social changes, which hadn't happened and were now being seen in reverse.'[16] In 1988 he confessed to being 'terrified' at the prospect of *Fanshen* being taken up by the National Theatre's Education department. 'Fifteen years ago I said in response to the theatre of the left, you can't write about politics without talking about the deep problems of reaction in this country. Why are the people so reactionary?'.[17] *Pravda* was the first 'Life under Thatcher' play and Lambert Le Roux is the question. From this point there were to be, as Hare confirmed, 'an awful lot of Tories in my work because apart from Leslie Titmuss, who is a brilliant example of the new Tory, there is almost no fiction about them'.[18] *Pravda* was followed by Tony Marchant's *Speculators* and Doug Lucie's *Fashion* as well as

Serious Money, but Hare was at another turning-point, again filling in gaps, and more interested in dissecting the charisma of the Right than in explaining the failures of the Left, more interested in drawing a map of this new world than in imagining the next.

7 Dreams of leaving

Love and existentialism

As the male voice-over at the beginning of *Dreams of Leaving* self-consciously (first person) looks back (past tense) nine years from the relative wisdom of early middle age, he declares his intention to select and interpret his life as the structure for the coming narrative. An innocent from the provinces, William arrives in the big city and finds sexual experience, the pick-up in a cinema intercut with steamy scenes from a South American movie to imply a casual sexual promiscuity.

One night, 30 feet across the newsroom, however, William (still unnamed) sees a woman, the object of his subsequent attention. As Colin, who is buying hash from her companion in the newsroom, asks, 'Are you going to tell me where it comes from?' and receives the teasing answer 'No' (p. 13), Caroline has entered the newsroom from behind a glass partition at the back of the frame. As Colin continues with, 'I'll just take a look', Caroline draws the eye from left to right as she passes behind him. She is followed in focus by the camera to the centre of the frame in front of the continuing deal and reaches a still point on 'This looks first rate' (p. 14).

From the first she has been admired and judged by men. The word 'look' then continues to be used at key moments and appears some forty-five times in the printed directions. John Caughie's illuminating essay on *Dreams of Leaving*[1] makes clear that it is the look – the construction of meaning by the variation of the visual field – which distinguishes cinema from other visual arts and goes on to discuss whether the pleasure of the look is as pertinent to (art) television.

As he had done with *Licking Hitler*, Hare chose to shoot *Dreams of Leaving* on film and deliberately foregrounds the fact; there are very few lines and the scenic structure is more oblique than in his earlier film, being distinguished by the change of Caroline's clothes; by cutting from outside the flat to inside the gallery, from night to morning and night to day; by the closing of a door or by a left to right sweep of the screen. Although transmitted as a *Play for Today*, *Dreams of Leaving* is, therefore, a film which happened to be produced for television rather than a television play, and, because of his own confessed inadequacy as a film director at the time, Hare described it as 'an honourable failure'.[2] As a result, *Dreams of Leaving* is often ignored in accounts of Hare's work but, broadcast in January 1980, it laid to rest the unhinged heroines of his history plays and prefigured many of the concerns of the decade.

If the look is at the heart of the aesthetic of cinema, it is also at the heart of Sartre's phenomenological ontology. In contrast to Barbara Dean, who introduces *Saigon* in the middle of an everyday action, William identifies a distinct beginning: the moment at which he first *looked* at Caroline, the moment at which he became conscious *of* something. In this light, William would seem to be the *être-pour-soi* (being-for-itself), consciousness aware of itself and perceiving of Caroline, the *être-en-soi* (being-in-itself), an object for an alien consciousness and significantly with aspects not immediately given to experience.

Through the voice-over William gains a stable career (journalism) and a stable personality; Caroline, in contrast, has three different jobs (fine art sales, photography and dancing) and is presented as a series of fragments. It is, however, Caroline who initiates him and the viewer into the ways of the art-dealing world. Just how else aesthetic value is to be justified was to form the basis for *The Bay at Nice,* which takes place entirely within the gallery, but here the paintings behind them in the final moments at the gallery are loaded: where William is, like the expressionist painting, strongly moving in blues and blacks, Caroline is apparently as receptive as the painting of pastel pinks behind her. Their personal lives are intermingled with their professional lives; as the romantic strings of Nick Bicât's music swirl in anticipation, Caroline declares 'I want to make love to you' (p. 18).

Caroline does not want to make love with him, but to him, because, echoing Susan Traherne in *Plenty* and Maggie in *Teeth 'n' Smiles*, she says, 'I love more than anything to make love to strangers. It's the only time I forget who I am' (p. 19). Just who she is, is explained later. She is the daughter of a disintegrating bohemian family, the apparent inheritor of Alice Park's bohemianism, and of Maggie's sixties revolution, saying 'People seem to want to drag you down with them. Why can no one be content with a night? When it's good?' (p. 28). Hell is not only oneself; hell is other people as well.

> CAROLINE: You have that look. I really can't kiss you.
>   When you have that look, it freezes me up.
> WILLIAM: What sort of look?
> CAROLINE: The look that says 'help me'. I'm sorry. I can't.
>   (p. 25)

In the seamless landscape of the modern professions, there is no transcendent value. 'Good Lord no' says Caroline (p. 16). When a good night is not connected to friendship, when there are no good jobs any more and a good sound goes unheard, clinging to anything beyond the profit-motive rules of the marketplace is 'mad'. Life is, as William defines it in a sequence of words which reinforces the invocation of Sartre, not merely 'shameless' and 'ugly', but 'absurd' (p. 15) – sexually, aesthetically and metaphysically promiscuous.

Dreams of Leaving might be 'an obsessive love story, that state you get into when sex is all you can think about all day',[3] but it is a love story without sex scenes. Unlike *Heading Home*, which revisited much of the same territory a decade later, the lovers of *Dreams of Leaving* remain clothed and there is a single kiss in 75 minutes of the film. The lack of consummation between them is expressed in the use of the telephone within the film. William had used it to commit his lying 'massacre' of former girlfriends; Stone uses it to dump a Hockney on his rigged market; it signals William's abandonment of Caroline, which expresses Caroline's independence of him, and it is the telephone – in the only call where we see both parties – which reveals William's desperation for contact with her. Where William has shown himself to be sexually promiscuous, Caroline will not cheapen their relationship with sex. It is Caroline – in her friendship and sincerity – who is the beautiful (as opposed to the ugly), and the good, laying claim to the word in describing her photographs chronicling the social reality of London brothels.

Caroline's confession that 'I'm in love with you' (p. 26) stands at the centre of the narrative. Feeling flattered, William seeks her approval by adopting her views on journalism in the longest speech of the film, and disrupts the editorial conference by identifying 'the smell of bad conscience heavy in the air', and then concludes 'Excuse me. I'm afraid I must go' (p. 32). When Caroline condemns rather than rewards William for his outburst, he becomes ashamed in front of her, the reverse of Andrew, who has gone from being ashamed to being shameless:

ANDREW: I used to feel some sort of shame in a way.
CAROLINE: Why?
ANDREW: Just because it's odd to like anything so much.
CAROLINE: Why be ashamed?
WILLIAM: I think you're lucky.
ANDREW: Well I admit I don't feel it any more.
WILLIAM: I think what you are is some sort of ideal. Andrew
    needs nothing. Just his work and that's all.   (p. 27)

Where William needs reward, support and comfort, Andrew is his own man. Where Andrew is free, William is in some sense guilty and can only apologise. The telephone call which was printed as shot sixty-two was moved to occur after shot sixty-seven precisely to underline his failure in the face of the challenge.

The bad conscience William has identified is not simply that which Susan Traherne had found amongst the men of the Suez crisis of 1956, or the public lying which was at the root of *Licking Hitler*, but the way that public lying is an externalisation of something inside us – our failure to take responsibility for ourselves and our lives, our abrogation of freedom. The loss is – as William expresses – inside and not outside us. This is Sartrean bad faith (*mauvaise foi*), a fleeing from anguish, and a denial of our responsibility for our situation, a form of self-deception. Bad faith is not simply wrong belief, but the search for excuses for conduct in a world we have in fact made ourselves and are therefore responsible for.

Shame in this context is, like love, a metaphysical rather than a moral feeling and it is the look, the realisation of another consciousness turning oneself into an object, which is the heart of the concept. It was only in introducing himself to Caroline in the art gallery (shot fifteen of the printed text) that the owner of the voice and body was named as William Cofax; it is in relation to her that he takes his identity. William, then, becomes 'ashamed' under the gaze of Caroline. In contrast, when William watches her with the secretary in the gallery, Caroline smiles, 'not knowing she's observed' (p. 17). In Sartrean terms, then, it is Caroline who is the *pour-soi*, Caroline who is free and anguished; it is Caroline who is the existentialist hero, the example of good faith, not whore but Madonna. All William had to do was keep his faith with her, then they'd 'be fine', and the phrase is recited throughout the film cumulatively to assert this point.

In *Dreams of Leaving*, like *The Secret Rapture*, love is not a form of salvation. It is rather the moment at which the individual surrenders autonomy to another, abandons freedom by becoming the object of another. When William does 'find' Caroline again he tries to make her a victim. He starts by apologising but then says he doesn't want to see her and if he doesn't see her, she has no identity. At the end of his outburst, Caroline gives him a single kiss with the words 'Well that's it. You better go now. I never loved anybody ... I only love you' (p. 35). Those are her final words and, at the moment at which she touches him, she loses herself. Caroline is unseen for the next seventeen shots. Following William's careful construction of himself as attractive to women, Caroline's refusal to sleep with him must be abnormal or 'mad' (p. 25), and anorexia is usually associated with adolescent girls involving the denial of the physical ideal of womanhood. In a reversal of the control of the gallery encounter, William walks down the corridor bringing the camera and the doctor with him. He leaves Caroline in a state of mental collapse and there is significantly no look between them.

When Hare returns to questions of relationships after *Dreams of Leaving* – in *A Map of the World* and *Wrecked Eggs* – his women are rejecting promiscuity in favour of permanent relationships. Kate Nelligan's place at the centre of Hare's work is taken by Bill Nighy, who moves from the journalistic cynicism of William in *Dreams of Leaving* to the earnest journalist with left-wing views in *A Map of the World*, the unscrupulous and voracious accountant Eaton Sylvester in *Pravda* and, finally, to the dissembling Edgar, the inheritor of the war-torn kingdom of *King Lear*.

If William's expression of relief at Caroline's madness had come as the ending to the play, the audience might have been left with some shock. Instead, William can return to his career in Fleet Street and the short reluctant kiss of a suburban marriage in which Laura and William 'look at each other' (p. 41) with passionless expression. In his cork-tiled, pine-furnished sleep of the epilogue, however, William, and Hare, is troubled with bad dreams. What we have taken to be his confidence now seems to be a way he had of hiding his fears, that Caroline was 'right'. If she had reached out to him, there is no guarantee that she would have been 'saved'. If she had reached out to him, William would certainly have been saved from his bad dreams, from the recounting which comprises the film. As it is, 'Our lives dismay us. We know no comfort. [Pause] We have dreams of leaving. Everyone I know' (p. 41).

The smell of bad conscience

Hare has invited the audience into a love story and given them no comfort. He has left unasked and unanswered questions of why William might be grateful, why William knows no comfort and what the implications would be if Caroline were not mad. This pointer does not, however, come until the final line of the play and, despite the title, the issue of *Dreams of Leaving* is whether the weighting is sufficient to rescue the film from relapsing into that same relief and gratitude that Caroline's madness lends to William.

By the time *Saigon* was made, Hare had dreams of leaving the tasteful minimalism of British television drama production within whose confines *Dreams of Leaving* operated; he also had dreams of

leaving the idea of the writer as teacher. The printed screenplay for
Dreams of Leaving totals only thirty sides of text. Such slightness is
not simply the result of transcribing a visual entity. Hare's own
Saigon, for example, amounts to some sixty-five sides. There is in
Dreams of Leaving a measured verbal economy which, together
with its profusion of ellipses and pauses, superficially resembles a
Pinter text. The work after *Dreams of Leaving* shows a level of self-
conscious doubt, a wrapping-up of the 'message' in layers of obfus-
cation, unknown to the writer of the three-page speech about class
war in *Teeth 'n' Smiles*. After *Licking Hitler* and *Plenty*, it seems, the
simple judgement at the heart of theatre no longer applies. Hare's
single explicit unanswered question in *Dreams of Leaving* asks simply, 'Who can judge people?' (p. 33).

Just as Sartre's Roquentin responded to nausea by abandoning
his history of the Marquis de Rollebon, so, for a period at least,
Hare abandoned his English history plays. William's comments on
Fleet Street begin to read like Hare's own comments on theatre in
his Lecture of 1978: 'I have got tired with the feeling that we all
end up writing less well than we can ... I dread a lifetime randomly
producing something which we all distrust and despise ... If we
who work here can't believe in it, how the hell can the people out
there? ... I'm afraid I must go' (p. 32). Hare duly went to America.

Dreams of Leaving is told in the first person by a man of Hare's
age played by an actor (Bill Nighy) of startling physical resem-
blance to himself, who came, as he did, to London for a profession
in media/art circles in the early 1970s after the May Ball days of
Cambridge. A *Radio Times* interview[4] of the time reveals that
William's flat was indeed a flat Hare once lived in and that
Caroline's clothes were those of Hare's female friends. This is more
than getting things right; this is veiled autobiography.

In *Dreams of Leaving*, William's wife is – like the abandoned
press agent of *Teeth 'n' Smiles* – named Laura; unlike Hare's per-
sona in the earlier play, William has made the comfortable marriage and (like Hare himself) has three children by 1980. Hare
could well agree with William when he says, 'Since that time I
haven't done badly' (p. 40) and with Lazar in *Plenty* who says, 'I
gave in. Always. All along the line. Suburb. Wife. Hell' (*Plenty*,
p. 83). The first-person voice-over begins to look like the same

faint-hearted attempt at distance as the projections in *Teeth 'n' Smiles*. Screened in the year his own divorce from Margaret Matheson was granted, there would appear to be direct parallels between *Dreams of Leaving* and his own life, with the title inviting the interpretation of *Dreams* through Freudian psychoanalysis.

'A dream does not simply give expression to a thought, but represents the wish fulfilled as a hallucinatory experience.'[5] In her first appearance, Caroline climaxes under William's very gaze with the words 'Yes I'm coming' and her first line, 'Yes, I'd like to' (p. 14) is delivered as she gazes levelly at William (out of shot in the position of the camera). This hallucination is directed at and shared by a male audience, whose sexual curiosity is assumed. 'Always implicit there was the promise, if I held on, the moment would come …' (p. 29). The promise is implicit to the very moment the closing credits have appeared over a painted image of a woman's body, until finally it reaches the face. This face is not Caroline's so that the film itself stands revealed as a tease, holding up the actress Kate Nelligan, Hare's specific choice for *Licking Hitler* and *Plenty*, as a sexual object.

The fact that the male viewer's consumption is ultimately denied does not let the film or its writer/director off the hook. Hare believes that 'a play is always what the author wants to write'.[6] The writer has elsewhere wanted to write differently: what is treated in *Dreams of Leaving* receives different treatment in *A Map of the World* and in *Heading Home*. 'A dream is a (disguised) fulfilment of a (suppressed or repressed) wish.'[7] If William's dream-story is taking place within David Hare's dream-art then it may be seen as a defensive fiction to protect a repressed wish to possess actress Kate Nelligan. The desire for her is realised in the circumstances of art against the background of belief that the perceiving audience operates on the basis of an internalised misogyny.

Dreaming and the making of art are, for Hare, a conscious and not, as they were for the Surrealists, an unconscious process. In both cases the role of Hare's art becomes less the explanation of despair, the relief of pain by historical analysis, but a form of catharsis for that despair and pain resulting not in a challenge to the ruling forces but in a comfortable sleep.

It is dangerous, perhaps, to mingle concepts of dream and of art, but, although Freud had no systematic theory of art, he did at various times in his writings use both dreams and jokes as suitable models for the interpretation of art as biographical evidence. Hare has made plain that for him 'it's worth remembering how often theatre has been compared to dream; for me the analogy is clinched by the way that, as with dreams, your own are so much more interesting than anybody else's'.[8] Freud's model of the mind is a useful key to the obsessions of *Dreams of Leaving* and to the structure of the coming plays of the eighties, all of which to a greater or lesser extent are built upon the opposition of the conscious and unconscious, and Freud's later model of Eros and Thanatos. While it is possible that we read this in, it is almost impossible to read it out.

When William finds Caroline in the dance studio and his voice-over is heard, the camera pans round to reveal that the previous shot was merely a reflection, that William was commenting not on reality but on illusion. The point is not, as it is for Pinter in *Monologue*, that memory is inherently unreliable or, as it was for Sartre in *Nausea*, that since we do not live an adventure, story-telling is a distortion. However tenuously ironic it may be, distance from William is possible and reveals that he is guilty of distortion.

'Time of course has cemented things over, so this now seems like the inevitable course' (p. 11), but – as Hare was to make clear in the final moments of the voice-over to *Heading Home* – meaning comes only from the end; it seems like the inevitable course but it was not. 'If I'd been wiser perhaps I would have known' (p. 41). The goal of art is, in some sense, wisdom, or, as Sartre writes in *What is Literature?*, to recover this world by making it seem as if it had its source in human freedom, appealing and demanding of the audience.

Unlike Barbara Dean in *Saigon*, William remains our only informant in the film, and in contrast to *Licking Hitler* there is no authorial interjection. Caroline's photographs were taken to provide a back-drop for a band's performance and they end up as little more in the film. The claim to fill the vacuum of television coverage of sex therefore leaves Hare guilty of either gross artistic failure or dishonesty. As Hare confesses, 'It's a film that was intended to have politics',[9] taking up from *Licking Hitler* the interrelation between personal and political promiscuity, 'but they are not to the fore-ground the way the sex is'. In that sense the political remnant is either a bad dream disturbing his sleep or an appeal made in bad faith.

'The only honest thing would be to confront them' (p. 31) and Hare does not. In the newsroom, political events are reduced to single clichéd headlines and background noise. Unlike *The Ploughman's Lunch* and *Plenty*, both of which focus on the Suez crisis, the journalism of *Dreams of Leaving* has no object. And if the promiscuity, loss of family, the madness and bad faith are a subjective response to an objective crisis of the system, if the loss of value implied by gossip journalism and the rigged art market is itself a propaganda, its causes are not clearly identified in any historical context. Where previously historical schema had laden characters, lack of social context makes them pale and empty existentialist ciphers. Caroline is deliberately classless and Hare does not exploit his own latent connections; what he dreams of leaving is not that decayed bourgeois life, not the system itself, but the anxiety and shame which awareness of the system generates. If his failure as a film-maker cannot relieve him of responsibility, neither does it strip the film of politics: it blunders its way through the moral miasma of 'the personal is political' to a statement which is highly reactionary.

It is the absence of information about Caroline which constructs her mystery. In contrast to Chesneau in *Saigon*, who escapes the gaze of Barbara Dean, nothing is seen from Caroline's point of view. The mystery of Caroline is created not by the impossibility of information but by its deliberate omission by Hare. In the hotel conference, she appears as a briefly glimpsed enigma only because we do not know where she has been or where she is going. In the viewing room Caroline stands lit by a spotlight beside the easel and painting that is waiting to be bought by the (male) client seeing from William's position. In the storeroom she pulls out a huge canvas and becomes part of the Lichtenstein. She is framed by it but, further, her white shirt and green skirt are in total sympathy with the coloured brush strokes, merging with them into a new construct, the unattainable and Platonic ideal. As she talks about the price and is viewed through William's eyes, she becomes the object for our admiration and consumption.

This framing of Caroline, making her into an art object, continues throughout *Dreams of Leaving*. Outside the gallery, Caroline is framed by windows – in William's room; in the doorway to the bathroom in both the hotel and the band's offices; in the window there; in the doorway to her flat and, finally, in the windows of the asylum. In Sartrean terms, it is David Hare who is simultaneously the *pour-soi* and the *en-soi*; it is the writer who is god, while his characters – in depending on the consciousness of the audience for their existence – are being-for-others, *être-pour-autrui*.

William's distortion can construct our lack of knowledge not because he is controlling the discourse, but because Hare allows little evidence which might contradict his story. Unlike Virginia, the ostracised daughter in Richard Eyre's direction of Trevor Griffiths' *Country*, there is no other perceiving subject. Where Virginia was documenting her family with her own camera, Caroline simply snaps William in passing and her photographs of the brothels are rifled through by him. Further, Caroline barely exists outside William's gaze; he is present in all the scenes in which she is seen and very little is given from her point of view except as she sits outside the newsroom, a point which serves to reinforce his vanity. As Caroline puts him off after their first date the camera stays exclusively on William and his uneasy wounded pride.

In *Country*, the camera moves restlessly through the great hall of the ancestral home to imply its unease and keep the subject-matter under control by its reflexivity. Stephen Frears tried to do the same with expatriate life in *Saigon: Year of the Cat*. In *Dreams of Leaving* Hare remains trapped in what he has described as the 'depressing grammar of so much British television – the master shot, the two-shot and the close-up'.[10] Its attempts at ironic distance fail and, as a result, it remains all too possible – if you assume William's expectation that his desire will be gratified as both legitimate and reasonable – to read Caroline as a 'prick-teaser', the femme fatale leading William on only to go frigid on him.

Where to be outside society is a positive thing for Sartre, it leads only to destruction for Hare. In *Dreams of Leaving*, as in *Plenty*, the cost of living an honest life in a corrupt system is madness. It is Hare's selection which presumes that Caroline's madness and William's departure are related. Her madness could be a province of the modern but it could be a direct result of women's liberation. 'I don't know what role I'm meant to be serving' (p. 34), complains William, and since Caroline is presented as well adjusted, William's (and implicitly Hare's) failure to understand Caroline becomes a failure to admit of female independence, to be unable to keep faith with her. Stated simply, because in this instance one consciousness is male and the other female, the assumption is that if a woman does not sleep with a man, he will leave and if he leaves, she will go mad.

After making a vigorous attack on the film for its moral evasion,[11] Ian McEwan reworked many of the same themes in *The Ploughman's Lunch*. At an exhibition of paintings, his own guilty journalist, James Penfield (Jonathan Pryce), forges his desire for the elusive television researcher, Suzie Barrington. The private immorality of James' rejection of the demands of his own working-class family and the deceit of his best friend (Tim Curry) culminates in the public immorality of James' reconstruction of the Suez crisis for the American college market, set against the wave of jingoistic fervour of the post-Falklands Tory Party Conference of 1982. As Suzie tells James, so McEwan is telling Hare, 'You're much too old to be making a drama out of alienation or whatever you want to call it. You've got to take responsibility for your own happiness.'

8   Drawing a map of the world

Lines of engagement

From the very beginning, *A Map of the World* has an argumentative tone. Two journalists meet casually in a hotel lobby and immediately become sparring partners. Stephen Andrews has a tendency to read situations wholly in terms of the jargon of political/economic analysis, to be impatient and intolerant where Elaine le Fanu, an experienced reporter for CBS, accepts and observes the process of politics. Hers is from the beginning the voice of the old hand, the voice of informed mediation between the west and the Far East, an influence for objectivity on the sidelines of a frustrating UNESCO conference on poverty.

This is established before the Indian-born novelist Victor Mehta, who is to address the assembly, swans in with an elusive waiter in tow, comfortable and in control. Talking of truth as his right, his is the carefully cultivated and precise language which belongs only to the foreigner writing in English. As Darwin said in *Plenty*, 'seen from Djakarta this continent looks so old, so beautiful' (*Plenty*, p. 27) and Mehta values all old civilisations over young ones. Stephen is visually boyish, proceeding by parody in a language buzzing with contemporary slang. He is thus aligned with the younger civilisations, whose aid he defends and on whose behalf he attacks the content of Mehta's books.

In their meeting, then, Stephen and Mehta draw the lines for the coming confrontation, the positions are given and entrenched – young against old(er), Left against Right, politics against art – the oppositions which stood at the heart of *Teeth 'n' Smiles* and would again preoccupy Hare in *The Bay at Nice*. Stephen and Mehta oppose each other like animals fighting for territory; their postures follow one upon the other in different styles of speech containing opposite perspectives. They are living different language games and can therefore barely enter into intellectual exchange.

What concerns Hare in the early part of *A Map of the World* is not poverty but the idea of argument, the very possibility of discussion and the notion of conference itself, and this was the initial idea for the play. Soon we see that beneath the posturing of the Right and the Left of politics, young nations and old, is one game that both men are playing – the seduction of women. The apparently public debate is based on a private quarrel; the apparently political is highly personal – the battle for Peggy Whitton.

As in *Dreams of Leaving* Hare puts the question of who sleeps with whom at the heart of the play, but Peggy is not the object of obsession. She acts rather the romantic and dramatic lubricant, tying the personal to the political. Without Peggy's intervention, Victor would never even listen to the statement on the inherent distortion of fiction that the delegation from the socialist countries has asked for. Without Peggy, the heavily contrived central debate of *A Map of the World* could not take place. It is not the moral blackmail of the west by the Third World which brings Mehta to negotiate, but sexual blackmail by Peggy after their one-night-stand together.

'Why did Victor Mehta read the statement on the nature of fiction at the UNESCO conference in Bombay in 1976? For thighs. For thighs and arms, and hair that falls across the face' (p. 37). The discovery that the writer of the statement is Stephen Andrews makes Victor withdraw the concession. The person is not separate from the argument, and Victor assumes that the motive for Stephen's display of principles is revenge for his association with Peggy.

When she offers herself as the prize to the winner of their argument and puts her body where her mouth is, it is her intention to demonstrate that such behaviour is out of date. Her offer, however, demonstrates that such behaviour is successful. Stephen had lost her to Mehta and now, suddenly, he is in with another chance. Mehta and Stephen are like knights in a medieval joust and – as his name guarantees him – Mehta is the Victor. Hare explained, 'One of the strands of the play is about that girl's growing up and she realizes that that peculiarly American way of looking at the world is inadequate to the world's problems.'[1] The letter home at the beginning of the second act provides a summary of the action for the audience returning after the interval. It also demonstrates that, even while the events are proceeding, Peggy realises that her action is recklessly foolish and that she must learn to live with her decision. The sincerity of that realisation is demonstrated by Peggy's presence on the film set and by Madeleine, the Peggy-actress, who breaks down with the realisation of her innocence (p. 63).

The problem with Peggy is two-fold. First, her six-pack hippy philosophy is inadequate to the task of suggesting that the American perception of the world is inadequate. The second part of the problem is the nature of that conceit. Just as Anna Seaton was to have learned through the passive acceptance of violent sex in *Licking Hitler*, Peggy is supposed to have learned by offering herself as a sexual prize. Hare is certainly guilty of the 'ultimate progressive offence' by refusing to be 'pro-women' – as he points out, that charge may be subject to 'merest fashion'. The charge against *A Map of the World* is primarily one of credibility.

The change in Peggy could be created – as indeed is shown – as part of the ageing process alone by understanding one basic fact, that she was young. Her maturing could be and is prompted by an intelligent relationship with a man she loved. Instead, as both writer and director, David Hare was either unwilling or unable to create a fully rounded character for Peggy Whitton. Even without a love scene, Peggy's offer provides a form of 'titillation' for just those men of the audience who would like to think they could win a woman's body by intellectual argument. It is intended to, and does, spice up a wordy debate between two men and, coming as it does at the midpoint of the action, is a pivot about which they swing.

In his redrawn *A Map of the World*, just as in his sixties revolution of *Teeth 'n' Smiles*, the role of women is still to adjudicate, mediate, offer motivation and decoration, but not to participate as equals. It is not that revenge or desire would play no part if Mehta's opponent had been female, but that a text delimits its possible readings, and *A Map of the World* admits of one which has Peggy

standing as a reinforcement of machismo. One might say of Hare
as Stephen says of himself, 'A shambler, a neurotic, almost by definition, I've accepted the picture the world has of an idealist as a
man' (p. 73).

The idea that a controversial writer would be invited to speak at
a UNESCO conference on poverty is equally implausible. The
idea that his failure to undermine the art for which he is known
would result in the breakdown of that conference is – or at least
was in 1983 before the Salman Rushdie affair – patently ludicrous.
If *A Map of the World* began as a satire about the way people argue,
it nonetheless developed in the writing into something more. At
the heart of the first act is a 10-minute speech in which M'Bengue
deplores the constant misrepresentation of Third World regimes in
the western media on the grounds that distortion is the price of
freedom. That there should be no doubt about the justification of
his complaint, M'Bengue's comments are supported by both
Stephen and Peggy and unopposed by Mehta, providing the only
consensus of political opinion in the play.

By exposing the pernicious aid machine on the stage of the
national theatres of Britain and Australia, Hare has reached precisely the kind of people who operate them; he has strategically
penetrated a mischievous statement on one subject into a play
about another. Since Elaine and M'Bengue are integral to the plot,
it is also out of political intent rather than guilt that he helps to sub-
vert the casting and playwriting prejudices in operation in British
theatres. Although Victor (as an Indian choosing to live in Britain)
could be seen as an 'honorary white', two unmistakably black per-
formers take sizeable parts and become part of a heavily white-
dominated company. The same cannot be said of the
homosexuality attributed to Michael, the Stephen-actor. *A Map of
the World* (and all Hare's plays) enshrine heterosexuality (and the
battle between men for a woman) as the norm.

After travelling, Hare has redrawn his map, putting the Third
World in proportion, putting British class differences to one side in
favour of the global ideology. The war which Hare is fighting is
not, however, the war against racism. Hare's discontent is still with
his own country and the war he is fighting is the white-middle-
class English war against despair. When Hare looks (or travels) to

the Third World, he seeks either solace or ammunition: 'I wanted to show that the current fashion for right-wing ideas in Britain is very parochial indeed, it's a period through which this country happens to be passing. If you go elsewhere in the world then you will find utopianism is still a vital force.'[2]

For this reason, Hare prefaces the play with a quotation from Oscar Wilde's 'The Soul of Man Under Socialism'. 'A map of the world that does not include Utopia is not even worth glancing at, for it leaves out the one country at which Humanity is always land-ing. And when Humanity lands there, it looks out, and, seeing a better country, sets sail.' If the quotation from Wilde refers to the need for idealism, it also — as Hare made clear — 'alludes to a line from the play's central character, Victor Mehta, an Indian novelist who complains that we only notice those things which fit in with what we already believe. For "everything that suits us we place upon our map".'[3]

Hare's Players' Scene (Scene Five) serves principally to reinforce the general demonstration that people do not answer a question; they make statements from their own vested-interest position. As the actors on the film set await the day's shooting, the Martinson and Elaine actors become involved in an argument over the answer, with seven letters beginning with Z, to a crossword clue: 'The plague of the earth?' The answer 'Zionism' creates a heated and unresolved dispute until, that is, the M'Bengue actor points out that the answer begins with S and is 'Slavery'.

In *A Map of the World*, it suits Hare to place M'Bengue and the struggle for change on his stage, but this should not be confused with any interest in the place itself. Hare presents the problems of the Third World through precisely the Eurocentric paradigm about which M'Bengue complains. The view of politics presented is pro-foundly medieval; it is a crusade, in which concern for others is a form of penance for sins committed. In claiming to write about the Third World, Hare is simply disguising the true agenda. For this reason, Mehta makes only one response to M'Bengue's complaints:

> MEHTA: People are venal and stupid and corrupt, no more so
> now than at any other time in history. They tell
> themselves lies. The writer asks no more than the right to

point those lies out. What you say of how the press sees
you is probably right, and the greater grievance you have
I am sure is right. But I will not add to the lies.
(*There is a pause. And then he gets up.*)
And that is all I have to say.   (p. 42)

In this way, as Hare describes, Mehta does not make the journalist's
claim to a good story, but 'the artist's claim that he is entitled to this
truth which is higher than documentary truth'.[4] For Mehta, art is a
way of setting the chaos of life into order; England stands for something positive, yet he found 'a deceitful, inward-looking ruling
class blundering by its racialism and stupidity into Suez. This was
bitter for a boy from an Indian village' (p. 66). This was bitter also
for that other immigrant – the boy from Bexhill. If Mehta had his
priorities clear to succeed in that society, so too did David Hare. If
Mehta found the tendency of the young to disown that success 'the
ultimate cruelty', so too did David Hare complain in *Teeth 'n'
Smiles* not about the failure of the sixties revolution, but about its
noise.

For Mehta the fact that aid occasionally averts crises is, as for
Oscar Wilde, merely evidence of the disease being prolonged
rather than cured. Against this disease, against journalism, Mehta
offers the artist. Where was a man meant to look for reason? To art
itself, pure form, an ideal form setting an example and owing nothing to the world, its very distance from the world the guarantee of
its usefulness. Even coming to the conference is a compromise for
Mehta. Like Stoppard's Lord Malquist, he stands aloof, contribut-
ing nothing 'Except by example. By what one is. One is civilised.
One is cultured. One is rational. That is how you help other people to live' (p. 19). He does not know how to solve the imbalance
between the west and the Third World: 'I tell you there is only one
thing I know, and one only: that in this universe of idiocy, the only
thing we may rely on is the lone voice – the lone voice of the
writer – who speaks only when he has something to say ' (p. 68).
So Hare had said in 1978, 'All a playwright can do is promise to
speak only when he has something to say.'[5]

What does Hare have to say in *A Map of the World?* It is Stephen
who is given the most debating time, he who has the greater

energy, venom and sexual imagery. In a play in which the audience is intended to agree with the last speech it has heard, it is Stephen who has the last word of the debate with his moral victory, clinched by his refusal of the prize of Peggy's body. Stephen tells Mehta that, 'What you must do only you can decide', and Victor makes a choice — if out of personal emotion and memory for Stephen rather than intellectual principle — to stay away from the conference because, 'This feeling, finally, that we may change things — this is at the centre of everything we are. Lose that... lose that, lose everything' (pp. 82-3).

Structural uncertainty

The argument, as contrived as it is interesting, over two days in Bombay in 1976 is the main substance (some forty-eight sides) of *A Map of the World*, but throughout Hare constantly pulls out of that action to reveal that these events of six years before are being filmed in the present from Victor's novel about them. Like a collapsing telescope, the film account folds inside the book, which is itself an account of real events, of life.

The overlapping fictionality is remarkably similar to Tom Stoppard's *The Real Thing*, which opened in the West End in 1982 while *Map* was in Australia. In both cases, the convolutions are much more difficult to describe than they are to watch, but they serve different purposes. Using layers of quotation, Stoppard's structure is simply the *reductio ad absurdum* of the play-within-a-play, collapsing, as the title of his character's play suggests, like a house of cards. If the conceit amounts to no more than 'all art and thought are biased', or 'reality might be a fiction', it is nothing very much to be concerned about, since audiences and writers have taken that for granted, at least since the time of Shakespeare and the players' scene in *Hamlet*.

The function of the overlapping fictionality in *A Map of the World* is not to imply that life is like a predetermined film script or simply to inject wit. Only two of the fictional actors are given names (Michael and Madeleine), but their tribulations comprise some twenty-eight sides of text, equal weighting with the proceedings in the conference room they are depicting. Hare is reflecting upon multiple misrepresentation – fiction of reality, the west of the Third World. The movie framework reminds us that all fiction is a manipulation by the writer for his own purpose and creates the vital link between the two concurrent plots.

It is because of this device of the play-about-a-film-about-a-book-about-real-life that the question of misrepresentation is inserted into the very fabric of the writing, and the subject of *A Map of the World* shifts away from the Third World to the very idea of representing the world at all: 'it's about the difficulty we have with meaning, the difficulty we have with the truth'.[6] At the centre in Hare's theatrical map is not aid allocation or racism, not sexism or socialism, but art.

In *A Map of the World* David Hare is not a historical witness. The conference in 1976 is not a real conference, the events did not take place. This does not mean, however, that Hare's play spirals into farce. The book is intangible; it cannot be read, but the audience is told and shown that the film is distorting the lives it purports to present. Peggy was an actress and not a jazz violinist. Clearly identifiable by being 'more heroic and heightened' (p. 25), the film is given only three sides of printed text. These takes are occasionally identified by quotation marks (the presence of scripts on the set), but usually overlap with conversations on the set. The difference is evident because the language changes to a more florid style.

Although the first interchange between the 'real' events and the film of them was rewritten to leave not Stephen but Mehta alone with Elaine, still, the lights concentrate, her acting is 'expanding alarmingly' (p. 25/*Asian Plays,* p. 171), 'sound men have edged on' and Elaine 'steps up into her highlight'. When Victor and Peggy walk on to the film set (at different times), they assert their independent existence. Hare is making sure that the difference between the film and the events it depicts are visible. The film Angelis is making is shown to distort, to romanticise and to add blatant inaccuracies for the sake of location shooting or Hollywood morals. Hare makes a truth claim – that he is presenting real life as it was. Unlike Stoppard, Hare is not sucked into an endless spiral where you cannot identify what the real thing is.

A Map of the World is a rejection of Martin Esslin's concept of the 'Theatre of the Absurd', the final nail in its coffin. Mehta does use the word 'absurd' repeatedly but, as in *Plenty* where the object of attack is the diplomatic service, it is a criticism of bureaucracy, the huge entanglement which is the United Nations. Like Franz Kafka, whose diaries Hare had adapted in one of his first writing attempts for Portable Theatre and who is quoted in the programme, Hare's sense of the absurd lies *within* a social and linguistic structure and is not a statement about the whole. Making a political statement may be fraught with difficulties, but it is possible and, if it is possible, then so is change. Because his trade is with words, the writer is in danger of climbing an ivory tower projecting his own isolation as despair.

For Hare, the absurd is not the reflection of a universal crisis, but the universalising of a limited one, and its effect is to suggest that change is either constant or impossible, and to contribute to laissez-faire, look-after-yourself capitalism. If absurdity had been in fashion in British theatre during the 1960s and 1970s, under Labour and soft-right Conservative governments, it was something about twentieth-century humanity and the social, economic and intellectual structures which was being said.

The absurdity has ever been the case – it can be read into/from every piece of fiction ever written. The sense of the collapse of character is engendered by the uncertainty of roles; the overuse of words in a media world intensifies the cycle of invention, use, misuse and disuse into a feeling of collapse, and leaves morality in one sense untouched and in another inoperative. If the relation of language to the world, contingency, has not altered, explanations must be sought in history, in psychology or in nature. What is treated in *Dreams of Leaving* as a crippling discovery is treated in *A Map of the World* as a malady with political causes and maybe even political remedies.

'A disputatious play, *A Map of the World* seeks to sharpen up people's minds, to ask them to remember why they believe what they do. To ask, in fact, whether they still do. Or should.'[7] Victor persuades the audience with charm as much as the content of his argument. The lure of the Right, its power to create and sustain a Thatcherite Britain into a second and third term, was to occupy Hare in the creation of Lambert Le Roux and in *A Map of the*

World, the final power of Stephen's conviction is only bought by the offstage and all too convenient martyr's death of his biblical namesake. Stephen's own decline into middle-aged doubt or right-wing complacency remains not only unseen but unseeable. Instead, it is Victor who, seven years on, visits the film set. For Hare, it seems, the end justifies the means.

Just as Angelis argues with Mehta (p. 30), Hare argues with himself, and as Victor makes his final revelation, the world is elsewhere and it is not listening:

> MEHTA: ... this feeling, finally, that we may change things –
> this is at the centre of everything we are. Lose that ...
> lose that, lose everything. (*He stands, the man who has
> lost*.)
> PEGGY: I'm sorry. I didn't catch what you said.   (pp. 82-3)

The telescoping device in *A Map of the World* does not cover Hare's tracks, but uncovers them, revealing a serious doubt about the viability of a belief in change. Like the dissident in Stoppard's *Professional Foul,* he seems to agree that 'In the end it must change. But I have something to say – that is all.'[8] Or at least, as Stephen says, 'I would if I could be heard among the clamour of voices' (p. 13). As Hare went on amending earlier passages, he told Melvyn Bragg that 'the ending completely satisfies me'.[9] If the ending expresses Hare's doubt, 'Then please remember that my case stands or falls here that often from the best intentions we tell ourselves lies ... I am told to point it out is bloody-minded and – what? – "unhelpful". And yet to me, I am telling you, not to point it out is worse' (p. 68). If not to point it out is worse, then 'the power of the theatre to detect a lie extends even to his own desperate belief in a socialist alternative'.[10] As Mehta says, 'The act of writing is the act of discovering what you believe' (p. 58) and Hare's lone voice will not add to the lies.

Just as Hare's autobiographical self quoted from Yeats' 'The Gyres' in *Teeth 'n' Smiles*, so, with his talk of merest fashion and of the irrational, in Mehta he has, as the title of Yeats' poem suggests, a 'Second Coming'. Yeats' regret was for the loss of ancient lineaments, social breeding and the cultural elite; he looked back to more ordered times and especially the Renaissance with nostalgia, and his conservatism found sympathy in fascism. Mehta looks to art and to the old civilisations and the result is a pessimistic conservatism.

Where Stoppard could be said to have moved from the existential and stylistic concerns of surreal absurdity towards a need to account for social reality, Hare has brought in the self-conscious and entertaining artistry of the Right in modern drama and become increasingly unsure of the Left. The attack which Stephen brings against Mehta can therefore be levelled against Hare himself: unless he succeeds in finding an emotion which is not disdain, he will attack others who still have ideals with a ferocity out of proportion to their crime, withdraw into his ivory tower and, by ordering with style the chaos, end up withdrawing with style from the chaos.

He does so in a high-flown language of rhetorical debate, in two or three side speeches, which is in part a reaction against the ordinariness of naturalism and television drama, in part a repudiation of the propaganda of their uselessness. So the apparent naturalism of the colonial hotel floats in the bare bones of the theatre machinery. The actors are shown to be performing for the 35mm camera (p. 25) and the audience is made to feel like a cameraman, reversing the common technique of adopting theatrical modes in the cinema by using cinematic ones on the stage.

> All too often the real pleasure of epic theatre – the easy movement of time and place – is lost in the gaps while the scenery is changed. In this way the flow is disrupted and the irony you intend by setting adjacent scenes in different styles gets spoilt as stage-hands in black clothing blunder about in the semi-dark. *A Map of the World* is a seamless epic. There are almost no blackouts. The changes themselves are written as part of the action. They have a rhythm which contributes to the meaning of the play.[11]

Long arguments between people in a hotel or conference room are not cinematic, but the merging together of time and place is.

For Hare, 'The essence of epic is that one image should be replaced by the next.'[12] His inheritance is not from the Brechtian epic theatre but from Sergei Eisenstein, a legacy he shares with Brecht. Eisenstein's theory of montage developed under the influence of the dialectic from the idea of attraction between shots towards one of collision, by which he aimed to produce emotional effects in the spectator to jolt him out of his ideological preconceptions and make him look at the world anew. So the final scene of *A Map of the World* takes place in front of Mehta on the empty film set, and we consider whether Victor's account of what happened in his book is exhaustive of the action we have seen.

The filmic approach to *A Map of the World*, however, also contributes to one of the weaknesses of the play. Hare's play is made undramatic by unseen events. Peggy's experiences on her mountain-top and the death of Stephen are told and not shown. Such description is at the heart of the novel and not of the theatre.

'Jealousy is particularly fierce in writers and contempt, disdain. These are the characteristics of the middle aged writer.'[13] As Hare has moved towards middle age, so his own 'jealousy' has become more evident − of John Osborne for writing *Look Back in Anger* after which theatre was never the same; of right-wing writers who can condemn people to the miserable inadequacies of their own lives. In 1981, Hare directed a revival of Christopher Hampton's *Total Eclipse* for the Lyric Theatre in Hammersmith, Hare's last work to date as a director on another writer's work. In dramatising the relationship between the poets Verlaine and Rimbaud, Hampton's play explored the search to answer the question to write or not to write.

In *A Map of the World*, Hare's acknowledged debate with himself is not whether to write, but how to write, how to reconcile Mehta's style with Stephen's passion while seeing the virtues and the flaws of both right-wing wit and left-wing commitment. In *A Map of the World* the map is not a plan for change, and Hare significantly misses out the final part of the quotation from Oscar Wilde. If he used to believe in socialist realism, the showing of how things are and how they can be, he no longer does. It is this which makes the play so significant a moment in Hare's writing.

9 All our escapes

Produced for the newly established Greenpoint Films during 1984, *Wetherby* marked Hare's directorial debut in the cinema. At the age of 38, a man who once claimed to have gone into the theatre as a substitute for working in the movies achieved an ambition and was set to join the ranks of England's auteurs. In weaving together the historical concerns of Hare's earlier work with the unravelling of a psychological thriller, *Wetherby* reveals him not as a Romantic optimist with visions of utopia, but as a pessimist with ultimately metaphysical concerns. The film had a twelve-month theatrical release before screening on Channel Four on 12 June 1986.

An inspector calls

As the credits roll over a black screen at the beginning of *Wetherby*, a conversation between two unidentified voices is reminding the audience of Nixon the liar/lawyer of Watergate and placing the coming events against a background of massive political corruption. It is only as the blackout is lifted that the camera focuses on Jean Travers (Vanessa Redgrave) and the first attributable line – the second opening of the film – comes from Stanley Pilborough (Ian Holm).

The Nixon they are discussing represents not the public face of scandal but its private face – the bizarre nature of the courtship of his wife Pat. The subject of the film is not lying on the grand scale of Watergate or of Poulson, but the distortions of story-telling and the daily inveterate lying of the ordinary contemporary lives of a small Yorkshire town.

The fabric of Jean's ordinary life is that of the jumble sale and beans on toast, the school play and parents' evening. At her dinner party, the guests are all, save one, in their late forties or early fifties – three men and three women balancing the suburban dinner table. The directions make it clear that Morgan's relative youth is inconsistent and when he does contribute to the conversation, it is to name the crime of the girl who has annoyed Marcia – being young. As in *A Map of the World*, *Wetherby* is creating an opposition between the young and the older.

At school Jean is teaching this other generation *Othello*, teaching an examination English class to consider the lines, 'Look to her moor, if thou hast eyes to see / She hath deceived her father and may thee', which are written on the blackboard. A woman who lies casually to her mother, saying she has seen *The Third Man* when she was making love to an airman, might deceive us or even herself, but we are reading Jean Travers as Langdon does later, as 'a teacher, obviously good at her job'.[1]

Challenging our reading and the classical liberal assumptions which underpin it as much as Othello's misunderstanding of Iago and Desdemona, she asks, 'Do we become the way we look? Or do we look the way we really are?' (p. 16). The unanswered question places *Wetherby* in the interrogative mood of the thriller and, as ever, signals the moral thrust of Hare's writing. Whereas in his earlier work that questioning had been devoted to more obviously political concerns, in *Wetherby* it is apparently devoted to a two-pronged and connected investigation into a psychological concern about the nature of individual character and into an exploration of the value of education.

As Jean sits marking schoolwork in the summer evening, she is interrupted by the unwelcome arrival of one of her earlier guests. Her tension is one of the carefully placed clues that something is amiss, and sure enough, Jean's polite question, 'Are you staying with Marcia long?' evokes the ultimate in disruptive replies, 'No. I don't know Marcia' (p. 18). *Wetherby* has begun as an Ayckbournian social comedy of manners with a joke about the English taking civilised manners to ridiculous extremes but, as John Morgan goes on to explain that he has come to dinner without being invited, he disrupts the normal present-to-future time progression of the film with flashback to the beginning of the dinner party. Jean's response is one of disbelief, that it is 'Absurd. Impossible' (p. 20). And at this point Morgan blows his brains out.

Shown in closeup and with the red blood spattering out of the top of his head and onto the white wall behind, Morgan's suicide is an act of extraordinary violence against Jean and against the audience. That Morgan was meant to be there, we, like Jean, had not questioned and Stanley's realisation on the doorstep that something was wrong is played back only later to reinforce our subsequent doubts. The acceptance of the stranger might seem ridiculous in hindsight but at the time is made convincing by the fragmentary representation.

As Jean cries out in horror, the shock catapults her thirty years back in time to 1953, and a moment of passionate lovemaking with a young airman. The film is then to manipulate three time zones in a densely overlapping web. These flashbacks and layers of memory in *Wetherby* have the same structure of containment as those in *A Map of the World* and *Teeth 'n' Smiles*. As in those plays, it is always clear where we are: there is no spiral into farce, and the idea that the time confusions alone signal the absurd has already been explicitly denied.

The lived and chronological present of the film with its talk of political lying and its quiet naturalism is the dominant discourse, moving from Jean and Stanley's lunchtime drink on the day of the dinner party to the same situation some three weeks after it. Any flashback to the suicide is unmistakable in its violence, and the events of the dinner party have a clear touchstone in the drip of water, and the liaison on the landing which follows it, as well as the progression of the meal.

The events from Jean's past (twenty-four shots) are similarly straightforward and have the heightened dream-like quality of the movie style of the fifties. Events from Morgan's past comprise only twelve printed shots and therefore have half the weight. They are non-sequential and, being shot from a hand-held camera, uneasy, so that like Morgan himself, they are disruptive of both the film's and Jean's normality.

Consistency of texture ties the time zones together with the candlelight of the dinner table becoming a romantic moonlight glow of a night-time liaison in a troop carrier. Played by Joely Richardson, daughter of Vanessa Redgrave, the girl is the right age and colouring to be clearly the young Jean as well as generating a good deal of positive pre-publicity.

Hare is careful to place such detail as the photograph of Jean and Jim on the mantelpiece, but the time of 1953 was put beyond doubt not by explicit reference to the Malayan crisis, the political and military events of which are not expounded, but by a feeling. 'About 15 minutes of the film is set in the fifties. But I'm not going back for political reasons. I've never been able to write about my childhood and, if anything, this is a film that comes out of it.'[2] *Wetherby* evokes the atmosphere of a small town in 1953, the landscape of semi-detached red-brick houses in Bexhill of Hare's own childhood.

Just as Hare and his generation had looked to the time of their birth and the Second World War in television drama of the seventies, the fifties were suddenly the new chic in British film of the eighties. *Insignificance* invented a meeting in a hotel room between Marilyn Monroe and Albert Einstein, and *Dance with a Stranger* used the incidents surrounding Ruth Ellis, who in 1955 was the last woman to be executed in Britain. It is fifties styling which creates a Kafka-esque vision of a decaying bureaucratic future in *Brazil*. Terry Gilliam, Shelagh Delaney, Terry Johnson and David Hare were all using the atmosphere of their childhood to illuminate their present, and *Wetherby* is based not on research but on intuition.

It is not, however, semi-autobiographical. As in *Plenty*, the past is subsumed in a fictional personal history and 1953 stands as a time in her youth when Jean was happy. The film is not so much an intervention into the process of making history, but into questions of verification and psychology. In *Wetherby* one finds the overlapping of memories and experiences as we have them in life – in bits – but, like all thrillers, *Wetherby* is built on the empirical assumption that facts – including psychological facts – are knowable.

In his top-ten-rating thriller series *Dead Head*, Howard Brenton used the working-class hero adrift in a sea of confusion and denied explanation at the final moment to make his point about bureaucratic conspiracy. For Troy Kennedy Martin, the answer to the thriller series *Edge of Darkness* was nuclear cover-up. The thrillers of paranoia might have touched the nerve of eighties Britain, but *Wetherby* does not – as is the norm of the thriller genre – ask 'who did it?' for the simple reason that there is no murder and no crime. It is not a crime to kill yourself even in front of someone else, unless your death is provoked. As Hare said while discussing *Fanshen*, 'There's a comment of Len Deighton's which interests me very much. He says "I have no interest in going to a debate – unless I know that the loser is going to get shot in the end. That is dramatic." I feel the exact opposite. I have no interest in who's going to be shot at the end.'[3] As a result, John Morgan shoots himself at the beginning and the question, as ever in Hare's work, is not 'what happened?' but 'why did it happen?'.

Hare once worked as a thriller reviewer for the *Spectator* in 1970 and, unlike *Knuckle*, which was a pastiche of a Mickey Spillane thriller of the forties, *Wetherby* is influenced by the psychological thrillers of Hare's own time, and specifically by Patricia Highsmith, in whose work 'there is no obvious mystery except the mystery of why we are alive'.[4] In *The Tremor of Forgery*, for example, Highsmith also starts with a suicide but it happens unseen in another country, and the book ends with the confession by the central character, a novelist, to a manslaughter which may never have taken place. As she says through the words of her novelist character, 'I'm not so much interested in the story as in people's moral judgements on the hero' (p. 159). It is that kind of exploration of social responsibility and moral miasma that Hare enters into in *Wetherby*.

The film provides objective evidence that Jean is not in a legal sense directly responsible. Morgan may well have been a determined psychopath before he met her, as is shown by retracing the police enquiry to his arrival. In *Wetherby* the question is not 'Why did he do it?' which receives an immediate answer of 'Depressed, I suppose'; the question is, as Langdon realises, 'Why did he do it in here?' (p. 25). It is not the dead person who is of interest, but the one left alive, Jean Travers. The mystery to be probed is a mystery of her character and it comes under investigation when an inspector calls into the social comedy of the dinner party to make it a thriller of manners reminiscent of J. B. Priestley. The film then retains two parallel forms of investigation, which reflect the two different drafts of the script in the writing process – the police enquiry into a suicide and a cinematic 'moral enquiry into why so many seemingly comfortable people lead such unhappy lives'.[5]

A first-year student also from the University of Essex, Karen suggests that Morgan wanted to do it to her, as some form of revenge for her lack of contact with him. Vague and distant, spending all her time watching television and lacking curiosity, Karen seems to resemble the girl that Marcia had objected to at the dinner party. It is not so much that Karen has no personality, but rather that she refuses to share it. An apparent lack of communication, an invasion of her room and space reads again like Pinter, but Hare explicitly denied the comparison, saying '*Wetherby* may sound like Pinter, but what marks it out is its emotional flavour, and that stems from these people whose lives are apparently ordinary, and who indeed are ordinary, but who, by means of the film, can be shown to be seething inside with passions and a sense of their own loss which they cannot express.'[6]

People select their memories, put them in order and edit them to their own ends. So Marcia tells Jean there is no newspaper when Stanley is seen holding it; and Langdon tells Jean he has given up thinking about her and yet discusses the case with Chrissie. When the police reconstruct the events of the suicide, the charge by Morgan of Jean's acceptance of him is missed out. Jean's articulated explanation may not have been a lie but it was not the whole truth. In reprinting a snatch of a television interview which Jean is watching when Langdon arrives to interrogate her, the script makes the point explicit.

The camera always manipulates experience. *Wetherby* – like *A Map of the World* – is deliberately foregrounding the means of manipulation. It presents an event (the beginning of the dinner party), and then, in flashback, offers both Morgan's and Jean's memories of it. In the same way, the audience is shown the suicide, the police reconstruction of it and later Jean's memory of it mingled with a parallel to another violent death in her past which she could not have witnessed. The audience – whether sitting in the cinema or in their home – is given information allowing it to make a judgement. Jean, unlike William Cofax, is not doing the selecting, and the film articulates what she can only half fathom. For Hare, character is not an endless series of masks; explanations can be and must be sought in the combination of past and present experience (even if they are partial and partisan). We must look to Jean's affair with Jim in 1953, to Morgan's failed affair with Karen at the University of Essex and to Langdon's failed affair with Chrissie.

The flashback to Karen's repulsion of Morgan's invasion of her room in the university residences and of his desperate and obsessive 'sexual' advances towards her explains that John Morgan's loss is partly physical. Karen is not only denying sex to Morgan, however. She is denying the entire game of dependency by lacking curiosity about him or anyone else and being completely self-contained and unapproachable. Morgan's outburst is the confession of a specifically male emotional demand rather than a more general existential need. Karen's failure to understand or to share it produces the same kind of extreme reaction from the parent Mr Varley at the school play.

Being of the same colouring, Langdon, Jim and Morgan are consistently men Jean might find attractive. By connecting them through one woman, the film creates an equivalence in reflection about a central point. Chrissie walks out of the Chinese restaurant at the moment Jean talks of Morgan's obsession for Karen. The 'coincidence' forges an equivalence (whether or not it is well founded) between the three women in the lives of the three men. Just as Karen and Jean denied emotional contact with John Morgan, so Chrissie is 'saddle sore' (p. 46) as Langdon lies precoital in the bath; just as Karen rejected Morgan's need of her, preferring the television culture, so Chrissie returns to her husband and the countryside, leaving Langdon as a 'sub-plot' while 'the real story was happening elsewhere' (p. 72).

All the men in *Wetherby* are experiencing dislocation and despair. Stanley takes refuge in drink, while Roger is obsessed with murder stories and visits the spot where Moriarty pushed Holmes over the falls with a colleague from home economics; upon losing Chrissie, Langdon says it has 'shaken my whole idea of myself' (p. 72). In this light *Wetherby* is a wade through male, middle-class and English *Weltschmerz*, and Morgan's suicide begins to look like an act of violence not only against Jean but against women in general. If Jean could have prevented Jim's murder (for the sacrifice of her education) by having kept him at home, Jean/Karen could have prevented Morgan's death for a sexual sacrifice. Karen has rejected Morgan and he comes to do violence; Jean has rejected him and he does it in front of her.

For the first time in Hare's work, however, the women are all survivors. It is in the ability to cope with loneliness that the opposition between male and female works within *Wetherby*. Morgan could have chosen Marcia, but he had followed her home and seen a bustling family behind the windows. Even though the word 'spinster' is cut from Langdon's description of her, it is clear from the old photographs of her and Jim together, which are examined by both Karen and Langdon, that Jean is alone, she is apparently like John Morgan, sharing eye contact with him over dinner and agreeing with his comments. Jean was singled out for what they apparently shared and it is something that Stanley – played by Ian Holm with a look of crumpled suffering – rather than Marcia understands:

> STANLEY: If you're frightened of loneliness, never get
> married.
> JEAN: I'm not frightened. (*Begins to cry.*) I'm hardened by
> now.   (p. 36)

Playing the part of Jean Travers from a position of strength, Vanessa Redgrave does not begin to cry as the direction in the printed script implies. Her face is rather weary and resigned – the loneliness is not 'trouble' nor a source of fear, but a constant in Jean's life, something she has gone through.

Where Jean has coped with despair and stands on the other side of Jim's death, Morgan's is an over-intellectualised wallowing, which, like Hamlet before him, lacks an objective correlative. When Morgan shoots his head off he might be, in an existentialist sense, denying his isolation and insisting his existence on other people, but to say that only begs another question.

> LANGDON: What happened? Was it your fault?
> (*She looks at him nervously, trapped at last. Then she goes and sits on the sofa. Her shoulders sag, as if the whole effort of the last weeks were over.*)

> JEAN: I think, in a way, it's because he was a stranger. I'm
> not sure I can explain. Because I didn't know him, now I
> feel him dragging me down. I thought I could get over
> it. But everywhere now ... the darkness beckons. (*Looks
> across at him*.) These things become real. He wants me
> down there.   (p. 73)

Othello kills Desdemona because he is deceived by Iago; John
Morgan kills himself not only because he sees that he is mistaken
about Jean Travers but – through making her suffer – to make his
own prophecy come true.

   The shock of Morgan's suicide forces Jean to relive events and
emotions from her past life. It is Langdon – showing interest way
beyond the call of duty – who is the catalyst. As Brock said to
Susan in *Plenty,* so might Langdon have said to Jean, 'And yet ... I
really shan't ever give up, I won't surrender till you are well again.
And that to me would mean your admitting one thing: that you
have failed, failed in the very heart of your life. Admit it. Then
perhaps you might really move on' (*Plenty,* p. 79). Jean admits it
and moves on to a new relationship with the inspector. The writing on the blackboard (in the most commonly used still of Vanessa
Redgrave) invites us to read Jean in terms of 'Experiment, experience, expiate, extraordinary, extreme, exhume, expose, extrude,
exclude and extra' as well as 'examination' (p. 90).

   It is at the moment of separation from Jim when Hare brings the
cinematic investigation of Jean's past together with the police
investigation in the present. Jean does not speak; she does not stop
Jim from leaving for Malaya and the lovers walk into the evocation
of *Casablanca* which had failed in *Saigon*, into the throng of servicemen boarding their planes.

   Jean can express quite adequately to Marcia what she was unable
to say to Jim: that there was a gulf between them. Where Pinter
would say that 'we communicate only too well, in our silence'[7]
and he would concentrate exclusively on the existential isolation
that implies, for Hare the characters are communicating only too
well in their Englishness. As Hare asks, 'Why are the people so
reactionary? What is it about them that is so reactionary? ... I've
tried to define it more and more as an emotional quality in them, a

racial quality in the English.'[8] He is less interested in the unavoid-able failure of language than in the social forms within which it takes place – not only in class but in nationality – and, unlike Pinter, Hare takes great pains explicitly to contextualise his charac-ters in their social niches.

In the ordered middle-class corner of the Thatcherite late eight-ies, the talk is of property prices and unemployment. Written as *Saigon* was completed, the title town of Wetherby is that province of tight little hedgerows which Barbara Dean left behind. Casting Judi Dench in both films – this time as Marcia Pilborough – re-inforces the connection. In *Knuckle* also Hare had investigated an apparent suicide and found an indictment of contemporary cap-italism. Hare confirmed that 'Although in *Wetherby* my political purposes are a great deal more concealed than in some of my stage work, they are there. Where *Wetherby* is different is that in the past I've always made the characters articulate, and actually I think that's been a weakness.'[9] It is, then, Jean's refusal to conform with the lower-middle-class expectation of Jim's parents that if they are to be married she should give up her intellectual independence, which has 'caused' the delay of their marriage and the death of her lover; and it is education which has 'caused' or reinforced their class rift. If love challenges these class boundaries, the English or at least the middle-class English are – as Hare put it in *Plenty* – 'love-less' (*Plenty*, p. 11).

As in all his work from *Licking Hitler* onwards, Hare's aim is to make the audience work for his political point by denying them easy handles. Where *Fanshen* had evaded judgement by declaring its credentials as political theatre, *Wetherby* aims to confound classi-fication by critics and audiences by mixing disparate genres. As an established figure with a considerable track record, Hare was, however, classified in precisely the way he wished to avoid, and it has obscured the fact that Hare's only 'political' answer to the intriguing enigma he has created in *Wetherby* is a simple statement: 'She's young. That's all you're saying' (p. 13).

If Suzie Bannerman remains a vision of a new future, she does not share Hare's sense of loss for either the socialist revolution or male certainty, and is as much a mystery to the writer as the girl in the library is to Marcia. If the next generation has a playwright to express its reality it is not David Hare, and the youth paper *New Musical Express* gave the film one of its worst reviews.

When Suzie Bannerman runs off with Alfred Egerton of Science Fifth, Hare is still in the pub with Jean and Stanley toasting 'To all our escapes'. He talks not of the rights of socialism – which were to surface in *The Bay at Nice* and *Wrecked Eggs* – but the escapes of conservatism. Talking ironically around the time of the revival of *Fanshen*, Hare explains that 'Because I started out by writing about politics, I got trapped in being thought of as a political writer and critics end up not noticing what the bulk of my work is actually about, like spirituality and romantic love. There's a way in which British critics can't believe that you can be a socialist and yet not write about socialism all the time.'[10]

Civilisation and its discontents

When Suzie runs away from school she leaves behind the idea of gaining qualifications which lead to the middle-class professions and makes the opposite decision to her teacher thirty years before by choosing passion over ambition. A way of being ordered, education is also one of those civilising impulses, part of the logic which holds society together. It is one of the culturally constitutive and regulatory institutions including the law (Stanley), the library (Marcia) and television (Verity) which, in a dinner-party civilisation, sit round the middle-class professional table of Jean's provincial kitchen and were to occupy Hare in a trilogy at the start of the nineties.

The law sanctifies and limits greed (Stanley); the police always bring sadness; the television is either a substitution for emotional contact (Karen) or the provider of racist and nationalistic humour (Verity). Civilisation therefore has its discontents, and Hare's model is not historical but psychological. It is John Morgan who expresses how inside the room of ourselves are passions – goodness, anger, revenge – bursting to get out and that 'We bury these words, these simple feelings, we bury them deep. And all the building over that constitutes this century will not wash these feelings away' (pp. 80-1).

Following on from *Teeth 'n' Smiles* and *Dreams of Leaving*, the crime is not only outside but inside. Even in England those unruly passions break out under the influence of drink and, as Stanley describes his unruly thoughts (p. 79), Hare is using the Shakespearian metaphor of the garden to tell of a nation not so much going to seed as tied too tightly to its guiding canes. The nation, he is claiming, is rotting with its own internalised desire. To make the point Stanley's speech is punctuated with the dishing out of salad. It is an example of the kind of interpretation of the text which Stephen Frears was unable to make in *Saigon*, and which makes Hare's own direction of *Wetherby* as richly precise and resonant as *Licking Hitler* before it.

Jean's house, her defence against the forces of nature which surround it, has a leaky roof. She tries to sleep but she has bad dreams. These are not dreams of leaving, some ideological bad faith. The object under attack in *Wetherby* is not capitalism, there are none of the money-marketeers and property-developers, gun-runners and drugs-pushers who had inhabited *Knuckle* and *Brassneck*. There is no expression of the 'socialist belief we all bear the guilt' (*Brophy*, p. 110), which marked Hare's *How Brophy Made Good* and J. B. Priestley's *An Inspector Calls*. The mystery of *Wetherby* is not the mystery of middle-class responsibility, but of middle-class repression.

By not telling Jim of her true feelings, Jean 'causes' his death; by not admitting John Morgan, she 'causes' him to kill himself in front of her. Death is waiting to burst through Eros, the urge to civilisation and to Life, which normally maintains control through the operation of the personal and cultural superego or conscience. 'What the film is claiming – which seems to me optimistic – is that people who are dismissed as bourgeois souls are as full of passion and feeling as opera singers but they happen, because they're English, to repress those feelings. You could accuse the film of being a romantic view of the world.'[11]

It is not, however, Romantic. Hare explicitly cut earlier drafted references to the countryside and its contrast with the city; rather than ending with Chrissie riding free across the English landscape, the final image is of Langdon ambiguously leaving his CID card behind but still walking through a modern estate of brick and glass. It was Howard Brenton who examined the positive spirit of revo-

lutionary nature through the exile/utopia of Shelley and Byron in
Bloody Poetry.

> BYSSHE: For a poet to despair? Obscene! We claim to be the
> poets of England. How dare we – luxuriate in
> denouncing the human cause as lost?
> The great instrument of moral good is the imagination.
> We must not let it become diseased! We must be
> optimists for human nature!
> We might be all
> We dream of, happy, high, majestical.
> Where is the love, beauty and truth we seek
> But in our mind?
> Poets are the unacknowledged legislators of mankind!
> BYRON: You talk Utopia ...[12]

Speaking about his own play *What Happened to Blake?* in 1975 Hare
had agreed that it is the job of artists to stay sane. A decade later,
however, he is Byron to Brenton's Shelley. In 1976, Brenton
included a flight to the countryside for the fledgeling revolutionaries from the crisp factory in *Weapons of Happiness*; more than a
decade later, he was talking still about beneficent human nature in
a utopian vision of a collective agrarian paradise in *Greenland*.

In *Wetherby*, there is only one shot which might be taken as
being visionary, of a bonfire on the street around which the children play with sticks. As in *Country*, it is an image laden with the
defeat of the gunpowder plot. For David Hare paradise is lost;
human nature contains not only the good but the age-old capacity
for evil, revenge, desire and his moral in *Wetherby* is not, as it is in
the film version of Victor Mehta's novel, that you should never
nurse unrequited desires (*Map*, pp. 25–6).

> ROGER: Logic also tells you that there must be constraints,
> and that if everyone went round saying what they feel,
> the result would be barbarism. (*Looks round the room.*
> *Quietly.*) And I prefer civilisation. That's all.   (p. 49)

This is not so much Pinter's room, the existential isolation and fear of invasion by other people, as Freud's extension of his psychological model to social interdependence, the enemy within the garden of the nation. It falls to the underwritten character of Verity – the bickering subset of Roger and the only character at the dinner party with no life outside of it – to make the point with her name bestowing a high truth value to it:

> VERITY: (*Suddenly shouting at him*): Life is dangerous. Don't
> you realize? And sometimes there's nothing you can do.
> ROGER: That's not true. I think you can always limit the
> danger.   (p. 50)

You can limit the danger by imposing a block on the side of yourself which is undesirable or what is too awful to contemplate, by keeping your eyes down under the privet hedge, but the price of this educated repression is emotional death.

Roger is a pedantic pseudo-philosophising teacher alleviating the stale bickering of his marriage with a half-hearted affair and talk of murder. For Stanley and Marcia, too, marriage masks fear and loneliness beneath the veneer of suburban ambition. Like William and Caroline some years after *Dreams of Leaving*, they are 'prisoners of our dreams' (p. 91). The middle classes and the middle-aged may be emotionally dead because their language and their ideology is stultified; but those who feel the full force of passion – John Morgan and Jim – are consumed by it and are literally dead. If not an example of neurosis, psychology and paranoia, then, John Morgan is evil, a darkness which stands outside class, immutable like death itself and the opposite of Jean's goodness.

> MARCIA: ... Stanley thinks good of nobody . . .
> STANLEY: Not true. I expect good of nobody. And am
> sometimes pleasantly surprised. And when I find good ...
> my first feeling is one of nostalgia. For something we've
> lost. Ask John Morgan.   (p. 79)

In this light, the corruption of *Brassneck* and *Pravda* in retrospect seem to stem from something eternal in human nature, from greed and envy, as much as from the late capitalist formation. That, as

Freud elaborated, merely dictates the particular form they take. There still remains the family, which had stood at the root of *Knuckle* and would occupy Hare again in *King Lear, The Secret Rapture* and beyond. You are trained into a form of life which contains moral, political and psychological beliefs, which certainly leads to the loss of passion, often leads to class alienation (not only in Jean but in Langdon), and may in itself lead directly to despair.

Hare has tried to define the reactionary in terms of the character of the English middle classes and the particular forms those beliefs take, but he has found that the cost of that protection against barbarism is, as Freud perceived it, an inevitable unhappiness. Nobody draws a moral in the film because Hare finds that lifting the lid of repression is inevitably destructive. Although the schools and the courts may be ideological state apparatuses operated by the dominant bourgeoisie, neither education nor the law are in themselves ideological; they are rather psycho-sociological necessities by which civilisation of any kind polices its discontents. Hare, like Jean Travers, sometimes has trouble seeing the point of school, but remains one of those 'maniacs, assorted oddballs, eccentrics, folk who still think education is worthwhile' (pp. 90-1).

If *Wetherby* is 'a dream-piece', it – like *Teeth 'n' Smiles* – comes not from the unconscious but 'from my subconscious'.[13] It can release the dangerous emotions for its own preservation only in a controlled and acceptable way, a fact which an earlier draft of the script articulated, but which is in any case reflected in the very fabric of the film which limits camera movement to demure and repressed style. Art seems not a revolutionary force but a regulatory one, which Freud included in his sphere of the cultural alongside science and religion.

Wetherby articulates Hare's suspicion that civilisation – wherever it may stand in the map of the world – always has its discontents; he suspects that the good old words describe not the product of historical circumstance but some innate raw material on which history works. In explaining what he saw as Mrs Thatcher's 'tacit admission that the savage materialism she had preached over the previous years was as unsatisfying to her as to everyone else', Hare 'can only direct Freud's words: "Art exists to reconcile men to the sacrifices they have made on civilization's behalf".'[14] Whereas in the history plays, from *Licking Hitler* to *Saigon*, the time was out of joint and the individual was a cipher for *ennui* as his/her experiences and breakdowns reflected larger disjunctures, in *Wetherby* history is contained within the individual brought into focus at a moment of passion, decision and loss. The individual is not a cipher for history but contains all history within herself.

If Hare's model from Shakespeare is not from the comedies, which he had parodied in *Slag* and *Teeth 'n' Smiles*, neither is it the histories. Hare's dramatic inheritance is tragic, and Aristotle maintained that all the parts of epic are included in tragedy while not all those of tragedy were contained in epic. If tragedy involves peripety, discovery or both, this discovery is, in Aristotle's terms, inartistic if it takes the form of a writer's device. So *A Map of the World* buys Mehta's discovery of the value of a belief in change with the train crash which killed Stephen. In *Wetherby* and *The Bay at Nice*, however, Hare introduces discovery through memory and makes Jean's 'crime' a hamartia, which brings in its train a disproportionate punishment.

What Jean experiences in the film, by being forced to articulate and confront the repressed passion and memories of her past, is certainly, in its psychological sense, a catharsis but it also almost approaches a catharsis in the tragic sense, evoking if not pity and fear then at least a certain horror. As Iris Murdoch explained, 'Oreste in *Les Mouches* remarks that "human life begins on the other side of despair". It begins with the denuding experience of radical reflexion. Till then, all is bad faith. The primary virtue is sincerity.'[15] The point for Hare, as for Victor Mehta in *A Map of the World*, is that 'Mankind has one enemy only and it is not poverty. It is self deception' (*Map*, p. 68). The plays of the eighties begin on the other side of the despair of *Dreams of Leaving*; they begin with the radical reflection of *A Map of the World* and *Wetherby*. Till then, perhaps, all was bad faith.

10 Painting pictures

Written as a double bill for the National Theatre, *The Bay at Nice* and *Wrecked Eggs* opened in the Cottesloe directed by Hare in September 1986 as *Pravda* concluded its run on the Olivier stage. Centring on the authentication of an unseen Matisse, *The Bay at Nice* continues the investigation of the art object begun in *Teeth 'n' Smiles* and *A Map of the World*, while the more immediately accessible but severely flawed *Wrecked Eggs* picks up from *Dreams of Leaving* the theme of sexual and moral promiscuity. What links them – and their settings of Cold War Russia and contemporary America – is a parallel structure and a dual exploration of the nature of freedom, and what they reveal is a further shift from history to poetry, from the epic to the tragic.

A matter of taste

On entering the theatre for *The Bay at Nice*, the audience is confronted with a large painting. Vivid against the total white of its four walls, it defines the room as a gallery and dominates the stage. The atmosphere is hallowed and apparently timeless, although the time and location are clearly given in the programme as Leningrad, 1956. The careful formality of speech which – by the placing of adverbs at the beginning of sentences or the use of the continuous present – sounds translated, and the accent of the players under Hare's own direction served as a constant reminder.

In front of the painting are Sophia Yepileva and her mother Valentina Nrovka. From the first, 'What does that mean?' is the chorus refrain of a profound difference. There is no physical con-

143

tact between them and the conversation progresses only in fits and
starts, punctuated with pauses, uneasy silences, and heavily laden
looks of disapproval, contempt, anxiety, anger and mistrust. It soon
becomes clear that mother and daughter are speaking different lan-
guages.

The issue of gender is explicitly raised but, where Sophia apparently speaks 'on behalf of' the then eastern bloc of Soviet Russia,
Valentina's anecdotal style is the language of salons, of fashion, of
individuality and of artists – a part of her mother's past, significantly inaccessible to Sophia. And so when Sophia describes the
painting before its arrival as 'A window. The sea. A piece of wall'
(p. 8) – a description which associates it with the suggested title *The
Bay at Nice* – Valentina replies that it sounds like a forgery. This
even though there may be lost work and, if there were, it would
almost certainly contain a window, a bay, and some wall because in
Matisse's so-called 'Nice period', the painter was most interested in
light and the window motif.

Henri Matisse first went to Nice in 1917 when he painted
Intérieur au violon. He spent every winter for four years at the Hôtel
de la Méditerranée where he painted *Intérieur à Nice* in 1921. The
two paintings are reproduced on facing pages in *Matisse on Art* by
Jack D. Flam, which was reissued in 1984 shortly before the writing of *The Bay at Nice*. The former painting shows a room dominated by the shuttered window (with foliage and the sea glimpsed
through it) while, in the foreground, is a blue violin case; the latter
presents an open French window with a woman seated on a balcony in front of the sea, while in the foreground is carpet, wallpaper and bedroom furniture, including – at the centre – a chair.
Hare has, then, described a painting which is consistent with the
preoccupations of the Nice period.

The tsarist count of the play claims the canvas was discarded in
Matisse's hotel in Nice (p. 15). Valentina does not consider this
hard to believe and neither would an art historian. Stchukine, an
importer of textiles, lived in the Old Palace of the Troubetzkoy
princes in Moscow. He left Russia after the revolution for the
South of France. It is from him, and from the other main Russian
patron of Matisse's work – the factory owner, Morosoff – that the
impressive collection of western art, which began to be shown at

the Hermitage Museum in St Petersburg from around 1956, was seized. It is therefore entirely probable that in 1956 in Russia a painting which does not officially exist could have surfaced.

To test for a forgery, the museum authorities have turned first to science but it can provide negative evidence but not positive proof; it can test for forgery but it cannot evaluate. The heart of academicians like the assistant curator himself is in the catalogue of existing recognised work, which leaves little time for looking at the paintings themselves. Art critics, who do look at them, are dismissed as subjective and contradictory. Valentina's authority appears, then, to be based on her subjective knowledge, because, as his pupil, she knew Matisse in Paris before the revolution. Her memories, however, like the facts surrounding the acquisition of the painting, can be historically verified. Matisse did run a school in Paris (1908-11) and 'Sarah Stein's Notes, 1908',[1] include an account of a lesson, bearing a startling similarity to the passage on page 30 of *The Bay at Nice*. Hare's source material for Valentina stands barely disguised.

The incidents from Matisse's life which are related by Valentina are all included in *The World of Matisse* by John Russell. The fact that these events could not be known to a woman who left for post-revolutionary Russia in 1921 is, however, unimportant, since it is not for an exhaustive knowledge of the work of Matisse or for her knowledge of the man that Valentina is considered an authority but because she understood his spirit. At the root of *The Bay at Nice*, then, is an opposition between the state authorities and Valentina, between the logic of science and the intuitive understanding of art, which is a matter of taste and it is for a preference of taste that Hare has chosen Matisse over, say, Cézanne or Picasso. The choice is the culmination of an admiration which hung a Matisse cut-out in William's bedroom in *Dreams of Leaving* and was expressed by Andrew and Rebecca in the abandoned first scene of *Pravda*.

When Valentina accuses the state of insulting the walls by hanging them with the whirlpools of mud of socialist realism, and talks warmly of Matisse, the evidence in front of the theatre audience is contrary. The only wall we can see is hung with 'Guérin's huge oil painting for "Iris and Morpheus", a triumphant nude sitting on a cloud over the body of the King of Sleep' (p. 5). Because most

members of even a National Theatre audience would not be familiar with the work of Baron Pierre-Narcisee Guérin (1774-1861)
and it remains unspecified even by the programme, the work
before us becomes 'typical' of a genre – melodramatic, idealised,
mythical with all the soft shapes, plump bodies and irrelevant
subject-matter of bourgeois indulgence.

The characters on stage ignore the painting, making such art
into mere wallpaper. At the same time, however, as they sit in the
theatre, the audience cannot but have the Guérin in their field of
view. As in the rock gig of *Teeth 'n' Smiles*, the audience is being
made to play a dual role – this time that of both theatre audience
and museum viewer – and with their inadvertent gaze they turn
stage scenery into art and authenticate the painting.

The same cannot be said of the Matisse. Even at the end the
audience does not see the supposed Matisse, which is picked up
and carried off by the assistant curator. It is for this reason, the lack
of need for visual judgement, which led to the play being recorded
for radio in 1987. The Matisse painting remains a verbal object,
described again by the assistant curator. The painting, however, is
neither a copy nor a beginning. It is, rather, an end – an ideal
which stands contrasted with the ridiculous tastelessness of Sophia's
ordinary life, an ideal of western civilisation.

The stage instructions in the printed text of *The Bay at Nice* state
that at the end of the play, 'The background fades and the stage is
filled with the image of the bay at Nice: a pair of open French windows, a balcony, the sea and the sky' (p. 48), much as the hills of
France in 1945 flooded the stage at the end of *Plenty*. Hare clearly
changed his mind in the course of the production. If the Matisse is
an ideal of freedom, then it underlines the absence of that pleasure
of life in Russia, the lack of freedom to exhibit experienced by
Valentina and the other Russian modernists.

By leaving the painting as a verbal object, Hare ensures that – as
opposed to Susan's dream version of her youth and hopes for the
future – Valentina's idea of freedom cannot be falsified. In another
sense the Matisse painting is unseen because it is irrelevant. The
mystery of *The Bay at Nice* is not the mystery of the painting, but
what lies unseen in Sophia's life (in her speech which she has prepared but is too frightened to deliver). Just as she decides about the

authenticity of the painting before seeing it (p. 8), so Valentina anticipates the content of Sophia's speech without hearing it– that Sophia wishes to leave her husband. The painting is a means of getting them alone with time for reflection; the window on their lives which pits Valentina's decision in a foreign country thirty-six years earlier (having her baby and returning to Russia rather than remaining with her lovers and her painting) against Sophia's present in an unhappy marriage in the east. Valentina is called to authenticate not only a painting, but her daughter's choice.

In both *The Bay at Nice* and *Wrecked Eggs*, it is women who face the decision whether to have an abortion and/or lack comfort, or whether to have the child and/or marriage and be burdened; it is the women who are outside the system and who ask questions about it. In *The Bay at Nice*, it is Valentina who understands art and she and Sophia who paint; it is the women who are the dissenters against a cold, unfeeling scientific belief. Whatever their differences, Valentina and Sophia stand against Grigor and the assistant curator. At 37, Grigor is a headmaster and Party member. Since he is not seen, Grigor has no identity and he becomes the representative of collective belief, the subsuming of the individual in the collective. In joining, it seems, the assistant curator loses his very name in the interests of his career progression.

In this way it becomes clear that where Valentina balanced Paris against Russia, self-expression against duty, Sophia balances Peter against Grigor, divorce against marriage amidst greater oppositions of youth versus age, lovers versus marriage, art versus science.

Unlike *Plenty* and *Dreams of Leaving*, the damage dissent effects on the women is not a form of insanity. It is not women who are said to be mad, but Party member Grigor, who considers that Sophia is in the grip of a decadent fantasy and inflamed by the morals of the west. Hare has begun to move away from the simplistic assumption that women, just by virtue of their gender, are somehow less implicated in the ills of society and therefore can be relied upon automatically to hold the answers to male problems and despair. This does not mean that Hare himself was thinking less and less of love as he worked on the love story, *Strapless*; it is simply that neither *The Bay at Nice* nor *Wrecked Eggs* is a love story. Uniquely in Hare's work to date, they foreground not love but the conflict between marriage and identity, the relation between the couple and the individual.

A question of rights?

For Sophia what is important is not a matter of taste but 'the right to live my own life' (p. 19), to express herself in the sense of having her own identity, and it is this freedom which the lovers and the painting of Paris symbolise for her. Sophia might be only an amateur painter, who paints merely for pleasure, but she is leaving for a man who, as played by Philip Locke, resembles the description of Matisse as the German schoolmaster, and not only listens attentively to Valentina's recollections but acts as a catalyst for them. Where Valentina and Peter were supposed (according to Sophia's instructions) to talk about the divorce, they instead talk about Valentina's past with Matisse; they talk about art.

Peter is (in contrast to the assistant curator) named, and (in contrast to Grigor) seen. He is also divorced and works not for the education system or the museum but for the Sanitation Board. The Party enshrines marriage; if Sophia leaves him, Grigor will lose position. Sophia's self-expression, then, means the assertion of the rights of an individual over those of others, her individualism becoming mere selfishness.

If identity is not fixed and immutable, but a function of the roles which others cast us in, any change is dependent on the approval of those around us. Valentina's 'western' lifestyle was unacceptable even on the station platform in Russia, and Sophia's decision to leave Grigor is – in the face of the impossibility of his approval – itself dependent on Valentina. Her 'approval' proves to have an economic content, since Sophia cannot succeed in the lengthy divorce procedure unless she has the money to pay for it at the end, but it is the contradiction between the individual and the couple which is important. Sophia is struggling for the principle of the right to live her own life in the only way possible, in private, and yet she is dependent on public approval. The individual is in constant tension with the collective. She has the choice facing us all, men and women, between selfishness (the literal denial of the other) and selflessness (the subservience of the self for another). As Valentina asks, 'In what way is she different from anyone in Russia? What is her complaint? That she is not free? That's what I've been told. Well, who is free? Tell me, am I free?' (p. 38).

Hare puts his declaration that there is no freedom at the literal centre of the play and makes no points about the specific tyranny of the Party hierarchy. He is not so much making a political point about the nature of the Soviet system in particular, but undertaking a systems analysis, and the same point is made in *Wrecked Eggs*. The geography in Hare's map of the world is not political but human.

Although the date is given in a programme note, it is allowed to float loosely in the production with a timeless setting and costuming. In addition, no mention is made of momentous events of 1956, such as the invasion of Hungary, or of specific leaders. Unlike Rebecca in *Pravda*, neither Valentina nor Sophia is the focus of political activism. Just as Valentina rejects the idea of exile, Sophia's is a rite of transference within the system and not a judgement on the whole. Although in the days before the Cold War ended, there was an obvious impulse to write about Russia and America, the freedom which Sophia seeks is not dissident and Hare cannot therefore be said to be engaged in an any explicit evaluation of individual political systems or a comparison of international human rights. As Valentina puts it, 'Don't use that word. You have the right? What does it mean? It doesn't mean anything. Be a person. Do what you have to do. Don't prattle about rights' (p. 24).

Hare's point is not one of absolute right and wrong, but of individual choice, which is rarely black and white but rather comes in shades of grey. The comment is repeated twice more in the text. In *Wrecked Eggs* there is no question that individuals have a right (in the sense of freedom) to do what they want, but there is still damage. Hare explained that 'I felt that freedom was a myth. There is no such thing as freedom, there are only different kinds of unfreedom.'[2] In *The Bay at Nice*, Paris is not better, merely different. Freedom is not happiness, it is a matter of luck and historical accident. As Valentina says, 'Your life is defined by absence, by what is not happening, by where you cannot be' (p. 40). If you are in a relationship, like Sophia, you are trapped; if you are single, like

Valentina after her return from Paris, or Peter after his divorce, then your life lacks interest. For Peter, then, Sophia is an escape, an adventure, a risk. Just as that which was desired (Grigor) has become intolerable, so might the new object (Peter, freedom) become stifling. And so, although an art student in Paris, Valentina was still a Russian yearning for home; the grass is always greener on the other side of the fence and when you get there that is still true. Because of this, 'To give up seems cowardly. Finally that is always the choice' (pp. 39-40).

In *Brassneck*, Sidney, Lucy and Martin as children are merely younger versions of their later selves and function within the traditions of the family saga, and in *Plenty* it is the inability to conceive which signifies the failure to give birth to the future. Peter's answer to Valentina's questions about happiness is to think of his children. Almost in judgement it seems, one was, like William's in *Dreams of Leaving*, 'born a bit slow' (p. 25). Children are sources not of love which, if sent to an adult, must either be faked or solicited like a confession, but of conscience and responsibility constraining the freedom of the adult. It is on behalf of the children that Valentina agrees to persuade Grigor not to oppose the divorce. Where Sophia previously rejected her mother's embrace, she now reaches out to her. Valentina's past is accounted to its future; mother and daughter make their peace. Like the romantic novels Valentina condemns, the play ends where it might have begun; the play ends where *Wrecked Eggs* begins.

Rite of passage

The programme for the premiere of the double bill at the National Theatre carries on its cover a framed photograph which conflates into one family group the players (and therefore the characters) from the two plays. Peter the father (Philip Locke) stands behind with Valentina the mother (Irene Worth) lower left. Around them, are, perhaps, son-in-law (Colin Stinton) and wife (Zoë Wanamaker) and (thirty years on) Sophia's daughter Alexandra (Kate Buffery). The present – 1986 in the theatre – is what became of what was desired in the past – 1956 in Russia.

The idea of the family bond may well have been preoccupying Hare as he prepared for *King Lear* but, although the casting occasions a link between the two plays, the photograph places centrally a character who appears in part of only one of them (Peter) and distorts the connections. Despite the apparent continuity between Sophia and Grace (Zoë Wanamaker), it is Loelia who is facing the decision of divorce and Grace who has, like Valentina, taken a decision on abortion.

Having wearied of her youthful promiscuity, Loelia thought she needed Robbie, 'a brown shoe' (pp. 73-4). After nine years, however, Robbie and Loelia, like William and Caroline before them, are only happy when other people are there. Loelia – like an underwritten Sophia yearning for the promise of her youth – has, therefore, decided to leave her husband. In contemporary America, there is no question of a wife's right to leave her husband. In contrast to the rigidly formal language of *The Bay at Nice,* which expressed the constraints of Soviet society, the language of *Wrecked Eggs* is, in expression of its promiscuous society, littered with expletives and casual repetition.

Far from evoking the degeneration of language and conversation, Hare indulges it. As Hare says, 'I had this idea I would follow a very sombre play with a pornographic play and the pornographic play just didn't work.'[3] The play lacks the 'authentic stink of pornography',[4] which was achieved in *Lay By,* and contains merely gratuitous snippets, which contribute little to character and nothing to narrative. If all the gossip and hoopla were taken out of the play, only a borrowed skeleton would remain.

A press agent in New York, Grace has remained unmarried and is hounded by the 23-year-old son of a client, the father to the most recent of her several aborted babies. In a series of distasteful references, the foetuses are the *Wrecked Eggs* of the title and her life is a dog's dinner of easy answers, messy relationships and meals alone. Grace, then, parallels Valentina, who has taken the opposite decision to stay in the west, to live her own life; the aborted babies are an indication of that 'freedom'.

Where, in 1956, Valentina was invited by her daughter to give her approval (and money) to her divorce from Grigor and conversely to authenticate her 'marriage' to Peter, in 1986 in New

York State, Loelia has invited Grace – the mother of her own free-love hippy past – to authenticate her decision to leave her husband, Robbie. *Wrecked Eggs*, which at forty-one sides of printed text is only two sides shorter than *The Bay at Nice*, is a mirror-image of it.

In both plays the stage image is similar – three (or four) people in a room which contains a frame on the wall behind. Where in *The Bay at Nice* the frame is that of a painting on which Valentina sat in judgement, in *Wrecked Eggs* Grace sits in judgement in a room full of excess food, and the frame behind her is a window. Apart from the obvious assertion that Russia is spartan and America is opulent, another parallel is being made: through the slatted blinds, the light and heat are glowing and the splashing of water is audible from the swimming pool beyond. The title of Hare's painting in *Wrecked Eggs* could be 'The Swimming Pool at Rhinebeck' and what Grace is called upon to authenticate is a realised (as opposed to the dream of the painting) way of life epitomised and created by Robbie Baker.

In *Wrecked Eggs*, as in *The Bay at Nice*, the intended divorce is from a system as much as a man but, unlike Grigor, Robbie is both seen and heard and the mirror-image is both inexact and distorting. Robbie's career might not, like Grigor's, be in education but Robbie represents the same kind of male success story of the money-loving, ball-playing American. His 'Swimming Pool at Rhinebeck' is the product of his American way of life in 1986, just as 'The Bay at Nice' is the product of France in 1919.

Loelia, like Sophia, however, is aiming for what Robbie calls a 'rite of passage' (p. 62), taking the same irreversible steps from one state to another, the most significant of which are birth (the christening) and death (the funeral). Marked by the legal and religious ceremony of the wedding, at which a man and a woman (the individuals) irrevocably become a couple, marriage is the assumption of sexual maturity. It marks the final passage from child to adult and the assumption of adult responsibilities, and is therefore a rite of intensification for society and for the legal and administrative structures which constitute it.

Divorce or separation is more accurately a rite of de-passage, at which the theatre audience – sitting in the pews – takes the inverted role as witness as a church congregation. Despite the attempted undoing, however, the couple cannot go from being married to being single again but only from married to ex-married (divorced). What the theatre audience is watching over is not a social rite of intensification, but a failure of a belief. If a rite of passage for the individuals is a rite of intensification for the system of which they are part, then a rite of de-passage must be a failure to constitute the identity of the individuals within it, a removal of their consent and therefore what Jürgen Habermas called a 'legitimation crisis' for the legal/administrative structure of the system which is suffering a potential breakdown.

Just as Valentina's painting hides the secret of her past and Sophia's present, so behind this façade of opulent successful marriage lies the secret of Robbie's past and Loelia's present discontent. During the cold war, Robbie's father, Bill Dvorak, had betrayed (unimportant) secrets to the Russians and become a traitor. The nature of Bill's choice (to betray his country) is not equivalent to Valentina's decision to return to hers. Bill is unseen and therefore occupies the same position in the narrative as Grigor – one a model citizen, the other a traitor, constructing a parallel opposition of west versus east in *Wrecked Eggs* as found in *The Bay at Nice*.

The young Robbie changed his name and it is this fact which has – we are asked to believe – lead Loelia to her decision. A childhood of betrayal by his father has led to a lifetime of betrayal of himself. Robbie's is the story of every American immigrant who denied his past only to strive to become integrated in the new culture by epitomising the all-American boy. While Loelia had fun, Robbie gave up his youth; he betrayed not his country but his father, whom he never sees. We never see him either. As in *The Bay at Nice* it is not the past which fills the stage but the present.

Loelia thought she married the son of a spy, a romantic exciting figure who significantly doesn't depend on approval, but Robbie Baker is not his father's son, he is a fake. Loelia wants to leave the new Robbie (Baker) for the old one (Dvorak). If Loelia is intended to signify a line of political dissent which stands, like the spy, as a traitor to Robbie's profession of the law and the American way, it is undeveloped. It is not Loelia who cares, but (as her name implies) Grace, and in the longest speech of the play it is finally clear that what disgusts her is not the brassneck of developers whose person-

alities the newspapers massage, nor the idea of profit and private
ownership, but the nature of the criteria by which we judge them,
the absence of the question 'Is this right or wrong?'.

Grace's position is dishonest. She writes to complain to newspapers but uses a pseudonym; in order to get into print, she turns
political complaint into humour and, as M'Bengue made clear in *A
Map of the World*, 'Humour, like everything, is something you buy.
Free speech? Buy. But what is this freedom? The luxury of the rich
who are sure of what they have' (*Map*, p. 41). Once published, her
letters remain an institutionalised dissent which we, like Robbie,
can ignore.

The dissenters of both *The Bay at Nice* and *Wrecked Eggs* may not
be mad as Susan Traherne in *Plenty* and Caroline in *Dreams of
Leaving* are, but they are all contained; their dissent is powerless and
the cost to themselves is unhappiness. Grace expresses none of the
shame which Caroline forced on William, which Peter has and
which it is Valentina's intention to force on Sophia. Grace envies
Robbie's apparent ease. Faced with Loelia's choice between her
own life and life with Robbie she would choose Robbie's vision. In
a repressive system where marriage is enshrined by the party,
individuals want divorce and personal liberty. In a 'free society',
individuals want the firm commitment of marriage. 'Loyalty.
Courage. Perseverance. If you don't use them you're going to feel
lousy' (p. 93). And as a result of her intervention, Loelia decides to
stay, if only for another night. It is not the divorce which is authenticated in *Wrecked Eggs* but the tenuously continuing relationship.
Despite the gibes at yuppiedom and the easy target of American
opulence and excess, Robbie's party is not a rite of passage but a
social rite of intensification. Eight years after his own divorce, the
middle-aged playwright, like Grace, seeks comfort, and Grace's
highly rhetorical speech is dropped like a stone in the middle of
East Coast chatter.

Hare's apparent preference for marriage and his foregrounding
of choice seems to echo the moral Right and the fashion for fidelity
creeping into a society unnerved by AIDS. The sense of unease
which William felt in *Dreams of Leaving*, which Janetta was to
experience in *Heading Home* and which Hare had seen as vital to an
ability to change, has changed. Asserting 'rights' of 'certain quali-

ties' of loyalty, courage, perseverance, judgement, quality of life, taste, relationships, over his 'wrongs' of cowardice, betrayal, and momentary sensation, he no longer seems to join Stanley or *Wetherby* in toasting our escapes.

Although it might seem in the decisions his characters make that Hare is asserting west over east, the morals are the same, 'People should stick. They should stick with what they have. With what they know. That's character' (p. 27) and 'Whatever you choose, you must bear the consequences of that choice' (p. 46). Hare went on to explore these themes further in *The Secret Rapture* and *Paris By Night* but, like Peter in *How Brophy Made Good*, Hare is 'saying liberty entails restraint. Not authoritarian, but self-liberating. The choice is paramount. That's what I believe' (*Brophy*, p. 90). In both systems, individuals feel themselves to be lacking some ideal of personal freedom, and Hare might agree with Stoppard that 'the point is not to compare one ruthless regime with another – it is to set each one up against a moral standard'.[5] As Grace puts it, 'There has to be something... I don't know some standard... If there isn't what are we? I mean, is there nothing? Is everything allowed? Well, is it?' (p. 79).

... or a rite of intensification?

In *The Bay at Nice*, the Guérin painting before us is owned by the state and decorates the walls of the state museum. In *Wrecked Eggs*, an image of ease and comfort stands before us. In both cases, however, they are part of a fiction, frames within a frame, and cannot but be fakes. Conversely, if the dissent of Valentina and Sophia is contained by the system, just as the Matisse is contained alongside the Guérin in the state museum, what contains both is the stage itself. If America and Russia are yoked together, what creates the mirror in which they can be viewed is the play itself. For this reason, aesthetics is not merely the context, aesthetics is the point: the standard against which the system, any system, can be judged is the aesthetic form itself. Hare's work, then, appears by the end of the 1980s to be a statement of faith in theatre not as society's court, but as its standard.

As a named artist Matisse has a different status within the text of *The Bay at Nice* from the fictional novelist Victor Mehta in *A Map of the World* or the poet-lover in *Heading Home*. That naming and the fact that Valentina's 'memories' enter the text in unassimilated chunks lead to the conclusion that Hare himself feels a particular affinity with Matisse.

'What I am after, above all, is expression', wrote Matisse in *Notes of a Painter* in 1908.[6] 'The entire arrangement of my picture is expressive; the place occupied by the figures, the empty spaces around them, the proportions, everything has its share. Composition is the art of arranging in a decorative manner the diverse elements at the painter's command to express his feelings' (*Notes,* p. 36). This expressionism is contrasted in *The Bay at Nice* with what Valentina describes as the 'whirlpools of mud', for which the museum has opened a new wing. The play stands, perhaps, as the culmination of Hare's attack on the British dramatic forms of socialist realism in his Lecture of 1978 for, in contrast to his open staged 'epic' plays, *The Bay at Nice* and *Wrecked Eggs* offer frozen images, fourth wall theatre, which preserve the unities of time and place. As Hare has explained, the proscenium arch is his 'natural place' and 'I think I write more pictorially than most people realise.'[7]

The man who once wrote seamless epics is now painting pictures; the man who wrote a classical play about revolution has now written a classical play about art. The reason for Hare's choice of Matisse is, then, that Matisse is not modern but a classicist. In contrast to the fragmented sense data of Impressionism, or the bizarre distortions of Surrealism, Expressionism is committed both to the individual perception and to the world outside the individual. In contrast to the content which determines Socialist Realism and the arbitrariness of Dada, Expressionism is committed to the tempering of content by the rules of the form. As Herbert Marcuse put it in different terms, 'A work of art is authentic or true not by virtue of its content (i.e., the "correct" representation of social conditions), nor by its "pure" form, but by the content having become form.'[8]

Within Matisse's theoretical framework nature is the ultimate source of art, and the act of painting is an act of belief, a synthesis (or 'condensation') of sensations into perceptions, and of perceptions into significant form. In the closing moments of the play, after Sophia has demonstrated her resolve to leave Grigor by leaving the stage, Valentina – who is tired of looking – looks at the painting. It is the light, and not the subject-matter of the sea, the wall, the window, which convinces her that the painting is genuine.

> A distinction is made between painters who work directly from nature and those who work purely from imagination. Personally', wrote Matisse, 'I think neither of these methods must be preferred to the exclusion of the other. Both may be used in turn by the same individual. (*Notes*, p. 39)

David Hare may write *Fanshen* and *Dreams of Leaving*. In this way Hare might well agree with Matisse when he wrote:

> I feel very strongly the tie between my earlier and my recent works, but I do not think exactly the way I thought yesterday. Or rather my basic idea has not changed, but my thought has evolved, and my modes of expression have followed my thoughts. I do not repudiate any of my paintings, but there is not one of them I would not redo differently, if I had it to redo. My destination is always the same, but I work out a different route to get there. (*Notes*, p. 35)

Hare's basic idea has remained the same but he does not think exactly the way he thought in 1968 when he founded Portable Theatre.

> I had an idea that it was possible to dramatize the decline of England by stripping away the problems of aesthetics altogether and that by tumbling out of a van onto any old floor and presenting urgent short, sharp works in people's workplaces or homes in order to shake them up and give them a new way of looking at the world. That's still my aim, but I choose different means.[9]

Hare's thought has evolved and his modes of expression have followed those thoughts; he does not repudiate any of his plays but there is not one of them he would not do differently if he had it to redo.

As Matisse 'sought to distil' (p. 46) by removing the woman, the violin and the chair from his pictures of windows, so Hare removes talk of classes. Finally, too, history is grounded in nature. As Hare took up from *Wetherby* the realisation of death in life and the conflict between the individual and (any) society, he was to seek to turn the hour hand of tragedy, and not simply to run with the minute hand of political theatre. While Hare felt that *The Bay at Nice* had a tragic theme, he had not yet taken that step. As Valentina says, 'If I couldn't throw money away I'd be really tragic', but she can (p. 45).

'Matisse told Apollinaire that the artist had to find his own inmost personality and rely upon it entirely, and that this could not be done through introspection alone. He had to pit himself against the giants of the past, and confront them directly.'[10] So, in *The Bay at Nice*, as in *Wetherby*, Hare pre-empts his own confrontation with Shakespeare and with the challenge of tragedy, in his production of *King Lear*.

> VALENTINA: As to teaching, yes, of course, his teaching was inspiring. But it was as if Shakespeare had taught. It gave you an idea. But then when you pick up your own brush, you're faced with the reality of your own talent.
> PETER: Frustrating?
> VALENTINA: Not always. But how do I say? It's a very different thing. Talking is easy. Oh yes, and Matisse could talk. But genius is different.
> (PETER *frowns for a moment*.)
> VALENTINA: No. I went on painting. Although I knew my limitations.   (p. 31)

11 The moment of unification

Paris By Night and *The Secret Rapture* appeared in the same year (1989). At the centre of both was a phenomenon of eighties Britain – the successful Tory woman politician. Because of this, they appeared to be companion pieces, one on film, the other on the stage of the National Theatre, as *Licking Hitler* and *Plenty* had been a decade before. In fact, however, *Paris By Night* is a thriller written shortly after *Wetherby* and delayed by a turbulent production process. *The Secret Rapture* is quite a different sort of play, Hare's closest point yet to tragedy, which marks his own moment of unification with his theatrical inheritance.

Paris By Night

As the titles to *Paris By Night* are pieced together like a jigsaw on the screen, the camera moves down a long wood-lined corridor towards a woman sitting alone. Over romantic music and a babble of voices, we hear the distinctive keywords of parliament promising and insisting on 'Order, order'. Where Archie Maclean in *Licking Hitler* was disrupting the country house setting by invoking the audience as loyal Germans, we are this time apparently firmly inside the corridors of power.

As the words of the title are finally spelled out, the camera comes to rest on a face and Clara Paige is revealed at the heart of the coming story. Where Susan Traherne in *Plenty* could respond to the stultifying code of manners of Sir Andrew Charleson's Foreign Office only with hysteria, Clara Paige is shown into the minister's inner sanctum to be given an assignment in Europe. Sir

Leonard Darwin in *Plenty* saw Europe after the war as a great challenge of reconstruction; in *Paris By Night*, whatever ideals it
embodies, Europe is simply a bureaucractic haggle over farm
prices, where the old nationalistic rivalries are constrained by
civilised conferences.

The film shows very little of the workings of the European
Community or its parliament. 'The Butter Mountain' was the
original title of the film; that it changed is a measure of a shift in
emphasis. Hare is not interested in the institutions of Europe, nor
in the corruption of politicians, which he had exposed in *Brassneck*;
he had already dealt with the idea of conference itself, which was at
the root of *A Map of the World*. While it is of little consequence,
then, that Clara Paige is specifically a Euro-MP, it is important that
she is one of 'us', a Thatcherite Tory and a rising star. Composed
and elegant, businesslike and attractive, she was duly compared to
one of the high-profile politicians of the eighties, Edwina Currie.

Paris By Night is the first of Hare's works to present a woman as
a winner in political life and in the course of the film Clara Paige is
accepted as the parliamentary candidate for a safe Birmingham seat.
Moreover, the Conservative ideology is naturalised: where
Rebecca in *Pravda* was the weakly drawn and supposed alternative
to Lambert Le Roux, no one in *Paris By Night* is to question the
spirit of the Right. Instead each character illustrates a different
aspect of the working of the party – Westminster MP (Gerald),
think-tank (Gillvray), constituency work (Mrs Swanton), successful entrepreneur (Wallace) and failed businessman (Swanton). The
story takes place entirely within an ideology which stands as the
context of the film. Far from being the story of spending your life
in dissent as *Plenty* had been, *Paris By Night* is the story of spending
your life in being accepted.

Clara draws back the curtains on her home life in the second
beginning to the film. In a richly furnished and diplomatic-style
apartment is revealed an unidentified male body sprawled on the
floor. It is again a mirror image of *Plenty*. In *Paris By Night*, however, the two beginnings express not fragments from different
points in the life-history of the heroine but two parallel and concurrent lives of the heroine – career politician and wife/mother in
that order. As one of very many changes to the published script,

Hare reversed the order of these two 'scenes' in the course of editing to shift the emphasis on to Clara's rising political success and away from the apparent 'death' of a husband and the end of a marriage.

Although Gerald is said once to have been a passionate man and a photograph later demonstrates a once happier time, Clara's relationship with him is now clearly based on convenience, absence and disgust. Hare expresses in four lines a burnt-out, long-distance marriage. The following expression of hatred, however, comes from nowhere. The camera examines Clara's face in close-up – as it is to do at each point of declaration – as if trying to gauge the real emotions and motives behind it. It is her disgust and not Gerald's actions which are foregrounded. Gerald has a haunted, angular look but, although it is referred to, his drinking spree is not seen. This is the first one of very few times we see Gerald and Clara together; such lack of context embodies the nature of their alienation, but it is one of the failings of the film that Clara's judgement on what he represents – 'drink and cowardice in equal parts' – is not fulfilled and the emotions expressed have no root in the action.

It is Birmingham where the professional politician reveals her sleek and well-honed skills – dishing out community awards to potential voters in an ethnic community, moving her chair closer to the questioner to feign intimacy towards people with whom she clearly has no real relationship. In shots which seem to come straight out of *Wetherby* and *Saigon*, the burning bonfire and the streets of the city are seemingly a foreign land through which Clara, like Barbara Dean, travels by taxi.

And it is in Birmingham, only a few shots into the film, that the first clues are given that all is not as it is seems: a man in a raincoat stands beneath a lamp-post apparently keeping watch on the rising star. The realisation causes the sophisticated smart-suited woman to leave by the back door. Then in the next shot, alone in bed, she is disturbed by a telephone call. The equivalence between the two events is made by her and for the audience by juxtaposition as an unknown and unrecognisable voice says, 'I know what you're doing. (*A pause.*) I know who you are' (p. 5). Charlotte Rampling's face expresses thoughtfulness rather than outright fear, but the idea that Clara might be doing something awry, that she has a secret to hide which might be leading to blackmail, takes us into the realms of film noir thriller. Clara is, it seems, intended to be the kind of ambivalent sophisticated heroine played by Lauren Bacall and Ingrid Bergman in the movies of the forties and fifties which filled David Hare's cinematic childhood, and it is a link back to *Knuckle* as much as to *Wetherby*. Precisely what will happen is not revealed; for once in Hare's work it takes until the final shots (both senses) to find out.

Next morning, daytime normality is resumed as Clara arrives late to collect her son, Simon, from her sister, Pauline. She fails to listen to his explanation of the train set with which he is playing in the garden. He is ignored as she discusses her diary with her secretary in the car. He sits on the kitchen table, sullen and isolated, as his father leaves and Delia, 'the very spirit of middle class motherhood' and an evident contrast to Clara, arrives with three other children.

Hare used the idea of the family as a warm mafia overcoat against economic cold in *Brassneck* but, increasingly in his work, the family (in the form of children) has become an important part of the moral framework for judging a leading character. So in *The Bay at Nice* and *Wrecked Eggs*, the children are the touchstone for decision in marital discord. It is by this measure that Clara's home life is shown to have been sacrificed on the road to political success. And it is for making the parallel between a successful woman politician and ruined home life explicit, as much as for the accusation of ruthlessness or shady dealing, which led to the successful libel action by Edwina Currie against the *Observer* for comments made in its interview with Charlotte Rampling.

The point being made, that the family stands at the heart of the Conservative philosophy of the eighties, is confirmed by Adam Gillvray in the context of a 'philosophical' country-house weekend which follows the same evening. The country-house setting has, of course, appeared before in Hare's work as the venue for the creation of war-time propaganda. In this fancy dress of party power, there is little explanation of where the conservatism comes from – beyond an oblique reference to Hobbes' *Leviathan* – but on the playing fields of right-wing philosophy, there are no children. In the extremities of this ideology the mother's place is in the home, along with Adam's wife Angela, who is about to give birth to their seventh child.

Upon her arrival, Clara learns that someone has been trying to contact her. At dusk she slips away. The narrative is chronologically straightforward, covering a total of six days and nights. Throughout the night is the time of mystery, the time without a diary entry, without an agenda. Although the detail of their relationship – that she and Gerald sold a lame-duck business to Swanton and it went bankrupt – is not clear at this point, their greeting implies that they know each other well from the past. In Swanton's description of a new business project and request for a loan is more than a hint of blackmail, and this brings Clara to the conclusion that he is responsible for the telephone calls. The location, a deserted cattle market, suggests the kind of free market economics which brought them together and which stands at the root of conservative economics.

Conservatism in the eighties is more than this, however. In *Pravda* the force of personality and the power of money were confronted through Lambert Le Roux. In *Paris By Night,* Gillvray champions conservatism as a release from the uncertainty and guilt of socialism, asserting the right of individual freedom, of following gut instinct. It is after this episode that Clara dials Michael Swanton and refuses his demand. When Swanton leaves his night-time world and threatens to come inside Clara's current daytime life by entering the country house retreat, a different and more threatening side of conservatism is revealed; the security guards descend upon him, the first 'scene' is over and she is gone.

The conference to which Clara has been sent could take place anywhere in Europe. Certainly it could have been Brussels or Strasbourg, the twin homes of the European Parliament; even the town of Maastricht now bears the name of a summit and its supposed 'agreement'. That it is held in Paris invites comparison with *The Bay at Nice.* Upon her arrival Clara does two things which are again linked by juxtaposition: she calls Gerald and asks him to read the promised story to Simon, then '*She stands for a moment as if a great weight has been lifted. Free at last*' (p. 20). At this point, she meets Wallace Sharp, a design entrepreneur whose business she had helped; by having a drink with him she begins a relationship based on a sense of freedom – from family, from political power-broking and from Britain.

> CLARA: I love being abroad. I feel safe. It's like aeroplanes.
> From the moment you get on, till the moment you
> leave, no one can get at you.
> WALLACE: I have.
> CLARA: Yes. But you don't want anything. So you don't
> count.   (p. 23)

Wallace is her escape, into the Zinyafskis' home and into Paris by night. That night – the longest 'scene' in the film – begins with a picture designed to make other people's lives seem so attractive, a family supper in a French-Jewish home full of eager debate, children on apron-strings, food, love and happiness. To mark out its difference, as much as in pursuit of realism, most of the scene is in French. The detail of the arguments might be lost on the audience, but as ever in Hare's work, the key moments – the integration or otherwise of Jews into other cultures – are translated. It is another weakness of the film that the relevance of the references, so carefully placed, are not themselves integrated. Just as the implications of Clara and Gerald being legislators, who make but do not obey the law, is not explored, so the difference(s) between historian Gillvray and historians Paul/Hector, the relationship between the Asian communities in Birmingham and the integration of the Jews in France, are not explored. The result is to leave the Zinyafskis as a somewhat simplistic image of all that Clara's life lacks, and the assertion 'We belong' implies merely 'in a home like this' and 'in Paris'.

Similarly, the Paris which Clara and Wallace enjoy is intended to be that of the café culture of the Marais which – it is claimed – is being lost to art galleries and banks (p. 27). Although the description of the shots is clear, they are visually blurred and indistinct in execution. *The Bay at Nice* picked up the idea of Paris as a symbol of individual freedom and artistic expression. In *Paris By Night* it is romance which is seen and which reveals a different side of a character. As Wallace draws Clara while they sit in the café, '*She looks romantic, a little haunted, tender*' (p. 28). As she embarks on her walk to watch the dawn from beneath the Eiffel Tower, Clara wears a bright red coat, and the lady in red marks the disjuncture with her political colour.

On the streets at night, Clara is literally outside in a film dominated by interiors, by soulless hotel rooms and formal houses. Although it is referred to as the preserve of England and in opposition to the mere landscape of France, the countryside which had become manifest at the end of *Plenty* and stood implicit in the picture of *The Bay at Nice* was cut from *Paris By Night*. This world, this freedom, is a fantasy or an unattainable ideal which Clara cannot realise and, as she walks across the Pont des Arts, she meets her 'blackmailer', Michael Swanton.

As Lambert Le Roux said in *Pravda*, 'You have to hit a man in the face if you want him to disappear' (*Pravda*, p. 108) and, before she can confirm why or how he came to be there, Clara tips Swanton over into the swirling waters of the Seine. Frustration, paranoia and anger, apparently, lead her to act on impulse. It might be deliberately unclear whether the lovers kissing on the toll-path have seen the incident, but we the audience have seen, we are witnesses to the crime. If *Paris By Night* is a thriller it is not one in which the detective or the audience must find the killer. This murder is instead being posited as the price of her freedom, of trying to avoid responsibility for a past of destructive individualism (rather than the creative individuality of *The Bay at Nice*) and we are being asked to play the part not of detective, but of judge and jury.

After running through the streets, Clara flusters over the loss of her hotel key. On the verge of honesty she draws back; Clara begins to lie, to start the process of self-justification. 'I have lost everything. Isn't it absurd? Bank book, traveller's cheques, credit cards' (p. 37). When the trappings of industrial civilisation have gone, life is again absurd. The reference does not take us back to *Dreams of Leaving*, however. The parts of Paris which are clearly visible are the dark and gloomy river over which man has constructed a bridge and on which the illuminated pleasure boat rides for only a few seconds. Reminiscent rather of *Death in Venice*, the watery depths of gut instinct eat away the apparent civilisation of the city, death eternally erodes the banks of life and morality rots with it. Hare is not concerned to wade in the *ennui* of modernist Europe, however. In the police station where the guardians of civilisation work, normality begins to be resumed. As in *Teeth 'n' Smiles*, the dawn brings the promise of a new tomorrow and, in this case, a government credit card.

In visiting the embassy to collect the credit card, however, Clara meets Swanton's daughter. A clumsy bearer of truth (that Swanton was in Paris by accident) and convenience, Jenny ineptly brings together Clara's past and present and the parallel strands of David Hare's mystery. As visualised in the photograph and in the text, Clara is trying to escape that past – an apparently lower-class upbringing, a failed business, a cosy family in Birmingham. It is Jenny who, bored with expressions of concern for her disability, 'justifies' Clara's harsh uncompassionate attitude, but this is an aside; it is Jenny who reveals that Gerald gave Swanton incorrect figures. It is this 'evidence' which leads Clara to reverse her decision to return home to her son, in hospital with appendicitis, and to telephone Gerald.

In *Dreams of Leaving*, the telephone was a symbol of lack of communication. In *Paris By Night* the sheer number of calls implies dislocation and isolation but here the telephone is the agent of blackmail and betrayal. It is first used by the anonymous caller to undermine Clara's sense of security; then Clara picks up the phone to refuse Swanton's attempted blackmail and to refuse the 'nightcap' with Gillvray. In using the phone to ask Gerald to tell the bedtime story to Simon, it expresses not concern but abandonment; when he pleads with her to return and she does not, it is a moment of betrayal. When the anonymous calls continue after Swanton's death and Clara realises that her assumption about his identity was wrong, she immediately calls Wallace in a gesture of vulnerability which starts their affair. And at this point, the crime of murder is compounded by the sin of adultery.

In a trend which continues from *Saigon* to *Strapless*, the affair is expressed in a different visual style from the thriller. The camera wanders over their bodies as it did in *Saigon*; the romantic music begins to express Clara's physical and emotional nature. It is Wallace who articulates this positive view of her, but he is not alone in this. Hare shows Clara under the light of the full moon in

her own bed when she is vulnerable to phone calls from anonymous callers. It was in this kind of moonlight in *Licking Hitler* that
Anna Seaton began to 'learn' from Archie Maclean; in *Saigon*
much of the truth of the American presence is revealed in the bed
of Bob Chesneau and Barbara Dean. After sex with Wallace, Clara
'confesses' the basis of her beliefs. People, she says, should make
their own decisions, and 'If you do something, you must live with
the consequences' (p. 58). In so doing, she invites him and us to
judge her in these terms.

While Clara Paige is in bed with Wallace, her son is lying in a
hospital bed. That she knew was clearly established; the news is a
pivotal moment in the film. It is Clara's question 'Was that the
wrong thing to do?' (p. 61) rather than the act of murder she commits which is the trigger to the moral questions which surround
her. The point about Clara for Hare is that she slips through your
fingers. At the moment of this question, says Hare, 'We were all
robbed of our usual reactions. This is something I have so long
wanted to do as a writer that a profound and lasting contentment
came upon me in that room and it persisted through the remaining
weeks of the shooting. For as long as we worked, the process of art
did what it has always promised: it comforted, it clarified, and set
everything in order.'[1]

Although Wallace does not reply immediately, the question is
not unanswered. In the next sequences, a man who has had an
affair with a woman he knows to be married claims to be appalled
that she should stay making love with him, then keeps her longer
with another act of love-making. The violence of that sex takes us
back to the same dubious territory as *Licking Hitler*. The sex does
not lead Clara to any education or greater self-awareness; it is a
penalty for the 'confession'. As a reminder of the crime which we
have witnessed, shots of Swanton's body floating in the river are
intercut and in this way the violence of the sex becomes a judgement on her. This judgement is made, however, not for the crime
of murder but for the 'crime' of not putting motherhood first.
Upon her return Gerald, as he promised, does not forgive her for
her failure to come home and punishes her by refusing a divorce.

In addition, Gillvray expresses his new theory – a vision of the
future which he must sell to the party from the right wing – that

women not only will submit but inherently want to submit. He will then squeeze the moist peach in his hands until it is bruised and consumed. Jenny in *Knuckle* might be resigned to the fact that she will be bruised and battered and offer solace to men throughout her life, but, having been followed, Clara Paige follows Gillvray. He is unaware of her presence and is, therefore, unthreatened by it. Having been the victim of anonymous callers, Clara Paige calls Gillvray. As she does so, however, Clara is outside the gentleman's club of which he is a comfortable member. However successful, even if she enters Westminster, Clara will never be admitted. As the photograph of the Euro-conference is taken, '*Clara is the only woman among them*' (p. 42). She might be inside the corridors of power but she is not behind the desk. The guiding hand which shows her into the minister's room is around her throughout and it belongs to the men. The 'we' they refer to is not a party but a gender.

In a pattern which is all too common in Hare's work, the apparent heroine sits at the base of a spiral of male creators. There are four stories with two parallel pairs of men and two sins – Swanton (past) and Gillvray (present) with two sides of blackmail in a pursuit/murder thriller, and Gerald (past and present) and Wallace (present and future), husband and lover in a play-for-today adultery triangle. All the men in various ways threaten her: with exposure, with submission, with custody battle and with honesty. When she barges her way into Gillvray's club, she does not change the rules but only breaks them. The result is dismissed as a failed joke (p. 69) and the association with the murder is made again as intercut shots of Swanton's body in the water remind us that the account is still to be settled.

Clara Paige seeks freedom in her physical relationship with Wallace, but when he realises that she killed Swanton (after seeing the story in the newspaper) he comes to challenge her. His concern, however, is not for the murder. Her crime is said to be insulting the intelligence. He does not call the police (from whom he has retrieved her handbag) and he comes because he feels used, he comes for revenge. In inheritance from *Dreams of Leaving* and prefiguring *The Bay at Nice* with its concern for identity, Wallace makes the ultimate accusation: 'You're corrupt. You have no character. That's your real curse. Words come out, but there's nothing in you.' His judgement is not legal or moral, but existential. Personality is the façade of politics; but Clara exists not so much in carefully constructed media opportunities as in a series of roles she is expected by others to fulfil. These are defined by men and, like Caroline in *Dreams of Leaving*, she is denied her own terms of reference. As her name suggests, she is a pa(i)ge on which the men – including the author/director – write. When she is alone, the camera explores her body as much as any supposed vulnerability.

It is precisely because Clara Paige has no character that *Paris By Night* fails to convince. Throughout, Charlotte Rampling's face is unexpressive: the audience cannot interpret Clara Paige as the text does and because of this they cannot care for her or be much concerned for the outcome of Hare's film. It was evident from *Wetherby* that expert editing and detailed placing of visual clues are required effectively to manipulate the multiple overlapping threads of a moral thriller. In *Paris By Night* the many changes from the printed script indicate (as they did in *Saigon*) lack of agreement between writer and director, even when they are one and the same person. Hare had not yet learned how to do outside shooting and the film noir elements – the strange crow of a bird, the man standing beneath a lamp-post – are simply too few to shift the balance. As Hare said, 'A work and its reception are entirely different things and its making a third.'[2] *Paris By Night* was received unenthusiastically and had only a short cinematic release. By the time the film was released the object of its attention – the successful breed of women politicians – was no longer new and Margaret Thatcher had won another term in office.

As Clara says, 'It's time to be honest. If we're honest, we can make a fresh start.' Her response to Wallace's judgement is to lie; a cornered animal, she tells him only what she thinks he already knows and tries several tactics in the manipulation game – an assertion of love, an assertion of some goodness and, finally, the assertion that Gerald too wants a divorce when the audience has specifically seen him refuse one. In this way, we know that no fresh start is possible. Gerald has seen the newspaper story about Swanton; when he telephones Clara and hears Wallace's voice, he puts the two crimes – murder and adultery – together and wreaks the ultimate revenge.

> INT. FLAT. DAWN
> GERALD: *still sitting. The sound of the front door opening.* CLARA *comes into the sitting room. She puts her bag down. Then puts a lamp on. She does not see him.*
> GERALD: You killed Swanton.
> *(She turns, startled.)*
> CLARA: Gerald ...
> GERALD: You're having an affair.
> *(She looks confused, begins to move towards him.)*
> CLARA: Listen ...
> GERALD: You think you can get away with anything. No regard at all for anyone's feelings but your own. You're trash. You're just trash. You're human trash. And trash belongs in the dustbin.   (pp. 81-2)

Gerald is a failed entrepreneur and declining politician with nothing to lose, contrasted in this (and implicitly his sexual prowess) with Wallace. Gerald doesn't ask for more than knowledge of her infidelity and it is for her failure to tell him, as much as murder, that he kills her. As the direction note informs us, Clara reels like the puppet she is with each shot.

For the only time in his work, Hare has gone the whole way and killed his leading lady. She does not get to *live* with the consequences of her actions at all so we cannot ultimately judge her by her own or any other terms. The ending is, therefore, the easy way out for a moralist who fears that Clara Paige might not otherwise have been brought to book. Mrs Swanton expresses relief that her husband is dead; Jenny has a good job and Swanton in any case wasn't happy and 'deserved' to die because he was soft and weak and he failed in the market economy.

Art did what Hare wanted it to do – it comforted and it clarified. There is no reference to the Tory double standard of male politicans who have had well-publicised affairs and continued in public life and the judgement on Clara is not extended to the party which used her. Hare is indeed putting things in order and this means not denying the audience their expectations, but reinforcing them. The scales have, therefore, been weighted against Clara. As a Westminster MP, Gerald too, leaves Simon sitting unhappily on the kitchen table, but this has been underplayed. It is he who reads the bedtime story and is seen at Simon's bedside in hospital. The judgement on her – from the violent lovemaking to the shooting – is the same length (seventeen sides of printed text) as the opening scene; the centre section in Paris is thirty-four sides. Paris and London are equally balanced. The final shot stands as a vindication of Gerald's action: the fact that Simon sits up bewildered and alone is an inadequate vehicle to counterbalance Gerald's relief at putting Clara in the rubbish bin.

A woman who committed murder is herself murdered. In a reversal of *Wetherby*, where the woman survives and John Morgan and Jean Travers' fiancé both die (but not by her hand), a kind of justice is done. Unlike *Wetherby*, this justice is apparently in proportion to the 'crime' and is not, therefore, tragic. The discoveries of Clara Paige's two wrongs are made by the same device of a newspaper clipping and not by any meaningful self-discovery on her part. 'It is a thriller, a murder story, and the sole purpose is to scare the hell out of people',[3] wrote Hare, but the death of Clara Paige, unlike that of Isobel Glass in *The Secret Rapture*, evokes neither pity nor fear.

Hare once said that he had no interest in who was going to get shot in the end, that it was the debate which was dramatic; in *Paris By Night*, it seems, he was only interested in shooting her at the end. Although Hare has claimed that 'If I've ever appeared to dislike a central character, it's only through failure of technique',[4] he has also confessed, 'I didn't want her to get away with it.'[5] He promised 'Order, order' and – clumsily executed and inadequately expressed – *Paris By Night* has delivered it without much regard for the consequences. The dawn has come on the nightmare and there is no character left behind, no integrity, no goodness. Was that the right thing to do?

The Secret Rapture

At the opening of *The Secret Rapture*, the darkness of grief is literally upon the stage as Isobel Glass sits at her dead father's bedside and her sister Marion enters the room to retrieve – for its real as much as its sentimental value – a ring she had given him. 'In *The Secret Rapture* I tried to write a play in which death is present', says Hare. 'I just was very conscious that we don't proceed on a line towards death and that the image is that we live our lives and then at the end death is waiting for us, whereas if you get into middle age which I am then you become conscious that death is in everything.'[6]

In the shadow of death, the first scene is a prologue establishing the core family relationships. Robert – an idealistic, non-materialistic bookseller and father of Isobel and Marion – had married in later life an erratic alcoholic of their own age. Even before she is seen, Katherine is the catalyst to the action, immediately exposing the differences between Isobel and Marion. Where Marion considers that Robert was taken for a ride, Isobel respects that the passion he felt for Katherine distinguished his later years (p. 5). Isobel has been 'heroic', caring for her father at the end and refusing to condemn Katherine for not helping. Isobel is a good, kind person, but her very tolerance and compassion infuriate Marion, even though she makes no attempt to impose them on her. Isobel's silence is constantly (mis)interpreted and her reluctance to judge others is perceived by Marion as disapproval.

Smartly dressed and crisply efficient, Marion is a career politician who is up at 6am and always contactable by the mobile phone, which rings in her bag even on the day of the funeral. Where Clara's confession to Wallace in *Paris By Night* is the kind of off-the-peg philosophy which had dogged Peggy Whitton in *A Map of the World*, Marion's is the well-thought-out and intelligent conservatism of a junior government minister. To make the point, she uses the house she hates as a weapon in her defeat of the Green Party, who make the mistake of underestimating her skills and knowledge.

Although her party's in power, she's in office and a 'cert for the cabinet' (p. 7), she is permanently angry. Marion dislikes the mess of feelings and seeks simple, ordered solutions to human problems. She is angry with Katherine because she drinks, and with Isobel because she resists such simple solutions as giving Katherine a job or at least lying to her in the meantime. Marion's husband Tom doesn't get angry. He is a born-again Christian and Jesus, he says, makes things incomparably easier. The jokes about his religion prefigure the tone of *Racing Demon,* and Hare was struggling to find a way of writing about the Church of England at the time. The references were cut almost entirely from the film version of the play, which was completed in 1993. In 1989, however, they are used to establish that if Isobel is a good person, this goodness is not derived from God or from faith. Tom's honesty is not at issue but the fact that his business practice – where the tax position determines when to invest and when to sell – on the bandwagon of eighties materialism means that Christian faith is not a vehicle of opposition, whether political or moral.

Although Isobel questions whether making money might turn us all into arseholes, she is not aligned with the Greens, the Left or nuclear disarmament, but with the idea of 'decency' and, as the word is repeated in the text, it stands revealed as Hare's core value:

> KATHERINE: ... It's why I love the idea of joining your
> business. I like what you do. Your designs. There's
> something decent about them. When I pick up a book
> with one of your covers – or a record – I always think,
> this is something which gives nourishment to people.
> (p. 14)

The meaning of 'a sense of value' is clarified in the film script but, in both cases, the idea is associated with Robert and through him with books. The link to literature and nature is strengthened in the film by the change of family name from Glass to Coleridge and the physical presence of the woods around the house, where both Katherine and Isobel seek refuge, and which had been a single emblematic oak tree in the National Theatre production.

In Scene Three Isobel's small design business, together with her relationship with her lover and partner, Irwin (renamed as Patrick Steadman in the film) are shown, in contrast to Tom's approach, to be based on mutual respect (p. 14 and p. 19) and quiet job satisfaction rather than financial reward. One of the first things Katherine is seen to do in her new job is to criticise Irwin's work. She also badly misjudges the nature of their most important client in bringing an inappropriate sexual brashness to bear, in an episode added and made explicit in the many revisions in the film version, which was released in spring 1994.

After the conversation with Irwin about this incident, Isobel no longer wants to make love; in this way Katherine has already climbed into their bed. When Irwin is bought off by promise of a double salary in Scene Four, the respect goes and love dies. As the guns of the countryside echo in the background, Irwin 'sells out' their business and implicitly their relationship for Tom's injection of cash. At the moment about which the play is symmetrical, Isobel, alone as the final obstacle, literally turns her back on him.

The effect on their business and their relationship is demonstrated in Scene Five, which follows the passage of time of the interval and which parallels Scene Three exactly. In more stylish and luxurious offices, Irwin is again 'working', this time entertaining Rhonda to a bath. Isobel returns from rescuing Katherine from a drunken outburst and they argue. There is no intimacy and no shared understanding; instead the exchanges are marked by the interrogative. And where Isobel sees in Katherine maladjusted confusion, loss and unhappiness, Irwin sees evil dreaming of ways to destroy:

> IRWIN: I know, you think she's just unhappy. She's
> maladjusted. She hates herself. Well, she does. And she is.
> All these things are true. But also it's true, Isobel, my
> dear, you must learn something else. That everyone
> knows except you. It's time you were told. There's such
> a thing as evil. You're dealing with evil.
> (ISOBEL *turns round, about to speak.*)
> That's right. And if you don't admit it, then you can't
> fight it. And if you don't fight it, you're going to lose.
> (p. 58)

In *Paris By Night* the conflict between good and evil was supposed to be within Clara herself; but she is neither a Dr Jekyll nor a Mr Hyde. The idea of goodness was weakly conceived in Wallace's drawing of her – he was in any case an unreliable witness – and it is far from clear that she is deliberately evil rather than merely ambitious. In *The Secret Rapture,* evil is manifested in Katherine as the temptation to sex, to violence, to drink, to freedom, and to death, but it is precisely the tyranny of weakness rather than the manifestation of the devil. Neither is the evil of Katherine of the same order as that of John Morgan in *Wetherby*; her manipulative dependence is not the same as his vengeful depression, but it is a serious point which Hare was striving to make about alcoholism. As he put it, 'to be kind does not help them because it feeds their habit but to be cruel to them does not help them because it makes them feel there is no hope and that double bind is what you call tragic. It may be that whatever course you take, you're damned.'[7]

Good and evil are human effects rather than causes and they lie in the choices people make. 'People say I took advantage of his decency. But what are good people for? They're here to help the trashy people like me' (p. 19). Robert had his eyes open and loved the excitement Katherine brought. Marion and Tom assume Isobel will take on Katherine, but it is when Isobel *chooses* to do so that her life is inexorably changed: 'whatever's happened is my own fault' (p. 69), she confirms. It is her decision, based on a single smile of shared understanding, rather than Robert's death, which generates the action of the play in a series of four pairs of parallel scenes. As Hare confessed, 'My subject is goodness. Yes, I was interested to show what choices good people might have to make in order to survive or prosper among some of the other typical characters of the age. But I was also drawn to a more timeless theme. I wanted to show how goodness can bring out the worst in all of us.'[8]

In an environment where the Greens are written off as a seventies problem (p. 37) and political morality has been rewritten as the search for cheap nuclear power, Marion attempts variously to redefine and explain Isobel's integrity as neurotic and unnatural grief, or as naive and old-fashioned. It is Isobel's generosity of spirit, the determination to see Katherine as the product of circumstance who will change if circumstances do, which is a fatal flaw and for which you approach the coming denouement with a sense of foreboding: 'Oh, god, it makes you feel so powerless. I saw it all coming. I saw it weeks ago ... And there's *nothing* you can do. You can see it coming, and you still can't do anything' (p. 16).

When Tom and Marion seek to inject the surplus from their cash-rich business into her design agency with little regard for its character, and Irwin is won over to the ideology of self-interest, Isobel cannot resist. 'I was weak,' she confesses, 'but putting that aside I have just been – what is the word for it? – I think I have just been *asset-stripped*. Isn't that the term for it? "Objectively", as you would say, I have just been trashed and spat out in lumps' (p. 69). *The Secret Rapture* is full of perceptive 'serious money' observations and Hare is deeply concerned at the emotional and human cost of the way materialism dominated the age. For him, 'A political author is no less than one who acknowledges this fact. An apolitical author is one who denies it.'[9]

Through the character of Rhonda, sexual gamesmanship is equated with political energy but, just as the conflicts which consume Clara Paige are personal rather than political, so Hare's attention here is elsewhere. The core opposition is not political/ideological, but moral, and 'the emotional roots of the play are in something completely different: the problems of good and evil. The source of my work is not political but my own emotional life.' It is one of the few weaknesses of the play that Hare cannot resist making the obvious party political points, which fall ineptly from Katherine's lips, and they were cut from the film script.

For Isobel, 'The great thing is to love. If you're loved back then it's a bonus' (p. 5). For Irwin, love demands response and is a form of salvation. Like Caroline in *Dreams of Leaving*, Isobel refuses to get angry and to play the parts written for her by other people, she refuses to provide that comfort for Irwin. It is Gordon who had loved Isobel and been ashamed, and he is unseen in the play and cut altogether from the film. Some of the ideas of love and existentialism which had emerged in *Dreams of Leaving* are re-treated here, however. It is when Isobel refuses to restore Irwin's worth and be dishonest in the meantime, refuses indeed to *look* at him, that he is driven to distraction, and Hare foregrounds the relationship between looking and seeing in two new lines.

Katherine is associated with drink and sexual provocation, with violence and emotional blackmail, but it is Irwin who names evil and it is Irwin who commits the ultimate violence. Hare's own choice in the script foregrounds this evil as a death-wish, through a quotation from Rebecca West on the title page of the play script. In a confrontation which parallels in length his 'betrayal' of her in Scene Four, Irwin comes to the house where Isobel is caring for Katherine and shoots her at the end of Scene Seven. If it comes with a sense of inevitability then it is as much in fulfilment of Marion's anger with her sister and Isobel's fear of his obsession as Irwin's desperation.

> ISOBEL: In my case there's only one answer. (*She looks absently at them, as if they were not even present*.) I must do what Dad would have wished. (*She turns, as if this were self-evident*.) That's it.
> MARION: You are insufferable. You are truly insufferable. Hide behind your father for the rest of your life. Die there! (MARION *is suddenly screaming.* ISOBEL *looks down, undisturbed*.)
> ISOBEL: Yes, well, no doubt I shall. (p. 71)

In the original production of *The Secret Rapture* Irwin's action was prefigured but not explained. In the film version Hare added short episodes to show the progressive deterioration in Irwin after his rejection by Isobel. The result of this fleshing out was, however, to shift the balance of sympathy between the two.

In *Paris By Night*, it was at the moment of Clara Paige's death that justice was done and order restored. To put it in different terms, the writer who quoted from Yeats in *Teeth 'n' Smiles* might say it is only at the moment of death that the past, the present and the future are reconciled and when humankind achieves what Yeats saw as the unity of being. In this way it is a moment of joyous unification or, in different terms, of religious fulfilment, and the title *The Secret Rapture* refers to the moment a nun is unified with Christ.

In Hare's play, however, goodness does not yield any joy, any rapture in this sense. By temperament, Isobel claims, 'I'm actually an extremely cheerful girl' (p. 56), but we do not see it. Neither is Isobel's life justified in the hereafter. Isobel says she is bored by the idea of suffering and specifically rejects the allocation of the word 'sacrifice'. If there is any salvation, it does not come from the church for, at the end, Tom loses touch with Jesus. Isobel is neither a Christian nor a Christ figure and in her death she does not so much absolve the family and the audience of sin or guilt but charge them with it.

When Isobel dies, Irwin declares, 'It's over. Thank God' (p. 80) with the same kind of relief as William had felt at Caroline's madness in *Dreams of Leaving*. Unlike William, however, he does not survive it and is not seen again. Once she has gone, Isobel not only withdraws her approval and his worth, but his very existence; he loved her and he lost himself. If there is salvation, it is not from romantic love, but from self-knowledge. As Hare acknowledged, it's not a religious view, 'It's a stoic view.'[10]

Unlike *Paris By Night*, which ends with the single shot of Simon sitting up in bed, there is a coda to *The Secret Rapture*. It is not Isobel's death which marks the setting in order but its effect. Marion for the first time turns off the mobile phone, saying she does not wish to speak to the ministry. Politics, it seems, must finally give way to human mortality (p. 62). In the garden of her father's house, Marion finds a more passionate expression of love for her husband and opens up the channels to her emotional life, to the deep old words of *Wetherby*. Pretending things are simpler than they are does not solve human problems, anger does not wash away the pain, only channels it temporarily in someone else's direction. It is, perhaps, in this discovery, in her plea for Isobel to come home, that salvation lies.

Certainly the implication of *The Secret Rapture* is that it is the particular nature of conservatism in the eighties which has destroyed the kind of goodness Isobel nurtures, and that if such goodness were to prevail, life might be improved. What marks out *The Secret Rapture* and what contributes to its maturity, however, is the fact that there is no clear and unambiguous pointer to this moral. Similarly, there is no evident gender distinction, nor any class division. Tired of what he calls shallow, pessimistic art, Hare is searching for something more than politics. 'When *The Secret Rapture* was first presented in London, it was inevitable that it should be seen by commentators primarily as a political play ... Yet when I finished the play, I believed it to be the most personal and private I had written.'[11]

As Marion asks, 'We live in this world. We try to make a living. Most of us just try to get on with our lives. Why can't we?' (p. 65). Where is the sense of meaning and morality to come from in the midst of human pain? We know from *Paris By Night* that honesty alone is not enough. Even if Clara Paige had been honest, she would not have had character. Isobel has character defined as 'kindness and tolerance and decency' (p. 14) with a sense of family, social justice and responsibility from which the other characters have cut loose (p. 31). It is these middle-class liberal virtues born of man's humanity to man which Hare is, tentatively, asserting.

In Jacobean revenge tragedy and in early work like *Brassneck*, hope lay in the confidence that evil will ultimately destroy itself. If goodness could not triumph except through death then it would not triumph. By ending the play with Marion's self-discovery, Hare overcomes the difficulty he faced in *A Map of the World*, when Stephen bought his victory over Mehta only through a kind of sacrificial or martyr's death. Grief, it seems, as well as love, can bring about great shifts in character in which the unseen funerals are the rites of passage.

For almost the first time in his work, Hare's women are not ciphers and they are not judged. If we are being asked to consider an intellectual question, we are also being made to *feel* our way towards an answer.

> MARION: I get the drift of your questions.
> ISOBEL: They have no drift. I've simply been establishing the facts.
> MARION: Oh yes, I know what you think of us.
> ISOBEL: What I think? Oh, really? How?
> (ISOBEL *is half smiling.* MARION *is angry.*)
> MARION: I just *know.*
> ISOBEL: I don't think so. Perhaps you know what you yourself feel. But that's different.
> MARION: What do you mean? (*She is panicking now.*) I've nothing on my conscience. I don't feel anything. (p. 68)

In the first scene, Tom did not feel anything in reply to Isobel and Marion's disagreement over their father's second marriage. By the final scene, he and Marion literally feel each other. On the eve of the 1990s, the two distinctive virtues of real plays for Hare were that 'they show us that feelings which we had thought private turn out to be common ground with others, and uniquely, they appeal as much to our heads as to our hearts. Or, rather, they send our minds and hearts spinning together, so that we cannot tell which is which.'[12]

The salvation is Hare's, a personal act, and the rapture is essentially 'secret', a change in the world certainly but one which takes place at a profoundly personal level. The true source of salvation is tragedy – not so much the pure form and order of art itself, but the emotion which it generates. In *The Secret Rapture* that emotion is one of pity and of fear. Just as Isobel feels pity for Katherine and fears for what Irwin will do, just as Tom fears for Isobel, so does the audience. And when Isobel turns her back on Irwin meaning to shock him out of his dependence, it results in a *peripeteia* which is her own death and Marion's *anagnorisis* or discovery. Together they offer a way for David Hare and for the audience of coming to terms not just with a particular ideology and set of circumstances, but with the eternal situation. And in this discovery and reconciliation is an optimism which is profoundly moving and which inspired not only *The Secret Rapture* but *Strapless*.

12 *Strapless*

Given extensive cinematic release after its completion in spring 1989, *Strapless* was finally screened three years later on Channel 4. It was, however, written alongside *The Secret Rapture* and features Blair Brown, to whom *The Secret Rapture* was dedicated. Although quite different in period and style, *Strapless* is Hare's most unambiguously optimistic film and can be seen as a culmination of his search for belief.

As images of crumbling statues, of '*dying blooms, mists in the mountains*' (p. 1) give way, *Strapless* opens to reveal a woman, Lillian Hempel, standing before a statue of the Madonna in a Catholic church. When she drops her handkerchief, a smartly dressed man kneels beside her and picks it up. The title song 'When I fall in love' ends as the camera focuses on his face gazing up at her. What Raymond Forbes, an ambiguous but apparently successful entrepreneur, is doing in this church is, like so much about him, never to be explained, but this is a carefully placed set of associations establishing that Raymond worships her and that romance is the context of the coming story.

From the outset it is also made clear that, whatever is to come, these people – unlike the faithful praying around them – take no sustenance from religion. It is said to be obscure that just by dying in some way Christ would make everyone's life better (p. 2). It is revealed over a meal on a hillside that – just as they are both alone, on holiday – Raymond and Lillian also share a liking for the early days of a relationship when love is given freely (p. 5). Lillian, however, rejects the proposition to proceed directly to bed. Despite Raymond's evident confident expectation, she fails to turn up at the hotel later that evening. He is left pacing up and down at the entrance. The enchanted atmosphere of a Mediterranean climate, of wandering camera and orchestral music is brought to an end and Lillian turns to go.

Part Two opens on the unflattering strip-lighting and harsh sounds of an NHS hospital corridor. This American works in England and is assured and needed by the team around her, the white coat confirming her status as she is formally introduced as 'Dr Hempel'. And, as she breaks the news to Mrs Clark that her husband has an inoperable cancer, the audience is confronted with a grim reality, a deliberate disjuncture marking the second of three intermingling strands in the film.

The coverage of the case of Mr Clark might comprise only a few pages of the printed text but the hospital is more than just the background to Lillian's life. Just as we were invited to consider the value of the education which Jean Travers expounded in *Wetherby*, so as a doctor in a cancer hospital Lillian is shown to be in contact with death all the time. The limits of our humanity stand as a constant challenge to her abilities and to mankind's battle against nature. It is the unremitting greyness of an emotionally exhausting and demanding job from which, we are to assume, she wishes to escape on her holiday to Europe and which 'justifies' her involvement and actions with the elusive and attractive Raymond Forbes.

Played by Bruno Ganz, an actor known for his appearance in such art-house movies as *Wings of Desire*, he is a precise, immaculate and appealing entrepreneur who avoids giving information about himself. His interrogative style reinforces an air of mystery, but Raymond is far from threatening: his questions have the innocent charm of childhood and Raymond lacks the cynicism of evil. As his second attempt at courtship, he brings a horse named 'Heartfree' – with all its associations of natural speed, sexual energy, extravagance and gambling – into the London streets; he brings his crisp suit and quizzical smile into the uncomfortable crush of an NHS waiting area; he brings the unexpected into the routine. His proposal of marriage challenges Lillian to leave behind the congealed uneaten meals and the demands of the medical bleeper and enter an idyll of fields and sunshine.

Raymond has understood that 'All your life you have to make

judgements, you have to be professional and capable and reserved. You have to hold your life at arm's length. And yet all the time, inside, you want to say yes to something' (p. 29). The idea of professionalism as a form of emotional distancing is picked up again in *Murmuring Judges,* but in *Strapless* it stands to contrast Lillian with her younger wayward sister, Amy. 'Wild, anarchic, natural' (p. 11), she is still asleep in the afternoon when Lillian gets home from the hospital. They share a flat and a boil-in-the-bag lifestyle, but Amy moves on the seedier side of life with the *paparazzi* earning money from voyeurism of minor royalty, posing nude for photographs, changing her 'profession' as often as her boyfriends.

Raymond is not inviting Lillian into the kind of promiscuity associated, through Carlos, as it had been in *Dreams of Leaving,* with South America. Lillian has clearly had lovers and Raymond's invitation is not so much to sex as to romance.

> LILLIAN: I don't get it. Who are you, Raymond? (*Gestures round the room.*) What do you believe?
> RAYMOND: I don't believe in sex outside marriage. (p. 33)

It is also a different kind of challenge from the one Ian Tyson offers Janetta in *Heading Home* or Archie MacLean presents to Anna Seaton in *Licking Hitler.* In the forties, young women were offered the chance for sexual and life experience; in the nineties, an established, professional, middle-aged woman is offered the chance to take a risk and to be an unreconstructed, romantic heroine. And, as Raymond touches Lillian for the first time, she responds sympathetically, allowing his hand to run through her hair. She is still not ready to marry someone she does not know, preferring instead to live with him, but it is she who leads the way up the spiral staircase to bed.

As he puts his arms around her, the music climaxes and the door closes with the seduction unseen. It is not the relationship itself which is the substance of the film, but its effect. The success of the sexual liaison is, however, implied as, radiant and happy, Lillian emerges from the mists of the early morning ride on the horse Raymond bought for her, saying 'Oh, it's wonderful. It's absolutely wonderful' (p. 35).

At the moment of consummation, however, the balance between them changes. They cannot leave the hotel room because Raymond – the man who cares nothing for money and behaves with an air of wealth – is unable to clear his gambling debt. As Lillian pays it, so Mr Clark is intercut, angry at losing control of his bodily functions. The juxtaposition does not, perhaps, go as far as inviting the audience to consider love as a sickness undermining the relationship. Despite the changes in sequence of shots from the printed script, the parallel between the death of Mr Clark and the relationship between Lillian and Raymond generates only the mildest sense of unease. When Lillian tells Mr Clark, 'Just trust us. We'll see you through' (p. 41), we know she can only ease the physical pain of dying; and we are therefore less inclined to trust Raymond as he meets his new temporary secretary in modern offices. The smallest trace of doubt is consolidated when the post-marital intercourse at the end of Part Three is followed by Lillian scrubbing up for surgery and forgetting her wedding ring at the opening of Part Four.

When Raymond leaves an ambiguous and inadequate message to account for his sudden departure abroad, it is with mounting anger that Lillian goes home to her own flat for the central confrontation with her now pregnant sister. The outburst is a string of rhetorical questions – contrasting with Raymond's own style; it contains one of only two profanities in the film, indicating Lillian's own loss of control and pointing to the disproportionate savagery of her assault on Amy. It is this exchange and this unanswered question which stands at the heart of David Hare's film, coming between the consummation of Lillian and Raymond's relationship and their marriage. Immaculately structured, the film is symmetrical about this point, built on three sets of parallel scenes which are punctuated – like *Licking Hitler* a decade earlier – with blackouts.

> AMY: I don't have it in me?
> (LILLIAN *just looks at her.*)
> What, you think people can't change?
> (LILLIAN *does not reply.*)
> Lillian?
> (*She is suddenly very quiet and serious.*)
> Can they? Please tell me. Can they?   (p. 44)

It is the confrontation with Amy and this challenge to change that prompts Lillian to shortcut the usual stages in building a relationship, to take the final step and marry Raymond. Their 'liaison' had begun in the remnants of imperial Europe. It takes place outdoors, in a restaurant, on Hampstead Heath, on the Downs. When they get indoors, into the Registry Office, into the normality of domestic life, and Lillian wants to stay in, the basis of their relationship ceases to exist.

If *Strapless* is another go at romantic love, it ultimately demonstrates yet again that romance cannot last. Having failed to entice her to continue the illusion of a continuing courtship with the gift of a BMW, Raymond leaves the room for the night and the outside; he disappears. When the debt-collectors start to call, Lillian denies she is a relative; as the music changes from swirling strings to insistent drip and she finds Raymond's offices and the picture frame from his desk empty, the full realisation dawns. Lillian's impregnable professionalism cracks – she makes errors, hides in the closet and bursts into tears:

> LILLIAN: Where am I? You know. Can I ask that? For years
> I've done nothing but give. Just give. Oh, I know, it's
> rewarding, of course. But there is something you're not
> meant to ask.
> (SABOLA*'s face, looking at her distress with great fondness.*)
> The giving's great. It's great. I'm sorry, but when do I
> get something back?   (p. 60)

The answer is quite soon. The apparently hard, bureaucratic Mr Cooper assures her 'It's good work. You bring comfort' (p. 60), and with faint humour says 'You can always have this cupboard. Whenever you need it.' This is not the place where 'We know no comfort. Our lives dismay us. We have dreams of leaving. Everyone I know' (*Dreams of Leaving*). This is not the existentialist landscape of the shameless, the ugly and the absurd, nor the cold calculation and compromised belief of the stale conservatism of *The Secret Rapture* and *Paris By Night*; this is a place and people of commitment and of values.

It is to explain her own conviction that a relationship based on intuition and trust rather than intellect and analysis *is* meaningful that Lillian traces Raymond's background. In the third part of the film and with an oblique echo of the opening, Lillian finds Raymond's disillusioned father-figure, who has lost his faith, and his adoptive mother's acceptance of a lifetime of romantic dreaming. Although going some way to justifying his actions as a positive love of women rather than a malicious maltreatment of them, the episode amounts to little more than a convenient link to Lillian's meeting with Raymond's first love, Annie. This provides final confirmation that Lillian's marriage to Raymond was a sham so that she is freed of moral obligation to him; it demonstrates that the women can be friends despite this and – in experiencing Annie's self-reliance as a single mother in a country cottage – provides the catalyst to Lillian's final (re)discovery.

The nineteenth-century Romantic view of the world of the opening, portrayed also in the rotting seedy grandeur of the hall to Lillian's flat and the school chapel, is dying as surely as Mr Clark. Women are now independent of men and the nuclear family is an outmoded institution. Changes to the script which cut Lillian's former boyfriend, Tom, altogether and reduced the presence of Carlos (the father of Amy's baby) served further to assert their positive independence.

As Mr Clark decides to reject drugs and die as himself, so Amy proves herself. In a reversal of control, it is Amy who decides to cancel the cheques Lillian has written to clear Raymond's personal debts. The world might not change, but people can and she demonstrates her character just as Valentina had done in similar circumstances some decades earlier in *The Bay at Nice*. The sterility of Susan Traherne in *Plenty* is banished and Amy quite literally gives birth to a new future of a child cared for in a community of support rather than a nuclear family. What was intimated in *The Bay at Nice* and in *Paris By Night* is made explicit in *Strapless*: motherhood is one source of value.

> MADELEINE: You must feel so good.
> LILLIAN: I'm so proud of her. Isn't it absurd?
> MADELEINE: She'll be a wonderful mother.
> (LILLIAN *stops, the champagne suspended.*)
> LILLIAN: Yes. I feel that. (p. 79, lines as spoken)

Although named Mary, Amy's baby is not christened as originally scripted, so that the religious connotations are further weakened; this is not Madonna, the mother of Christ and the route to Man's salvation, but the daughter of self-supporting humanity and the new relationship between independent women.

> LILLIAN: ... When did you do these?
> AMY: Oh, while I was waiting. I'd been fiddling you know all kinds of support. Straps and little bits of things.
> (LILLIAN *smiles at the drawing.*)
> Then, you know, I decided, what would be easier? And what would look better?
> LILLIAN: Nothing.
> AMY: Exactly.
> (LILLIAN *looks at her, then bends down and kisses the child.*)
> LILLIAN: Goodnight, Mary.
> (*She stands up, right by the window, moonlight on the side of her face.* AMY *smiles at her.*)
> AMY: Let them stand up on their own.   (pp. 79-80)

Let them stand up on their own and let them also stand up and be counted. Although not the main focus of the film, Mr Clark's disease is a potentially fertile if underwritten political metaphor. As the NHS, it is said, faces a period of almost infinite contraction, Lillian – an American in Britain for twelve years – nonetheless considered it was not her fight. At the opening of *Strapless*, she was hardworking but unengaged, but, as Mr Clark achieves his wish and dies as himself with some dignity, so Lillian accepts her responsibilities. Countering the English disease, Lillian decides to join the fight for the NHS, so offsetting the apparent negative ending. It is the women, Ramone and Lillian, in stark contrast to an administrator's incomprehension and Colin's drunken celebration, who understand that 'If we do nothing – don't protest, don't organize – then we collude in the system's decline' (p. 82). And if we do this, Hare asserts, then our faith will, like Lillian's, be repaid (p. 83): Imre duly visits to bring to Lillian the little silver horse which proves the emotional substance in her relationship with Raymond.

David Hare is, then, not concerned to criticise Raymond. Lillian was not betrayed; the clues were there to be discovered in retrospect by her and the audience and, as she explicitly acknowledges, she knew he was running on empty (p. 62). As Lillian sits waiting for Amy's fund-raising fashion show to begin, Raymond is intercut walking down a station platform and being presented with the chance to repeat the pick-up process with another woman who has dropped a handkerchief. Happy and with a spring in his step, he turns back, but Hare does not end there. It is Lillian and Amy, and David Hare with them, who move forward. Raymond was a catalyst to Lillian's self-discovery. As the classical music triumphs over the modern, Lillian draws back the curtains to the catwalk and breaks the black-out with the startling light of a new beginning. Hare may not follow Lillian through the curtains, he may still not know quite where the women are going, but David Hare, like Lillian and the dress she is wearing, is strapless, self-supporting and taking responsibility for his own actions and feelings.

> LILLIAN: I've been very arrogant. I thought I was exempt.
> No one's exempt. You have certain feelings. And then
> you must pick up the bill.
> (*She looks lovingly at her sister.*)
> You've always known that. But it's taken me time.
> (p. 79)

13 Heading home?

As the 1990s dawned, David Hare stood on the verge of something new: he had taken on Shakespeare and reclaimed tragedy. *Heading Home* was, however, the first film for television in a decade he made for the BBC and, screened in January 1991, it appeared to be taking him back to the forms and agenda of the history plays of the 1970s. Although *Heading Home* filled in the gaps left in Hare's previous accounts of post-war history, it also comprised another go at the themes of love and existentialism which had stood at the heart of *Dreams of Leaving* and concluded his discussions of the eighties on the purpose of art. In that sense it provides a reconciliation of the two major strands in his two decades of writing for the national stages.

At the opening of *Heading Home*, an unseen speaker identifies a special moment from her own past. As in *Dreams of Leaving* and *Saigon*, a voice self-consciously looks back to earlier times from a position of relative age and wisdom, but in this case the view is neither chronological – since the moment in question is identified as being too far on – nor part of an everyday occurrence. 'That particular road was quite extraordinary, even at the time' (p. 5) and what made it extraordinary was that it opened out so that 'You saw the beach and the bay.' Here, at the very opening of the film, is the promise of the 'perfect contentment' (p. 6) of a young woman and her lover in somewhere which 'never seemed like England' (p. 6), a concrete realisation of the image of freedom which remained unseen and elusive in *The Bay at Nice*.

Where, in *Dreams of Leaving*, William Cofax first came to London in 1971 and found a series of grim girlfriends, Janetta Wheatland is escaping the stultifying security of a middle-class provincial home clearly visible in her family snapshots (p. 14 and p. 31). Sitting with a group in a smoky pub she is recognised from the earlier shots and she soon accepts the invitation to share a bedsit with a journalist/poet, and a sculptor and her baby at the real start to the film. As in *Plenty*, the flash forward gives way to a chronological narrative starting in the post-war austerity of 1947; as in *Licking Hitler*, the young woman at the centre of the story is an innocent seeking experience, because 'it's time I learnt one or two things about things' (p. 13).

With the film apparently awash with references to Hare's own previous work, he appeared quite literally to be *Heading Home*. Published in 1991 alongside *Dreams of Leaving* and *Wetherby*, the associations were deliberately reinforced. Either Hare was, as he confessed in 1989, 'too old to change',[1] or he was having another go at the themes and styles of his own writing history.

Where William embarked on a difficult relationship with the enigmatic Caroline in *Dreams of Leaving,* Janetta finds a kind of extended family; where William was initiated into the style of tabloid journalism, Janetta enthusiastically takes a job at the local library where she soon sets about reclassifying and simplifying the processes, and is received as an agent of change. 'We've not thought about change. Just about survival', says Mr Evernden, Janetta's boss, 'Now here you are to shake us all up' (p. 17). She is also the agent of change in the domestic life of those around her for, in the next shot, we hear that Beryl and baby Sam have left the flat. Janetta and Leonard are alone, knowing that their friendship will soon become physical.

Her seduction remains unseen and it is rather the second stage of Janetta's learning curve which Hare chooses to make the subject of dialogue, as she struggles to come to terms with the sudden death of her boss.

> JANETTA: I went to his flat. There was nothing there. It was awful. At the end, he had nothing except a few objects. And a collection of books.
> LEONARD: Well? So what?
> (JANETTA *frowns, not understanding.*)
> You can't judge people's lives by the surface. (*He smiles.*)
> (p. 23)

It might be a cliché to say that a library of knowledge and culture is no defence against mortality and that you can't take it with you when you go, but each person has to learn these lessons, learn that this, in itself, does not make life meaningless.

What is also made clear here is that, having reached a pinnacle of achievement and self-discovery with *The Secret Rapture*, Hare had turned back from his recent preoccupation with death and from the view of life as inherently tragic:

> LEONARD: ... You can't judge people's lives by the surface. (*He smiles.*) I mean, look at us, what do we have? (*He pauses.*) Well, as it happens, we do have a salami.
> JANETTA: Really?
> LEONARD: Yes.
> (*He rises and goes over to the desk.*)
> I sold a poem.
> (*He picks up the salami from the desk.*)
> About my ship going down.
> (*He puts the salami down and faces* JANETTA.)
> But if a stranger walked in and looked round our lives, they'd say 'Do you realize what they had? Between them? A single salami. How tragic!'
> (*Moving towards her.*) And yet we're not tragic at all.
> (pp. 23-4)

Neither does the turning away from tragedy signal a return to documentary: there are no 'real' events in *Heading Home* and the whole is clearly filtered through the memory of one witness who, in the final assertion of the film, explicitly acknowledges her own partiality, saying, 'These events, I suppose, detain me and me only. No one else remembers them, or if they do, then quite differently. To them, they yield a different meaning' (p. 66). These are the lessons of representation and of propaganda, of significance and assimilation, which Hare had learned through *Fanshen*, *Licking Hitler* and *A Map of the World*.

And in answer to the question of what plans she might have, Janetta and Leonard head out of London to the beach of the opening. 'Summer came as we were driving. The winter ended in front of our eyes. And, for the first time, he talked about the war' (p. 25). In a few brief lines, Leonard describes his own confrontation with violent death. He does not talk about it much because, in a reference which takes us back to the expressionism of Hare's own early work, 'That's what poetry's for. To say what can't be said' (p. 25). That's what art is for, to rescue us from despair.

None of Leonard's poems is heard, however, just as none of Victor Mehta's novels is read in *A Map of the World* and none of Matisse's paintings is seen in *The Bay at Nice*. What enables them all to speak is David Hare's film, and that film chooses to demonstrate not so much the horror of war, but emotional frankness and physical joy which is fluently consummated on screen with passion and laughter. It is the only time to date that Hare has shown sex on screen which is unequivocally associated with happiness, and it is because of this that *Heading Home* does not present the feminist problem of *Licking Hitler*. Indeed, Janetta declares, 'I do remember I'd never felt closer to anyone. I felt I was wholly alive. I was free' (p. 26). As with Valentina in *The Bay at Nice*, her assertion of freedom occurs only in retrospect, in voice-over, but the specific repositioning of the line in the final edit after the script had been published served to strengthen the assertion.

As the chambermaid interrupts Janetta and Leonard as they continue making love during a fire alarm, she accuses them of 'behaving like animals'. In the next shot, Ian Tyson offers an explanation of the reaction: 'It's the English, you know. They're frightened of energy' (p. 27). It is also through Ian Tyson that Hare explicitly makes the connection between building bricks of property, the flow of history and repression which has recurred in his work since 1973. 'No more incidents. It's all they want, now they're back from the war. Build a little box and shut yourself in. (*He smiles.*) Everyone's had enough of events' (p. 31). The Englishman's home is his castle, which, in the 'Freudian' visions of *Wetherby* and *Dreams of Leaving* can be seen to constitute a fortress against the kind of energy which Ian embodies: 'Security? I have no idea what you mean', (p. 31) he confesses. It is through Ian Tyson, in *Heading Home*, that Hare fills in the gaps left in his first history play by examining the operation of the property market, which had also made Alfred Bagley's fortune in *Brassneck*. It is the central point of the film when Tyson explains 'Everyone is going to want property. They just don't know it yet. It's the Englishman's dream. Buy a house, close the door, stop history' (p. 30).

This is not to say, however, that *Heading Home* is the same kind of repressed wish-fulfilment of *Dreams of Leaving*. The casting of actress Joely Richardson as Janetta reinforces links to *Wetherby* and themes of emotional freedom and *Heading Home* does not, as *Dreams of Leaving* had done, make either character or actress into an object of obsession. Where, in *Dreams of Leaving*, Caroline had existed only through William's eyes and the camera had framed her as an object for consumption, it is Janetta who looks at Leonard writing through the night and declares at the outset that she will stay with him 'Just while I'm looking' (p. 13).

If the word 'look', which was so important to *Dreams of Leaving*, appears 110 times in the directions and 25 times in the spoken script of *Heading Home*, it is this time focused on moments of development in the relationships. In his opening line Ian Tyson declares of Janetta that 'It looks to me like you're too good for this place' and it is Janetta who is controlling the discourse (p. 19). Rather than referring exclusively to Sartrean phenomenology and theories of consciousness and identity, *Heading Home* contains a new imperative to *look*:

JANETTA: ...He's trying to work out what he believes.
    (IAN *just nods slightly*.)
IAN: And you think that matters?
JANETTA: Of course. More than anything.
    (*She looks at him a moment*.)
    What we believe? Yes of course. *Of course*.
    (*She stops, her disbelief growing. The two of them standing apart in the alley,* IAN *by a metal staircase, she in the middle of the alley*.)
    It's terribly important.
IAN: Is it?
    (*He looks at her a moment, as if really taking her in for the first time. Then he moves decisively away from the metal staircase*.)
    I must go home.
    (*She suddenly begins to panic at the idea of the conversation*

> *being left where it is.*)
> JANETTA: Now look ...   (p. 35)

In the year when *Racing Demon* appeared on the stage of the National Theatre, the question of the value of belief stood at the heart of Hare's work. It was picked up explicitly in this context in the script for the film version of *The Secret Rapture,* where many lines begin with the imperative and where Marion makes explicit the fact that 'People don't see'; 'they look but they don't see'.

When Janetta/Hare enable Leonard to talk about the war for the first time (p. 25), he talks equally about his own English background and the false expectations of his middle-class upbringing which the experience of the war shattered. Leonard is the epitome of the English middle classes; he was, he says, trained to be brilliant, to play cricket and have a proper career running the country and is now enjoying the luxury of being a poet, sitting in his metaphorical ivory tower expressing emotion and thinking about life rather than getting on with it. In contrast, Ian Tyson has come up the hard way and provides cheap houses for the poor, whom he knows well. He does business by telephone from a pub and deals in the alleyways of post-war business. He believes in action and is afraid of emotional commitment and kindness. In this way, emanating firmly from the characterisations rather than being an explicit point of them, the concept of class difference, if not of conflict, reappears in *Heading Home* for the first time in Hare's work for a decade.

Repression is, then, for the first time explicitly explained not as a psychological eternal but as a cultural constituent – a particular characteristic not just of the English but of the English middle classes. Psychological and linguistic models which dominated previous work are still visible, but are no longer given primacy. In the Nietzschean terms which informed *Teeth 'n' Smiles*, Leonard can be seen as embodying an Apollonian ideal of art and civilisation, represented by indoor locations, where Ian is associated with the Dionysiac revelry of the street, where violence, energy and ultimately death rule. In the Freudian terms which informed *Wetherby*, the regulatory forces of the BBC, of cricket and of art are the forces of Eros ranged against the destructive death-wish of Thanatos. It is the upbringing, class determinacy, rather than the eternal make-up of civilisation and its discontents which Hare cites in *Heading Home*. This does not mean that Hare rejects psychological eternals; it is rather that they are *ever*-present and, therefore, explanations still need to be sought elsewhere.

Where Leonard states, 'I'm going to write. It shouldn't disturb you' (p. 10), Ian disturbs Janetta from their first encounter in the library. Following through the keywords from *Dreams of Leaving*, it is Ian who causes Janetta to be *uneasy* in London (p. 29) and she paces the streets in physical manifestation of her distance from the cosy, sedentary bedsit. Where Leonard sits at his desk moving only his writing arm, Ian drives around London in pursuit of Janetta and of property. Ian is not illiterate but he reads only property surveys. He talks a different language and in their first encounter Janetta confesses, 'I'm sorry. I'm afraid I don't know what you mean' (p. 19). As a result of the meeting, however, 'Something had changed' (p. 20) and in the next shot Janetta takes Leonard to bed.

In their next exchange Ian goes further and challenges Janetta to step outside of the ideas of politeness (p. 27), decency and self (p. 35), to live without such nonsense (p. 36) and to become a 'normal person' (p. 19). 'And so things changed' (p. 39) again. Janetta is confronted with a clear choice between men, between thought/feeling and action and between two value systems, a choice which is made explicit by Ian.

> IAN: It's up to you. You can waste your life sitting there
> with your poet. I've met these kinds of people. 'Oh I
> think this; oh, I think that …' (*He spreads his arms,
> dramatizing.*) 'Oh, I feel; oh, I don't feel …' Of course it's
> fine. It's a great game. Especially for two players. (*He is
> suddenly serious.*) But don't ever kid yourself it's anything
> else. (IAN *suddenly seems almost angry.*) You're lucky,
> you're privileged. Spend your life asking 'What do I *feel*
> about this? Do I *feel* I'm doing the right thing …' (*He
> pauses.*) Or else you can just do it. I know which kind of
> person I like.   (p. 36)

The choice is very deliberately between equals. The relationships between Janetta and Leonard and between Janetta and Ian are of the same length in the printed script and follow the same pattern of development and decline. After the introduction to Leonard's bohemian lifestyle (eleven pages), the relationship blossoms and culminates at the beach (eleven pages); after the introduction to Ian and his business operation (twelve pages), Janetta's 'relationship' with him takes her into the auction room and alleyways (twelve pages). The opposition between city and country, bombed-out destruction and creative expression is there, but both are experienced with both men. If, in 1973, in *Brassneck*, Hare despised the property-developer, by 1991 the energy of the action man seemed much more attractive.

There is, however, an important difference between the two men. 'The difference is', as Ian puts it, not just that he had a good war where Leonard had a bad one but that 'I believe women can actually do it' (p. 42). Leonard claims Janetta as an inspiration for his poetry. As he confesses, 'My goodness, it's you' (p. 12) and she is indeed 'the perfectly discreet literary girlfriend' (p. 52) to be seen with at the poetry reading, the only woman present, silent and owned. The fact that Leonard's poetry is not heard is, then, at least partly an expression of Janetta's exclusion from it as the speaker of the narrative.

In contrast, Ian declares 'I believe in you. You could make a contribution. I mean it. You could be someone in your own right' (p. 42). And he acts on this belief, giving her rents to collect and then giving her the bidding to do in the auction room where she is the only woman present. What she gains from Ian is not the joy of sex and emotional freedom – since sex with him results in his sitting naked playing patience – but the joy of learning about her potential to act in the world. 'And so things changed' (p. 39); Janetta lied to Leonard about visiting an aunt in order to spend three days with Ian. After the fervour of the auction house and the agitation of the meeting with Ian's rival (Derek), Janetta returns home and lies to Leonard. She hugs the cat and not Leonard and the line 'You look well' (p. 51) was cut from his scripted response. It is in these ways that *Heading Home* fulfils the political responsibilities of the writer which were evaded in *Dreams of Leaving,* and leaves behind the concerns of Sartrean existentialism.

The turning-points and explanation of the two relationships

come not in exchanges between Janetta and her lovers but parallel exchanges of equal length between Janetta and their friends. It falls to Beryl to challenge Janetta herself to 'look'. 'If you'd looked once ... (*She pauses.*) If you'd looked at Leonard, I mean really looked, looked deep, you'd have understood' (p. 55). But she didn't because she was too busy looking at Ian's physicality rather than Leonard's beautiful mind (p. 27). When Janetta first sees Ian she remarks 'Goodness. Who was he?' (p. 19). She has assigned a value judgement which is never applied to Leonard. When Janetta returns home after her first evening with Ian, Leonard is in bed and not writing. She is not looking at him and instead tears fill her eyes. And, because she – the controller of the memory/discourse – was not looking, Leonard ceased to exist; it is only her looking in retrospect which (re)creates him.

'Leonard said nothing, I'm sure. For at least two reasons. For a start, he's English (*She stops, fighting back feeling.*) And for another he's a very nice man' (p. 55). He said nothing because he had no poetry outside of Hare's discourse and that discourse is 'owned' by Janetta's voice-over. He said nothing because he was powerless; it was his own inability to act, to return to the beach, which resulted in Janetta's initial liaison with Ian. The question in these relationships is not, as it had been in *The Bay at Nice* and *Wrecked Eggs,* who the other person makes you but who has least to lose. It is friendship – between Leonard and Beryl and between Ian and Juliusz – which is *easy*, rather than love, and Janetta never finds it. Janetta hurt Leonard because she knew she would get away with it, because she had nothing at risk (p. 56). It is with this realisation that her innocence ultimately gives way to experience and she learns the lessons of *The Bay at Nice* and *Dreams of Leaving,* about love as power, about shame and bad faith. The question remaining to be answered is 'Which way is the balance this time?' (p. 57).

Left the flat by Leonard when he leaves, Janetta provides sanctuary to Juliusz after he is beaten up by Ian's enemies on the streets. She rolls out the mattress in a reversal of the opening, when she had first stayed with Leonard and Beryl. She puts an end to the relationship between Juliusz and Ian just as she had 'caused' Beryl to leave Leonard earlier in the narrative. Battered and bruised, Juliusz is ashamed; he is not, like William had been in *Dreams of*

Leaving, ashamed in front of the woman he loves for the lack of principles he holds but ashamed for Ian that his territory has been attacked, that the rules of the game have changed. Lying in the darkness, Juliusz says 'If he sees me, he'll go crazy' (p. 58). 'I know Ian. He's going to get himself killed' (p. 58). And in this way he makes explicit the connection in the film between Dionysiac elements of energy, madness and death.

If Susan Traherne in *Plenty* was in some sense mad, Janetta is not. When she asks 'Am I being crazy?', Leonard's reply is, 'It depends. Do you have somewhere to go?' (p. 13). He then provides somewhere for her to go. And if Caroline in *Dreams of Leaving* lost her mind for not sleeping with William, Janetta sleeps not just with one man but with two. 'What's crazy is, I've been thinking, we discussed fidelity. He was quite clear. He said it didn't matter. He said you should never feel tied down. He said we should be free' (p. 54). What's crazy is that she believed him.

When Janetta knows about Juliusz's plans to return home and about Ian's vulnerability, when she realises the real basis of the relationship between her and Ian – that she is useful to him – the scales tip irrevocably in her favour. 'It's fine' (p. 15) for Janetta to enter while Beryl is in the bath and to be with Leonard; Juliusz reiterates that 'We're fine' about Ian's business (p. 19; 22; 23). At the poetry reading, Leonard claims 'Everything's fine' (p. 52). It is when Janetta emphasises herself and says '*I'm* fine' (my italic, p. 40; 60) as she returns to Leonard from Ian and later to Ian from Juliusz, that a decisive change occurs in both relationships.

Juliusz was Ian's 'property' and now he has returned to Poland and Derek has seized control of the street. Where Ian played cards, Derek plays golf and the horses; where previously their battleground had a front line, now Derek's patch extends 'Everywhere you look' (p. 50). 'Jesus Christ, Janetta, this fucking city! There's nowhere. There's nowhere. It's like I'm hemmed in' (p. 61). Ian, however, will not, like Derek, make the compromises of age and of profession. 'It's like, I tell you, I don't understand the species. I mean, by twenty-five, you can reproduce yourself. The job's done. Then what are we meant to do for the rest of our lives? Just sit around and get boring? *Just be boring?*' (p. 61). He would rather die and to do this he needs her to leave. At the moment Ian weakens, when he needs Janetta to give him the comfort of thinking that she belongs with the likes of Leonard, she refuses to tell him what he wants to hear (p. 62). 'That's when you grow up. When you know you have power. And you use it deliberately for the first time' (p. 56).

In fact, however, in one sense she cannot give such comfort. Earlier, the inexperienced Janetta had said 'I must go home'. Now, however, she realises 'I've left it. And I think it may be hard to go back' (p. 58). She has undergone the rite of passage from innocence to experience, from girl to woman, and can't go back to Weston-super-Mare. She can't go back to the poet, as Ian suggests and as she has done before, even if she wished, because he isn't there. And it is in this sense perhaps that 'Looking back, he had a triumph I'd say' (p. 52): he might leave and he might be unseen but – unlike Ian Tyson – Leonard is known to survive.

It is not only in this way that the choice between the two men (and two ideologies) in *Heading Home* appears to be between equals, but upon closer examination proves not to be. If the question to be answered in *Heading Home* is 'which way is the balance this time?' (p. 57) then the answer is, ultimately, in favour of the artist. 'I loved Leonard. I know I loved Leonard. I knew I had loved him all along' (p. 65). She gave herself to him in a way which she denied herself to Ian. Leonard, it is said, gave up on Janetta because 'You never get it back when it's perfect' (p. 57). The flash forwards to the beach at the start of the film is not to the *end* as it was in *Plenty* but to the middle, to a single moment of perfection which can be experienced but cannot be held on to and cannot be reclaimed. When Janetta goes to the beach again with Ian, no sex is seen and it is a form of compensation and farewell rather than freedom.

If Janetta cannot return to Leonard, to Ian or to the beach, she can, however, return to her job at the library for the simple reason that she never left it. When Ian challenged her to walk out, she did not; she only reclassified it to make life easier. And it is through her work that the epilogue, familiar from Hare's earlier works, brings the central character up to date, taking her through an unseen marriage and widowhood, when 'It was as if I were numb, my feelings long locked inside me. And they could not be released' (p. 64).

The beach where Janetta made love is built over, the bay has gone; her youth and the hope of the post-war period has passed.

At the end of *Licking Hitler* it was the author whose voice interjected to tell the audience that Archie MacLean never replied to Anna Seaton's declaration of love. At the end of *Heading Home*, Janetta speaks for herself. 'I knew what I had done. I had no illusions. All the time I had my reasons. But that is not always enough' (p. 65). In this way, she achieves the kind of self-knowledge that Anna lacked at the end of *Licking Hitler*. 'You're free', says Ian. 'Tell yourself stories. Why not? Most people do' (p. 36). Janetta, however, does not. Like William Cofax in *Dreams of Leaving* she has made excuses for her behaviour; unlike him she admits them.

'I understand to this day that people like Leonard do not speak their feelings. But I still to this day am not wholly sure why' (p. 65). David Hare understands to this day that the English middle classes do not speak their feelings. He knows it has something to do with the necessity of civilising impulses, he knows it has something to do with class and with nationality. Art for Hare is, then, not a dream or wish fulfilment as *Dreams of Leaving*, not a catharsis or escape in the psychological sense of *Wetherby* or in the tragic sense of *The Secret Rapture,* not just the historical explanation of the history plays but a process of learning, of coming to terms. Hare no longer seeks to teach a lesson, however, but to enable the audience to learn about their own beliefs. And, as Hare put it in *Plenty*, 'then perhaps you might really move on' (*Plenty*, p. 79).

At the end of *Heading Home*, Hare scripted to portray the same kind of housing estate with which he had ended *Wetherby* and which would have reinforced Janetta's own conclusion that there are no second chances in life. In the finished film, however, he showed instead the open spaces of the English countryside and the sea, which are outside her gaze. The film deliberately creates an ironic distance from its narrator, it forces a disjuncture between the memory of the individual and how it is portrayed by another. The result is a brief glimpse of freedom, the assertion of nature over civilisation, implying that things might not have turned out the way they did and might not always be as they are. Janetta might not be able to make choices differently except through art, but the audience can.

It is, then, not just the increased maturity of age or a violent shock which brings distance, as Jean Travers had found in *Wetherby* – that leads only to loneliness; neither is distance to be found in the recollection in tranquillity of the voice-over speakers of *Saigon* and *Dreams of Leaving*, for they result in self-delusion and bad faith. The historical distance which Hare had sought throughout his history plays – like the literally geographical distance of *Fanshen* and *A Map of the World* – either leave the relevance of the piece unguaranteed or verge on propaganda. Using women because they are less implicated in the crimes of the present has provided Hare with a lever on his own times, but one which, until the end of the 1980s, tended to lead to madness or despair. In *Heading Home*, he finds a new balance.

In *The Bay at Nice* and *Wrecked Eggs*, differing positions were presented within the same programme but in separate plays. In *Heading Home* Hare creates a classical balance within the film. In this way, art itself creates the space for choice and challenges the audience to 'learn something about where your own sympathies lie'.[2] In this sense, it is art itself which answers the question of how to find a distance on one's own life and times. The audience can choose, indeed must choose; it is not the writer's belief which is at issue but their own, and in this lies an invitation to responsibility which was evident also in *Strapless*. This realisation stands at the heart of David Hare's plays of the early 1990s.

> LEONARD: ... People claim poetry doesn't *do* anything. They say, what does it get done? (*He moves forward and starts to cross the room.*) Isn't it *weak* to sit around thinking and writing when there's been so much destruction in the world? (*He pauses a second*) I say no. It's strength. It's true strength. Truly. The hard thing is not to do, but to see. It's seeing that's hard. You get strength from looking things full in the face. Seeing everything, missing nothing, and not being frightened.   (p. 52)

14 Stepping into the future

Hare claimed that *Pravda* exhausted his impulse to write on large public themes and he concentrated for the following five years on plays in the private tone of voice of *The Bay at Nice* and *Wrecked Eggs*, of *The Secret Rapture*, of *Strapless* and of *Heading Home*. Having concluded his own reclamation of tragedy, however, Hare turned his attention outward again and embarked on his most ambitious theatrical project – to write a trilogy on the great British institutions of the Church in *Racing Demon* (1989), the Law in *Murmuring Judges* (1991) and the State in *The Absence of War* (1993).

Racing his own demon

Racing Demon begins in the interrogative. Unlike *Wetherby,* however, this does not mark the start of a thriller and a mystery to be solved. Kneeling in a darkened church, the Revd Lionel Epsy is beseeching, 'God. Where are you?' This is direct address of a very special kind – prayer. The question is not 'Does God exist?' but where he is to be found in the context of the inner city. He is presumed to be there and this is not a question of whether to believe, but how to believe and what, if any, is the value of belief. It is for this doubt that Lionel has an uncertain future in the church, but David Hare has a far from uncertain future in the theatre.

The middle-class rump in Lionel's flock, those who have been coming to the church for a very long time, are no longer sure that Lionel Epsy believes – as the Bishop of Southwark puts it – in the rules of the club. Amongst a squash-playing, gentrified Oxbridge-educated clergy, Lionel Epsy is singularly inept, unable even to play chess effectively let alone the card game of speed which is 'racing demon'. He is, they claim, undermining the show of the sacrament which is the only union within the Church of England, 'a disparate body held together by a common liturgy' (p. 4). In putting it in these terms, Hare invites comparison with his earlier work where the billiard table was the setting for propaganda, and victory on the golf course led to membership of the Masonic as well as the political club; Hare has returned to the English establishment, but in this case the game is one of advancement and regression within a guaranteed job-for-life.

Racing Demon followed swiftly on the report by the Church of England Synod on the role of the ministry in the inner city. It was, therefore, touching on a contemporary debate but makes no claims as fact. As his work focused increasingly on questions of belief, Hare had been looking for a way to write about the church for several years, and it was not documentary which provided his solution, but that unique private aspect of confession/prayer.

To reflect the diversity of the Church of England, Hare punctuates the play with short soliloquies given to the four members of the inner city parish team – Lionel, Harry, Streaky and Tony. For Lionel, the shared basic belief in the Father, Son and the Holy Ghost is much less important than the fact he and his colleagues in the parish are friends and that they are striving to help battered wives, such as Stella, without selling Jesus to them.

The Revd Donald 'Streaky' Bacon might be absolutely certain of God's goodness but he is the only member of the parish with no story, no independent life in *Racing Demon*. His faith brings him a simple joy; he loves being a priest and, although he attempts to help by talking with Kingston and Tony, Streaky makes it clear that ultimately he will not lay his job on the line for Lionel. He stands merely to ask why people find it so hard to believe. Harry in part provides the answer – that there is a gap between how people are and how they could be. He, however, has another question: how do you fight without hate? When the answer comes it is that you don't: you either get persecuted or you run away.

These are not left-wing extremists who want to change society; they just want something a bit fairer. Hare has claimed that during the eighties the failure of political parties of the centre and left to organise meant that the church at times seemed like the only voice of opposition. For its refusal to sanctify the Falklands War, for example, its passive dissent, Hare felt the Church of England was to be respected. As a man of conscience, rather than a man of faith, however, Lionel is no longer fulfilling his job description.

Tony, the young curate in Lionel's parish, is damned if he knows what is going on and will not accept the disjuncture between theological college and the reality of the inner city. He rejects the social work theory of the ministry, which finds Lionel giving communion to the housebound, sitting on the board of a housing charity and organising discussion groups for ex-prisoners and the mentally ill, in favour of an increasingly evangelical faith. He wants to fill the churches and preach the gospel; 'He wants to get hold of people and solve them' (p. 34). He is like the radical of any faith, be they the angry young playwrights of the late 1960s or the angry middle-aged Tories of the late 1980s, and he is prepared to give up his relationship with Frances because it distracts him from the cause. In Act One Scene Three, Tony leaves behind the sins of the flesh and breaks off his relationship with Frances in favour of total spiritual dedication.

Coming from the kind of influential lay families which invite bishops round for dinner Frances has, like Rebecca in *Pravda*, an insider's knowledge of the church without being part of it. Although there are jokes about the church's internal tussle over the ordination of women, when the play was written and first presented she could not be a parish priest. Nonetheless, it is Frances who warns Lionel of the seriousness of his position; it is Frances who reveals the dangerous thrust of Tony's faith and it is Frances, the familiar character of the woman who is right for no good reason, whom Hare, as ever, charges with opposition.

Out of the ninety-seven pages of the printed script, only twelve take place inside a church or cathedral. The church in David Hare's play is a place where people come to question; the cathedral is the place of professional assassination where Southwark and Lionel finally disagree; no services of worship are seen. The first act might build up to the Lord's Prayer at the end of Scene Eleven, as Kingston goes into Synod, but Hare does not break for the interval there, but with the unresolved difference between Tony and Lionel. Hare is not interested in the theological issues of Christianity but the value of faith in society and its effects on the individuals within the church. The play is, then, structured around three parallel pairs of scenes of almost equal length – between Tony and Frances, Frances and Lionel and Lionel and the Bishop.

The final image is of a plane taking Frances into the sky and into the sun in search of heaven or another country of values. We know from *The Secret Rapture* that Hare doesn't really believe that one.

> ISOBEL: Paradise. I took all my clothes off and walked along the beach. Lanzarotte was paradise. But unfortunately no use to me. (*She laughs.*) You can get away. You think you can. You think you'll fly out. Just leave. Damn the lot of you, and go. Then you think, here I am, stark naked, sky-blue sea, miles of sand – I've done it! I'm free! Then you think, yes, just remind me, what am I meant to do now? (*She stands, a mile away, in a world of her own.*)
> (*Secret Rapture*, pp. 70-1)

Expressing an agnostic belief in social justice, the absence of which invalidates the idea of the moral and good God, it is Frances who says, 'If there were justice then I'd believe in you. I like the idea of justice better than God. Because God is arbitrary' (p. 38). In private there's still some decency (p. 40); in the outside world it's quite a different matter. It is in front of the church's new advertising hoarding that Frances turns her back on Tony, and throughout the street is the place of conflict. It is on the rainy tarmac of South London that Tony hits Jabbai Marr for his abuse of Stella; it is on the darkened doorstep that Harry confronts the journalist who is trying to expose him and homosexuality in the church.

In *Racing Demon*, there is no justice, precious little love, and Frances's doubt is justified: Stella's face is burned, Lionel will lose his parish, Harry and Ewan must leave not because the church disapproves of homosexuality but because the Sunday newspapers smell a good exposé. The relationship between Ewan and Harry comprises only a few pages of printed text; it barely has time to develop. And the appearances of Jabbai and Stella amount to even less. If social justice is soon to be on the agenda, neither the church nor the theatre has anything to say to such people. The playwright who weighted *Heading Home* in favour of the artist against the man of action now demonstrates that the belief in action is an illusion and the biggest temptation of them all. Tony's attempt at intervention does not change Stella's future; she simply becomes a cleaner at the church with her soliloquy an expression of loneliness rather than of prayer.

As the strangle-hold of Thatcherism finally comes to an end, doubt, pain and suffering remain. 'We live here. On this earth. That's where we have to love one another' (p. 77). What unites all the characters, the price for all of them of their 'faith', is failed relationships. Lionel's and Heather's marriage is cold and empty, their children, like so many, it is said, are angry, absent and alcoholic. Jesus always gets in the way between Tony and Frances and Ewan goes back to Glasgow because Harry cannot overcome his sense of necessary discretion. Lionel and Heather have only a few minutes alone together; by the time Lionel realises he has neglected his wife, she will no longer let him touch her. The fact that Heather is the only main character in the parish not to have a soliloquy stands as a measure of her isolation from Lionel and from the church.

In *Racing Demon*, it is, of course, as a comment on the wide church itself that Hare does not resolve the co-existence of solo voices in the final scene into any single solution, but playwriting, as well as Christianity, is about avoiding the crunch (p. 44). Yet Hare, like Lionel, wants more than silence in answer to the question: 'Do we just suffer? Is that what you want? Fight and suffer to no purpose? Is everything loss?' (p. 97). That sense of loss, articulated in his lecture of 1978 as relating to an historical context, is given its spiritual/existential basis. And as Hare explored in *The Secret Rapture,* the answer to that loss does not lie in salvation from outside but from inside the theatre and inside ourselves.

If the audience is like a congregation literally sitting in the shape of the transept in the Cottesloe, they are not there to celebrate a communion with the Holy Trinity which is, by definition, unseen and unheard, but a different kind of communion. It is the audience to which Lionel addresses his prayer and they alone who can fill in an answer to his questions. Hare has concluded the debate which was foregrounded in *A Map of the World* and continued in *The Bay at Nice.* But art for Hare is not just for telling the truth as it was for novelist Victor Mehta, nor is it just an image of freedom which Matisse's painting represented, nor again the poetic expression of feeling. 'The job of theatre is not to trap the audience in a stale political rhetoric which will be dead in ten days, but to liberate them from it by showing human beings who are more than mere slogans, who are seen and felt to be so much more than the nonsense that sometimes comes out of our mouths.'[1]

What Hare is worshipping in theatre – as opposed to the novel or poetry – is not just the aesthetic form itself but the collective situation which is unique to theatre, because 'the theatre remains, in its ideal form, one of the few places where people of dissimilar views and backgrounds may come together and, in their shared response to what they see, find what they do and do not hold in common. I would define a good play as one which enables these acts of discovery. A good play, in the truest sense, ventilates democracy.'[2]

The means to that ventilation may be laughter, a democratic laughter which takes Hare back to *Pravda.* Hare is no theologian, just as he was no journalist; what made *Racing Demon* his most successful play since *Pravda* was the laughs. Although the working meeting of the parish team demonstrates the kind of sheet-of-A4 bureaucracy which now besets even the good amongst us, and the meeting with the Bishop of Kingston, similarly, conveys the insidious connection between church and state, the accommodation of the church to the 'harmless' eccentricities of the Masons, which Hare had exposed in *Brassneck,* they are both full of wry laughs about Streaky's name, about Macdonald's, about cycling. In *Racing Demon,* however, the emphasis is on the democracy and not on the laughter, and Hare resisted his first impulse to write a satire of the church on the grounds that the Synod was too easy a target. The elements of the play-that-might-have-been do, however, remain visible in the longest scene, set in the Savoy Hotel, where Streaky and Harry intercept Tony on his way to have a 'Last Supper' with the Bishop of Southwark.

Although people of dissimilar views and backgrounds may come together in the theatre, the fact of the matter is that they tend not to. Hare's theatre is precisely for those people who like the sacraments to be a good show and their theatre to have plenty of jokes.

In the early days, Hare claims, 'Both Howard Brenton and Trevor Griffiths seemed to glow with vocational confidence which I entirely lacked.'[3] Hare is now absolutely fulfilling his job description and glowing with vocational confidence, which was rewarded with four Best Play awards for 1990.

Murmuring judgements

The opening of *Murmuring Judges* has many similarities to that of *Racing Demon*. Gerard McKinnon is 'standing here, I'm thinking, oh God ...' and, with seven questions in the first thirty-two lines, the tone is similarly interrogative. With the emphasis of light falling upon him as it did on Lionel Epsy, he is being given a special status in whatever is to come. Gerard is not praying, however, but anticipating the judgement imminently to be passed upon him by the court of law which surrounds him on the stage. Almost twenty years after Hare declared that the theatre is the best court society has, he had, apparently, turned the stage of the National Theatre into one. This is not, however, to become the kind of courtroom drama of *Twelve Angry Men*.[4] The audience is not asked to hear the case and the play begins rather than ends with the judgement and sentence of five years in gaol. *Murmuring Judges* is, then, not so much a trial as an appeal, and one which is made not to the judge in the courtroom, nor even to God, but to the audience in the theatre.

Gerard might be the stuff of the legal profession, but as the courtroom dissolves and he is taken to gaol, the play moves on to another courtyard and another language-game. Where Gerard's stream-of-consciousness soliloquy is based upon phrase repetition and imagistic references, the language of the judiciary is well constructed, pompous and self-righteous. The Inn is a club where friends and colleagues meet and exchange a few sparring phrases over their recent appearances on *Desert Island Discs*, the ludicrous rationalisations of that programme made all the more perceptive by Hare's own experience as a 'castaway'. Even then their conversations, packed with words like 'remarkable' and 'extraordinary', are full of judgements.

It is here that leading advocate Sir Peter Edgecombe QC introduces his tenant, Irina Platt, saying 'She seemed to have all the assets we need in a forward-looking bar' and receives the acceptance from Judge Cudderford of 'Yes. I see those. Most clearly' (p. 5). '*She is black, in her mid-twenties, neat, well-presented, open-faced, with a quiet politeness which is hard to interpret*' (p. 3). She is a Commonwealth scholar from Antigua, and a woman who made the *faux pas* of turning up for court in a green dress, where the judge has a sense that 'I'd hear you more clearly if you attended court wearing black' (p. 6). It was Sir Peter who suggested she change (p. 6); in his chambers, however, it is Woody, his clerk, who initiates Irina into the underlying rules of their professional game: 'You see, the thing is, Irina, the point is, it's a team. There's a lot of latitude. But you play in a team. You want to start inside, not outside' (p. 11). It is for this reason that she is advised to accept Sir Peter's invitation to the opera, for 'the social is the professional' (p. 57) and 'It's good advice. Fight when it matters. Because surely to God, that moment will come' (p. 10). In this way, the audience is forewarned of the battle to come.

The play in its opening scene presents the murmuring of judges. In the very title, explained in the author's note, the play was positioned unequivocally as a crime against the judiciary. The evidence for the prosecution is, however, far from clear-cut. The initial introduction sparkles with humour and, from very early on, it is made clear that enquiry of the play is not to be into legal behaviour. Sir Peter is 'flash. But he's decent' (p. 13) and, as Gerard enters prison, he is advised by the warder that 'Society's put you in gaol' (p. 13). At the time of first staging, the Bar was under attack in the form of proposals for reform, but in *Murmuring Judges* it is shown to be putting up a spirited defence. The Home Secretary is entertained to dinner in Lincoln's Inn, the silver cutlery and the silver tongues are on full display. The infinitely precious richness of culture, the depth and breadth of vision of an Inn are extolled. 'What would you call it? The slow *silting* of tradition, this centuries-long building-up, this accumulation of strata, which makes the great rock on which we now do things' (p. 52). The Home Secretary's response is to concur that 'An independent judiciary is perhaps the most important bulwark against chaos this country has ... But we've nowhere to put all these bloody prisoners you keep sending us' (p. 53).

Prison, it is generally agreed, serves little positive purpose, but the question is not how to change the legal system but how to work within it. The focus of both the first and second acts and the longest scenes is not Gerard's initiation into prison survival nor the luxuries of the Inns; it is rather the daily grind of a local police station. In a second direct address to the audience, announcing her own kind of special status, Sandra, a young and upwardly mobile WPC, explains the 'stuff of policing'. There is the white stuff (p. 41) of drugs dealing, the fishy stuff (p. 49) of dubious evidence, and the stuff that makes you cautious (p. 65) – the daily abuse from the stream of petty thieves, drunks, traffic offences and domestic violence cases which spew out of the inner cities. It is a view of policing rarely seen inside the English theatre, a place where banter, racism and sarcasm get you through the day and the main professional skill is cutting down the bureaucracy which surrounds the administration of justice. It is a world where only 3 per cent of criminals get caught, so that achieving a result is a cause for celebration. Celebrating Gerard's conviction alongside two other unseen but certain villains is Barry, an experienced detective, whose own relationship and argument with Sandra over McKinnon parallels that between Sir Peter and Irina.

Sandra's compassion for an ordinary lad is brushed aside by her hard-bitten colleague: 'Just lock them up, Sandra, and get on with your job. We're not playing God' (p. 30). When Gerard made his appeal to God in the first lines, it was not the police but a judge who had his life in his hands.

> BARRY: ... The judge thought, I'm being nice, I'm being decent, I'm giving him less than the others. In *spite* of the fact that he's Irish.
> SANDRA: He isn't. He isn't Irish.　　(p. 29)

Decency, then, is constrained; a delusion which depends on where you stand. Barry has the same view of professional life as the Bar, 'Didn't they tell you? It's a team game' (p. 30) and the hardest rule is sticking up for your side. No one wants to know about the fact that Barry already knew the other villains and that he lied about it. 'It's clearer that way. It's simpler. I like a clear pond. Not muddy' (p. 31). But that is not the point for Sandra. That bit's easy; the unanswered question is 'Why did they pretend not to know you?' (p. 31). Something about Barry's defensiveness over the case and the excess of the five years sentence lead Sandra to investigate the cause of McKinnon's suffering for being, if not entirely innocent, then naive and afraid, for being a victim.

As Sandra conducts her own investigation, Irina visits Gerard to discuss the possibility of an appeal against the length of the sentence. She cannot help him in his enquiries about improving conditions inside the gaol.

> IRINA: I'm just a lawyer. (*She hesitates a moment, then smiles.*)
>   We say goodbye to you when you go through the court's
>   doors. (*He nods.*)
> GERARD: Is that a good thing?
> IRINA: It's the system. We're all in different compartments. The
>   judges used to visit the prisons in the old days. But now
>   they say it affects their independence. If they knew what the
>   prisoner was in for, it might affect their judgement.
> GERARD: Yes. (*He nods, for the first time beginning to loosen
>   up.*) Too right it would.   (p. 37)

In this way Irina is compared with the Something-Must-Be-Done brigade who visit prisons and, alarmed by the conditions they find, set off in a flurry of good intentions which lead to no action but, from this point, there is an easy intimacy between them. It leads as much to an explanation of why it is that she is interested in this case as the reasons for Gerard's involvement in the crime.

> IRINA:... People always tells me I'm unrealistic. Not just
>   about love. In everything. They say all or nothing's no
>   way to live.
>   (GERARD *has turned and is looking at her thoughtfully.*)
>   But so many people seem to settle for so little.
> GERARD: Maybe. Maybe most people don't have a choice.
>   (p. 39)

Most people don't have a choice; some people do. Judges might not enter the prisons, but Irina has. Similarly, the theatre can look at the operation of the court, the Inns, the chambers, the police and the prison. And having seen them set out next to each other, the judgement of the audience just might be affected. Through Irina's visits, the audience can witness Gerard's decline, his attitude hardening against his incarceration in the face of the loss of his family. Through these visits, Hare can force an appeal to the emotions of the audience as much as to the arguments in the court of law.

In Sir Peter's professional judgement, the case is unexceptional. Gerard has, as he admits, lied (p. 38); he had pleaded not guilty. He was beaten up in prison but there were no witnesses. To accuse the police of planting evidence or doing a deal would not, he believes, help the case. For these reasons, Sir Peter will only run with the 'lame-dog' appeal.

> SIR PETER: If we go for a lesser sentence, we've got a good chance.
> (*He looks to her for a response.*)
> IRINA: It's just… I can't explain. I don't want to do that.
> SIR PETER: No? (*He waits a moment.*) What's your reason?
> IRINA: I know this is legally meaningless. I do understand that. (*She looks uneasily between them.*) I don't want to do it because it isn't right.
> (*At once* SIR PETER *explodes.*)
> SIR PETER: Right? What's right got to do with it? (p. 81)

The system cannot admit of right or wrong, but she can. 'Your profession after all is the judgement of people' (p. 84) and not the judgement of the system you serve. The government's concern is how many prisoners have to fit into how many prisons. The concern of the upper echelons of the police is the crime figures. As exposed in the final direct address, 'It's public relations. We know that. So does everyone. Except for the public, of course' (p. 56). His point in general may be well made; to suggest that the National Theatre audience, comprising PR men, ad men and journalists alongside the lawyers and the literati, do not know this would appear naive in the extreme. In giving Jimmy the precious status of direct address, Hare is over-compensating for the fact that 'When you're name is Abdul, and they call you Jimmy, it does give you a certain perspective on things' (p. 63).

Judging might bring you in touch with ordinary people – 'Ordinary, common-as-muck individuals, some of them quite ghastly' (p. 52) – but Sir Peter has withdrawn from the human stuff of the real criminal world, preferring instead civil cases, and he has withdrawn from the ethical into the merely professional. To undermine his certainty in this convenient professional judgement, Irina posits the idea that she might have been lying when she said she enjoyed the opera; the price of the tickets being no guarantee of her veracity. 'These judgements, these "judgements" you make all the time, these judgements which seem to be graven in stone, they have only the status of prejudice' (p. 85), a prejudice based on the innately human qualities of rivalry, lust and greed. All the rest is simply the anaesthesia of appearances, a professional alibi rather than a genuine defence against chaos and insanity. In articulating this, Irina breaks the rules of the personal as well as the professional game – she has shattered the glass wall dividing the legal profession from the real world and entered the gaol; she has broken down the relationship between them, and by becoming emotionally involved she has also justified their arguments for the very professional distance she despises.

The psychological model which Hare had used in the plays of the eighties is still visible here. Emotion is set against intellect, chaos against civilisation. Classes are, however, significantly not set against each other and no political or historical models are invoked. As ever, the male-dominated establishment is infiltrated by a woman, or rather in this case two slightly different women, whose only meeting takes place in the outdoors of Crystal Palace; but it is not a meeting of minds. Sandra and Irina are not the familiar and unhinged voices of conscience from the seventies; they are deliberately intervening at different points, and with different reasons.

Irina is not only a woman, but black, giving her a double distance from the elitism of her profession. She is bright, she is a scholar and it therefore strains credibility that she should, by this stage of her career, lack professional distance by becoming personally involved in Gerard's case. Sandra is, in contrast, a copper's daughter. What they share is the commitment to the principle of right and wrong. For her it 'isn't right, Barry' (p. 71) that McKinnon and the others should go down the 'curly way', even if the faking of evidence in fact resulted in the stopping of another crime. 'What you've got is an unsafe prosecution. It's crazy' (p. 71).

What the women achieve is less clear. 'Parade your conscience', challenges Barry. 'If that's who you are. But all you'll do is make yourself despised by a lot of decent people. Me, I stopped going to the movies' (p. 72). Irina's intervention leads to Gerard's assault and subsequent solitary confinement in prison. 'Walk in. Upset them. Leave them. That's lawyers' (p. 45). This, in turn, leads to his becoming interested – as he never had before – in Irish history. The appeal which Irina struggles to obtain results in a six-month reduction of sentence, not enough to save him from absorption in the university of crime. Being right is no guarantee of success just as being wrong does not necessarily lead to punishment.

> IRINA:... You broke the rules. You did. The police have got
> to do better than that.
> (BARRY *smiles*.)
> BARRY: You may be right. It's not important. It doesn't
> matter, you see. Call me stubborn, or what. But I tell
> you what, I tell you. I don't take lectures on ethics from
> lawyers.
> (*He looks up at her, closer now.*)
> Put your hand on your heart, could you say I was
> wrong? (p. 85)

When Irina visits Gerard in prison for one last time, their exchange lacks the intimacy of their earlier meetings. Gerard has accepted the role offered to him.

> IRINA: Do you remember? I said I'd be your friend. And I
> will. I'll keep coming. It's something I want. Not to say,
> 'Oh, we're all in separate compartments ...'
> GERARD: But we are, aren't we.
> (*He just looks at her.*) (pp. 97–8)

In *Racing Demon*, Lionel was replaced and Harry driven into exile but, where Frances set sail for a foreign land as Hare himself might once have done, Irina remains on the legal team. Institutions are required to achieve effective change; the question is which ones? By moving to radical chambers, Irina becomes a striker and not a defender. As Irina claims that the radical bar is 'exactly the kind of pressure we need to try and make sure the public understand that the legal profession at large is infinitely more sensitive and responsive than perhaps some of the prominent dinosaurs make us appear ...' (pp. 101-2), her words are lost in a cacophony of overlapping voices.

The very difficulty of hearing the people talking in their different compartments on the stage is not, as it was in *Fanshen*, a measure of the difficulty of understanding, but of the difficulty of making a judgement between the conflicting positions, and of persuading others. What Hare does in *Murmuring Judges* even more explicitly than in *Racing Demon* is to show the differing and overlapping sides of an issue. The distance from the positions is created by the very juxtaposition between them. The positions have equal weight and it is 'almost impossible to say where right and wrong reside because to me that's what most of life is like'.[5]

It was also a way of pacifying people, preventing the kind of negative reactions which other plays and notably *Plenty* had generated. 'This "even-handedness" you commend was partly a question of refined technique', confessed Hare. 'I did have to look at the technique of my playwriting, because I was *not* seeking to judge people. I was trying to dramatise dilemmas which I believed to be common. Unfortunately, I gave the contrary impression.'[6] In his effort to be even-handed, however, and his determination to focus on the positions rather than the people, there is a real danger of turning characters into ciphers. The result − in stark contrast to, say, *The Secret Rapture* − is that *Murmuring Judges* fails to engage the audience at anything beyond a level of mild interest. Because of this, Hare might be accused of murmuring judgements where they should be shouted loudly, but he might well reply that 'It is my nature to sit in judgement. To be above the battle. To allow all points of view' (p. 5).

In the final moments of the play, the sound of overlapping

voices does give way to one single voice. There is no *Guardian*-reading section of the police force to which Sandra can transfer, but she has the final line: 'I wonder. Could I have a word?' (p. 102). Hare has serious doubts over the audibility of the challenge and the result of her appeal to the Super is not seen. The question itself, however, is heard and, as the final direct address, is made to the audience itself.

'That stuff is so easy. Me and my conscience. That's the easy route' (p. 69). The difficult thing is to find a route to something shared with others. It is in this search that the attraction of the great social institutions lies, for they create and define the environment for the whole of English society. The church − its congregations diminishing and split apart by the ordination of women − is, however, still an embodiment of the struggle for faith and morality in action. If the church is divided and declining in influence, the reputation of the law has been rocked by a series of highly publicised unsafe prosecutions. The subject of the play is, however, not the law; there is no suggestion that the law was administered incorrectly just as there is taken to be no question in *Racing Demon* that there is a God. These facts are constitutive of the game and form of life being played. The question is not what basis there is for our beliefs and our society, for that question cannot even be asked. The undeniable ethical issues of the nineties and the great unanswered question of the trilogy is 'So how do you choose when it's time to say no?' (p. 91).

The Absence of War

The opening of *The Absence of War* sees politicians of all parties gathering around the Cenotaph to lead the annual tribute to Britain's war dead. In this image lies the complex framework of historical inheritance and institutional respectability which has stood behind Hare's work since *Brassneck* in 1973. In *The Absence of War* he concludes that journey to explain the loss of faith in the possibility of change since 1945, while drawing the story of an electoral defeat of the Labour Party in terms of the tragic personality of its leader.

In time of war people do what needs to be done; in its absence there is only loss of purpose and keeping busy. The pressure on politicians' time and the relentless flow of meetings are succinctly expressed in the plethora of overlapping questions and sentences without endings which comprise Scene Two. In anticipation of a forthcoming election, the private office of the Labour leader is hiring a new advertising agent and preparing the campaign strategy. As the Labour campaign manager, Andrew Buchan, introduces Lindsay Fontaine to the workings of political life, George Jones, the leader of the Labour Party, is not there; indeed his office does not know where he is.

> ANDREW: Where were you?
> GEORGE: I was in the park. I went for a walk in the park.
> ANDREW: How was it?
> GEORGE: Fine. It was like spring. I looked around. People
> were walking. And kissing. And talking. I thought, you
> lucky people ... (*He pauses a second.*) You're free and I'm
> not.   (p. 9)

The fact that George Jones is trapped is established in his first remarks. As leader, he has brought the party to the point where victory might again be possible. He has streamlined and image-built and is aware of his burden:

> GEORGE: ... Like Pilgrim, this is the course I am on. (*He is
> suddenly firm.*) You can never let go. You can never lose
> sight of the problem that when this Party fell into my
> hands, it was torn, disfigured, unelectable. With a
> matchless capacity for meaningless squabbles and fights.
> So changing that culture, changing that disastrous habit
> of anarchy, controlling the Party, getting it to speak with
> one voice, this has been my historical legacy. Meaning:
> something I had to do. (*He nods and looks at her.*) I had to
> make this Party respectable.   (pp. 47–8)

As a result, the front bench uses the words 'fiscal' and 'responsibility' a lot and when there's a run on the pound, 'George goes pinstripe at least' (p. 23). Senior figures keep in touch by mobile phone and script their speeches to ensure that they all speak with one voice. It is 'Games theory! If you don't take risks, then you don't make mistakes' (p. 31). Dissent within the church and within the law could be seen, but the Labour Party cannot afford to appear split. Where in *Paris By Night* the different aspects of the Conservative Party (constituency worker, MP, MEP, Think Tank) were evident, in *The Absence of War* constituency parties and the Labour voters are noticeable by their absence; even senior members of the party are shown only in relation to the staff of the leader's private office, existing around him and in anticipation of his arrival.

In the minds of the private office is the clear-eyed appreciation that Labour could not win, can never win, on the Tory high-ground of the economy, especially by telling the truth about it. That would be portrayed as unpatriotic. The strategy therefore is to play to the party's strengths and minimise its weaknesses by invoking the principle of fairness in society embodied in education and the health service.

> OLIVER: Elections, you see, people think they're about
> arguments ...
> (ANDREW *shakes his head at the absurdity of the idea.*)
> They think when politicians speak it's an act of sense.
> But it's not. It's an act of strategy. It's taking up a
> position. It isn't like debate. We're not actually debating.
> ANDREW: Far from it.
> OLIVER: The only true analogy is with waging war.
> (*He cracks open another beer, excited, as they go into a self-
> supporting ritual, repeating the rules of the game.*) (p. 46)

And at the end of the twentieth century that party-political war is waged through the media. At the centre of *The Absence of War* is not the great debate which had fuelled *A Map of the World*, but a televised interview.

As Jones is grilled by Linus Frank the audience simultaneously sees the reactions of Jones' aides, reminding us of the relativity of (re)presentation while demonstrating the scale of the blunder he makes. George Jones walks into the trap, triggered by a leak, that Linus Frank has prepared; he breaks the first rule and gives way to anger. As the TV programme title declares, the 'Nation Decides' that Jones is lying, for we have already heard that there were plans to abolish mortgage tax relief and that Jones himself had them removed from the manifesto. Jones did not listen to the briefing his political adviser, Oliver Dix, tried to give him and in the scuffle between them is an image of the Labour Party tearing itself apart in its frustration.

'Like all Labour Leaders, I don't quake before the enemy', declares Jones. 'It's friendly fire that destroys you. We all go down to the shots from behind' (p. 84). And these shots were fired by Malcolm Pryce, the Shadow Chancellor, the clever Oxbridge leader-in-waiting. He exhibits the classic number two positioning tactic, a calculated distance from every decision so that he is not implicated in any mistake the leader makes. He had expressed his scepticism about Lindsay Fontaine's modern campaigning techniques as early as Scene Two and does not join the campaign team at George's flat on the night the election is called. Yet it is to Malcolm that Jones must turn in his hour of need, interrupting the campaigning to confront him with his inability to talk up the leadership. Just as Jones gradually lost the initiative of the TV interview to Linus Frank, so it is Malcolm who 'decisively winds up the meeting':

> MALCOLM: All right, thank you, George. I'll do what you
>   ask of me. I'll go round the country and tell everyone
>   that you're a very fine man. If that's what you want, then
>   that's what I'll do for you.
>   (GEORGE *looks at him, shaken.*)
> GEORGE: It's not for me. It's what has to be done.
>   (MALCOLM *nods slightly. Then he stops and looks hard at*
>   GEORGE.)
> MALCOLM: It isn't the Party. It's not that the Party don't
>   believe in you, you know. (*He moves across and puts his*
>   *hand on* GEORGE's *arm.*) I say this in love. They smell
>   that you don't believe in yourself.   (p. 86)

To achieve respectability, George Jones has suppressed the very quality which had made him leader in the first place – his elo-quence in expressing a passionate belief in hope. In the attempt to claw back lost ground in the face of worsening opinion polls, Jones takes a risk: he is tempted by Lindsay Fontaine's analysis to abandon the disciplined campaign which Oliver and Andrew have masterminded and to return to his old campaigning style. Addressing the theatre audience directly as if it were at the rally in Manchester, he seeks to tap into the old well only to find that it has dried up. The longest speech in the play slips away into repetition and hesitation as George returns to the script in his pocket. It is, however, the failure and not the script that has been heard. The new style is not working and the old has died. As Yeats – a poet quoted by Hare in earlier work – wrote in 'The Second Coming', it is in this position that 'The best lack all conviction, while the worst / Are full of passionate intensity'.

When George Jones loses the election the audience does not see him concede. It sees instead a waitress in a Birmingham hotel tell him that 'You're not anyone special' (p. 107); it sees a mirror-image of the play's opening; with Malcolm Pryce standing as Leader of the Opposition at the Cenotaph ceremony and George Jones commenting on it as Andrew Buchan had done at the open-ing. Where *Brassneck* ended with a toast to the last days of capital-ism, the audience of *The Absence of War* is left with a series of questions: 'Is this history? Is everything history? Could we have done more? Was it possible? And how shall we know?' (p. 110). And in these questions, the play falls into a trap of its own making.

In researching *The Absence of War*, Hare secured privileged access to the campaign meetings of the Labour Party before the 1992 election. 'Obviously Kinnock's dilemma is what moved me and which provides the emotional spring for the play',[7] he con-firms, and it is in the audience recognition of the parallel that the great strength of unfalsifiable action lies. Just as Roderick Bagley's career traced that of John Poulson, and Lambert Le Roux 'was' Rupert Murdoch as he took over *The Times* so, despite the many deliberate differences, Jones 'is' Kinnock for as long as audiences draw the parallel. The difference between the plays is not in the nature of the relationship between the character and his real-life counterpart, for none of Hare's plays are documentary, but the nature of that character: 'To me, now, at this moment, it's all about character' (p. 16).

The point about George Jones, as Bryden, the campaign chairman, makes clear, is that 'He's decent. He has total integrity. Underneath his manner, he works like no man I've seen. His authority stems from his personal character' (p. 33). The key value words from *The Secret Rapture* have reappeared and it is made explicit of Jones early on that 'He's got a fatal weakness. You know that. He likes to take one step back from things' (p. 20). When the play finally asks 'Is this history?' (p. 110), the answer, for Hare, is 'no': 'To me, George Jones makes a tragic pact, and the pact is with respectability ... So, for me, the play is a tragedy; a classical tragedy.'[8]

The deliberate balance of fact and fiction was evident even in the staging of the whole trilogy at the National Theatre. Directed by Richard Eyre, as *Brassneck* had been twenty years before, each scene was played within a detailed but minimal setting. These settings 'floated' in the foreground while behind were huge projections of photographs – of Whitehall, of a church window, of the Inns of Court. The photographs secured the necessary fast changes between time and place and continuity across the three plays. Being of places and things rather than recognisable people they did not, as they had in *Brassneck*, make any truth-claims for the plays.

If Hare was given privileged access to the campaign meetings of the Labour Party, he had gained similarly privileged access to Clapham police station in researching *Murmuring Judges* and to the Synod in writing *Racing Demon*. Relatively few people in the audience would have been familiar with the personalities involved in these professions and there was little speculation about the match between Hare's characters and his possible sources. As *The Absence of War* opened, however, Hare's collection of background interviews, *Asking Around*, was published. It is the book, rather than the play, which lays claim to being historical record, but the timing of its publication reinforced the public tendency to read *The Absence of War* as a documentary re-creation of the 1992 election. As Hare concedes, 'There could be no worse way of convincing people something is not a documentary than to simultaneously publish a documentary book.'[9] There could be no worse way than to conclude with the question 'Is this history?'

If, for Hare, the Kinnock–Jones argument is a 'journalistic confusion,'[10] it is one which he failed to dispel. Where members of the clergy wrote David Hare ten-page letters about *Racing Demon* and a party of twenty-four chief constables attended *Murmuring Judges* and invited Hare to discuss it with them afterwards, the Labour Party was largely silent except on matters of factual accuracy. The party took considerable exception to the implication that John Smith, then Shadow Chancellor, in any way 'betrayed' Neil Kinnock, and a flurry of discontent followed Hare's invitation to be guest speaker at the Fabian dinner in November 1993, when he felt moved to defend himself by claiming 'a strange equation between what the play itself was saying, and how Labour politicians were reacting to it'.[11] The fact that the television discussion of the play by 'liberal' commentators could focus so strongly on this issue demonstrates how serious the problem was.

'As far as I'm concerned,' said Hare, 'the play will fail if people see it as just being about the Labour Party.' In his own terms, then, the play must have failed but, if it failed, it was because Hare stabbed it in the back. As Michael Billington perceived, if George Jones was to be seen as a Faustian figure being untrue to himself, 'you would have had to have some evidence of the passion that was being suppressed',[12] yet the Manchester speech demonstrates precisely that the passion or its expression has been lost. If Lindsay Fontaine came 'like temptation with the impossible message' (p. 94) she nonetheless remained 'who people are' (p. 17): it was not the devil but the people challenging the Labour strategy to keep Jones in a box. Put another way, the problem of the play is that if George's political instinct is brilliant, then 'why are you still failing to get him across?' (p. 31).

It was the tragedy of the first production that John Thaw also became a victim of the very phenomenon he was there to present, for he did not find a way to portray the sparkle and the presence claimed for George Jones, but Hare's evident determination to make Jones into a tragic figure is insufficient to achieve it for him. In contrast to *Racing Demon* and *Murmuring Judges,* direct address grants no special status to George Jones, since minor characters use it to move the action fowards. The audience may *pity* Jones as he heads for an election they know he will lose, but, despite Oliver

Dix's expressed foreboding, it does not *fear* for him as it does for Isobel Glass in *The Secret Rapture*. There may be fear *of* market research and of the Treasury's real figures but not *for* George Jones.

'The fact is, he was free. That was the irony' (p. 101): as the electorate decides his fate, George Jones walked in the park and, at the moment of his defeat, his humour returns. As Linus Frank's commentary at the cenotaph reminds us, however, the price of freedom is death, yet George Jones lives. Like the play itself, Jones is self-knowing from the start; he does not gain the kind of self-knowledge which provided salvation in *The Secret Rapture* and *Heading Home*, but starts with it. The very references to Jones' love of theatre (p. 4) and to tragedy release the audience from the experience of it. 'I've done it consciously. Knowing just what I was doing. And knowing the price as well. (*His gaze is steady.*) It's been my decision. I'll live with it' (p. 105).

The Absence of War is not just a play about the loss of an election; it strives to present universal issues of leadership. If the situation of opposition is a general one, the explanations offered for its failure are historically specific. The Labour Party has lost its roots without sending out new shoots. For the Tories, with their shared basic belief in money, things are incomparably easier than for Labour whose belief in justice causes more argument (p. 18). Where Tories go to the right schools, Labour has no organisations. 'It did have once. They were called unions. But the communities that produced them have gone. The industries have gone. So now justice recruits from the great deracinated masses. The people from nowhere. Who have nothing in common. Except what they say they believe in. And that doesn't always end up being enough' (p. 18).

George Jones says he believes in the party and, like the party, he cares for what is right rather than for power. He says he believes in socialism as 'the way in which we go forward now to make this country one in which everyone is helped' (p. 95), but no one can define it further. As Oliver Dix explains, 'It's a big disadvantage. If you're a progressive. We're meant to believe in the wisdom of the people. "The people! The people!" we say. But the truth is, the people do stupid things. Like wear your bloody T-shirt and then vote against you' (p. 15).

The problem is not that 'you're not allowed to say *anything*' (p. 98). 'We can't speak of history, you can't say Britain happens to be trapped in historical decline. But it's true. You'd only have to say it to blow the bloody roof off!' (p. 98). Oliver Dix says it and nothing is changed; David Hare says it and the roof of the National Theatre remains resolutely intact. The problem is not that politicians are corrupt. Where *Brassneck* presented politicians of both parties corruptly involved in property deals and *Paris By Night* had a Tory woman committing murder, *The Absence of War* presents only hard-working and committed people.

The problem is that 'You once had the words. Now you don't' (p. 97), you once had a source of belief and now you don't. 'A politician can only deal with his inheritance' (p. 48) and, as the revolutionary words of Vera's generation grow old and ridiculous, the party has no language of its own. 'Fairness' has replaced 'equality' and the very obsession with the enemy leaves nothing distinctive. As they stand at the cenotaph with their backs to the audience, the politicians from the three political parties are 'indistinguishable' (p. 1). All that's left is playing the game (p. 98), but 'We're not bloody Tories. And so it's a game at which we can't win' (p. 92).

In the absence of war, there is no cause to ennoble our sentiments and unite the people. As Hare had put it in *Plenty*, when 'There is little to believe in. Behaviour is all' (*Plenty*, p. 72). In this sense, therefore, David Hare remains nostalgic for the past. He would agree with George Jones when he confesses 'I'm afraid there's a sense in which I even quite like a war' (p. 40), because people come back radicalised.

In *Murmuring Judges* and *Racing Demon* Hare created the theatre of juxtaposition, balancing positions without the luxury of an historical perspective and deliberately refusing to offer a resolution. In *The Absence of War* Hare balances these different explanations of Labour's dilemma. The explanations are all given by members of the party themselves. As Oliver Dix says, 'We're not complete idiots. We've read this sort of stuff. We do it ourselves' (p. 30). Perhaps the Labour Party was silent about the play not out of fear of the issues, but boredom with the issues they had hoped to leave behind. Hare too has explored all of these possible reasons for the failure of opposition previously in the history plays of the seventies.

In that sense the answer to the question 'Is this history?' in *The Absence of War* is 'yes'. The problem is not the absence of war but its eternal, recurring presence.

> GEORGE: We live in a country which is spavined with
> ancestor-worship. This country will never, *can* never
> prosper until it escapes from its past. (*He turns and
> addresses them all.*) Why can't I say that? You tell me.
> What is this? Is this my fault? Or is it the public's? (*He
> turns back away from them.*) Why can't I speak of what I
> believe?   (p. 99)

What is clear throughout the trilogy is that the questions of belief are not ones for the lawyers and clerics and politicians alone to address. When Lionel Epsy prays at the opening of *Racing Demon*, his prayer is heard by the audience to the play. It is not the author who is God, who ultimately guarantees the existence of the fictional characters, it is the audience. Similarly, when Gerard McKinnon says 'God it's coming', he is not heard by the court around him but by the audience in the theatre. George Jones' parliamentary question 'How long?' is addressed to the audience, an audience which comprises the very 'professionals' who, like Lindsay Fontaine, have replaced the old Labour communities and who are 'a bit lost. Not knowing what they think. Used to affluence. And things not being difficult' (p. 17). They are there to find out what they think, to make a choice.

When Neil Kinnock allowed Hare into the campaign meetings, he was expecting a friend of the Left to generate a play on the transition from opposition to government. In Labour eyes the fact that Hare has written a play at all might be seen as betrayal. In fact Hare's own allegiance is clear and his overall project to make the audience responsible is compromised. Just as the existence of God and the necessity of the law are not questioned within *Racing Demon* and *Murmuring Judges*, so the value of the party is not questioned within *The Absence of War*. This time, however, the institution is assigned a value:

> MALCOLM: But some of us – that includes me – believe if

> your policy is right ... if it corresponds to people's own
> experience ... if it will fulfil a real need in people's lives –
> as I believe ours will, Andrew ...
> ANDREW: No question. No one's questioning that.
> MALCOLM: Good. (p. 7)

The word 'good' is cumulatively asserted throughout the play. Hare, like George Jones, believes that the Labour Party remains 'the only practical instrument that exists in this country for changing people's lives for the good' (p. 105).

If George Jones is trapped, then so too is the rest of the party which is also 'decent' (p. 86). Malcolm Pryce's leadership does not constitute a new beginning: at the end he is just a different player in the role of a recurring ritual at which the audience too is still sitting in silence paying tribute to the dead. The cenotaph service traps the action of the play in an eternal cycle which can never be escaped. In this sense it may be that 'The play is a tragedy and tragedy is out of fashion',[13] but tragedy itself is part of the stasis. George Jones is defeated not only because *he* is insufficiently ruthless but because he can be written up as a tragic personality even by his adversary.

> OLIVER: It's the bloody theatre. He likes tragedy too much.
> I don't. To me, tragedy's just a posh word for losing. (*He
> nods slightly.*) This movement's had too much tragedy.
> (p. 20)

If the invocation of the movement of history, the evidence of change shown in the passing of time had been a new beginning in *Brassneck* in 1973, *The Absence of War* reflects an end. David Hare has done it consciously, knowing the price he would pay for the mingling of past and present, fact and fiction, and attempting the historical explanation of a contemporary phenomenon within the timeless sweep of tragedy. He must live with the consequences.

Conclusion: a statement of arrival

As the National Theatre's first-ever *King Lear* and Hare's first direction of a Shakespearian text, the production of December 1986 witnessed an extraordinary air of anticipation in the press and a television documentary. If Peter Brook's production of *King Lear* in 1962 'made a whole lot of people my age – me among them – decide they wanted to work in the theatre'[1], then Hare's production, almost twenty-five years later, was a statement of arrival. It was also a culmination of his concerns of the eighties. Further, however, 'People always temperamentally prefer one play and I'm a Lear-ist', Hare announced in the programme to his production of the play. In analysis of Hare's production, it is not surprising that one finds the progress of Hare's own writing to date made clear. The production is, therefore, used to structure this conclusion as a way to summarise the approach of each of Hare's works.

The stage for David Hare's production of *King Lear* was dominated by three huge white motorised canvases billowing above it. Into this bleak and unremitting whiteness (designed by Hayden Griffin) – as sanitised as the gallery in *The Bay at Nice* – stepped a court differentiated from the common people by a grey militaristic uniform and from one another by coloured sashes of rank. Hare did not intend to create the historically accurate, and the ancient in his ancient Britain was evident only in the final battle scene, where dismembered corpses lay around medieval battle trucks of spikes and shields.

David Hare might have stepped into the past with his production of *Brassneck* in 1973, leaving behind the extremist ends of Portable Theatre in favour of the aesthetic lessons he had learned at the Royal Court, but he did not step into a documentary theatre.

Inspired by Angus Calder's reinterpretation of the Second World War, Hare examined the recent past to explain the causes of his and his generation's disillusionment with the possibility of change, which followed the failure of the sixties revolution. The use of documentary evidence of the Poulson affair in the structuring of *Brassneck* did not amount to the adoption of documentary theatre. Unlike Piscator, Hare was not trying to turn the stage into a political meeting; he was, rather, searching for a perspective from which a judgement on contemporary life could be made in the court of theatre.

Just as, for Peter Brook, the only way to make *King Lear* into a world the audience believed in 'was to look for one's reality not in terms of history, but in terms of geographical conditions',[2] so, in *Fanshen* (1975) Hare had found a geographical distance. The fact that the play – adapted with Joint Stock from William Hinton's documentary history – appeared to be the model of a successful revolution, which put the people on the stage, and the apparent adoption of Brechtian techniques of alienation and historicisation, led to the incorrect assimilation of the work in the tradition of epic theatre. In fact, *Fanshen* was a classical play about revolution which asked classical questions about the relation between leaders and the led, and – in contrast to Marxist expectations – was unable to give an answer to the question of whether we should be any happier if the criteria by which we lived were collective.

What geography meant for Peter Brook was not distance: 'It's about the warmth of interiors and the desperate, barren cold of being out of doors.'[3] Hare, however, rejected the dialectic of indoors/outdoors within the play (although he has used it in many of his own). His interiors were subject to the same unremitting sky and the same cruel desolation, the same remoteness as his outdoors with the white screens merely lifted from the corner(s) to create different locations and standing at their height for the storm scene.

If Hare's *Lear* had a time or a place at all, it was given in the padded shoulders and tight waists of the costumes as a landscape of European post-Nazi austerity chic. When Lear divided his kingdom between his daughters, he leant over an unmistakably modern jigsaw map of Britain and, when Cordelia appeared with liberating troops at the end, she was a French Resistance saviour reminiscent of Susan Traherne in *Plenty*. For Hare it is the Second World War which remains the touchstone of the modern.

In *Licking Hitler* (1978) that war had two fronts – the world war and the class war – but Hare's intention was not to effect a 'strategic penetration' of a socialist message into a hegemonic form of television, nor to reach a mass audience, but the better to explore the relation between despair and propaganda by using the greatest propaganda medium of them all. In the authorial voice-over, Hare sought to distance his own work from the corruption of the truth which had resulted from the Allied victory and the media explosion, but it was in the use of a female central character that he sought to gain a perspective on a history in which he perceived women to be less implicated.

The process was continued through the people's peace in *Plenty* (1978), where it became clear that, far from being feminist, Hare's use of women concealed at this time an ambivalence towards them. In his shifting of the ground from the war through to the Suez crisis, it also became clear that his disillusionment disguised a nostalgia for the Edwardian certainties of empire. In *King Lear*, female Innocence is not merely (like Susan in *Plenty* or Caroline in *Dreams of Leaving*) sent mad, it is mercilessly killed in a manifest apocalypse for the splitting of the kingdom.

In *King Lear*, 'There are so many different themes in the play you may choose to emphasise'[4] and yet Hare went on to list 'Family, religion, politics, madness, sex'. In earlier days, Hare's list might have read politics, madness, sex, family, religion. Instead, as Lear blocks Cordelia out of his life with a raised hand, so he chokes back the tears when he speaks of 'our youngest born' and *King Lear* became a play about a family, a subject which was to stand at the heart of Hare's next stage play, *The Secret Rapture*.

On the *South Bank Show* on *Lear*, it was not Hare but Jonathan Miller who – as in his two television versions of the play – emphasised the political theme of social distance as the cause of the tragedy. Hare's reading of *Lear* was incompatible with a supposed genesis within a tradition of political theatre and, as a result, reviews of the production did not follow any clear ideological lines.

It was in *Teeth 'n' Smiles* (1975) that Hare himself had traced the failures of the British political fringe and in his Lecture of 1978, he accounted for his own move away from the categories of political theatre. He rejected them not simply because they didn't work but because they could never work; they were games played within a linguistic system which might ultimately be absurd. In *Dreams of Leaving* (1980) – at a time of great personal suffering with the breakup of his marriage and a self-imposed exile – Hare claimed to have abandoned the role of the moralist. The work stood in both Sartrean and Freudian bad faith, however, and the filming of the relationship between William and Caroline was part of Hare's debate with himself – between his head and his heart. He concluded that argument with a victory for artistic ideals over passionate conviction and laid the absurd to rest by redrawing *A Map of the World* (1983).

In *Wetherby* (1985), Hare consolidated this position by subsuming politics within the memory of the individual, and relegating history to the forces of nature. In his vision, there is no Romantic utopianism, only the realisation of an eternal struggle between good and evil, the individual and (any) society. In *The Bay at Nice* and *Wrecked Eggs* (1986) Hare yoked opposite perspectives – in the form of Russia and America – into one whole to make the point. In inviting consideration in relation to an expressionist painter, he stepped into a classical inheritance. He stood on the verge of tragedy and took the final step by pitting himself against his masters – Peter Brook and Shakespeare – in the production of *King Lear*.

The difference between Hare's reading and that of Brook's version (inspired by Jan Kott) lies in the use of the Fool as conscience rather than Lear as Fool. For Brook and Kott, the cold night of Lear will turn us all to fools and madmen, and turn tragedy to farce. Without the humour of a court jester and without any sense of pantomime clowning, the Fool in Hare's reading – as played by Roshan Seth – was an admonitory voice of conscience. At the moment Lear accepted that conscience as his own, the Fool could make a positive decision to leave him.

From *Plenty* to *Heading Home*, Hare showed an increasing interest in ageing not as a process of self-deception and disillusion, but as self-discovery, as Jean Travers – prompted by John Morgan's suicide – comes to terms with her part in the death of her lover in

Wetherby and Janetta accepts the implications of her feelings for Ian and Leonard in *Heading Home*. The lesson Lear learns under the vault of heaven is not so much social, emotional or political humility, but Christian humility; he learns to love for the sake of loving and not for a reward. The same lesson was to come to the characters of both *The Secret Rapture* (1988) and *Strapless* (1989).

Lear's fall is not from king to pauper, but from god to man, from immortal to mortal, and it is the idea of death which stands at the heart of Hare's vision. 'I had a view about Lear,' he explains, 'which was that basically the play is about a man who knows he must die and makes a preparation for death. Why does he give his kingdom away? Because he knows he will soon die.'[5] In his own plays immediately after *Lear* − *The Secret Rapture* and *Strapless* − death is central and, like Janetta and Lionel in *Heading Home* − only once he had confronted it could he move on.

For Hare, the key moment of Shakespeare's play does not come in Lear's railing at the elements, not in mere survival, but after it. The episode on Dover beach for him offers 'the statement of a very, very sparse Christian ethic, the Christian ethic of the sermon on the mount. You would have to be poor in order to be rich, to be a fool in order to be wise, to be blind in order to see. And that proposition seems to me to be at the very centre of the play.'[6] Hare would no doubt agree with Jan Kott that 'The theme of King Lear is an enquiry into the meaning of this journey [from cradle to grave] into the existence or non-existence of Heaven or Hell',[7] but for Hare the poignant parable lies not in the Old Testament Book of Job but in the New Testament. The wilderness is, then, the place of Christ's temptation, and the lesson to be learnt that 'Men must endure / Their going hence, even as their coming hither, / Ripeness is all.' (KL v.ii.9) Having laid to rest the sense of loss which had driven the history plays, Hare had, by the end of the eighties, found something positive.

Where Jonathan Miller and his Gloucester are looking down from a position of power to the bottom of the cliff, with prevailing pessimism Hare, like Edgar, is on the other side of despair and looking not down from the top of the cliff but up from the bottom. Hare, who until the age of 14 had thought he wanted to be a priest, who attended an Anglo-Catholic school, had not lost his faith but found it in a form of agnostic stoicism which he made explicit in 1991.The very title of *Strapless* refers to the leading characters having to survive with no outside means of support, without God. In *Lear*, too, as Hare explains:

> The characters suffer the most terrible hardship, and because of that they question whether God, or the gods, exist. I don't think you can infer Shakespeare's own views on the subject. What he wants to show is what life is like when people have no way of knowing whether their faith might or might not be well placed. That's where the terror comes from. This doesn't, as some critics have argued, make it an 'absurdist' play. Not at all. In fact what I most remember of Brook's supposedly 'cruel' production is its exceptional sweetness.[8]

His universe might be full of human cruelty, but it is not grotesque and if it is not grotesque, then it can be tragic.

In *The Poetics*, Aristotle identified several types of tragedy – the complex tragedy (which is all peripeteia and discovery); the tragedy of suffering; the tragedy of character; that in which the spectacle is predominant, and all plays whose scene is the underworld. As Hare invites consideration in relation to tragedy one can see that *Wetherby* was, perhaps, all peripeteia and discovery; *The Bay at Nice* and *Plenty* were, perhaps, all suffering, while spectacle and even the underworld predominated in *Teeth 'n' Smiles*. It was to be in *The Secret Rapture* that Hare prepared to step into his true inheritance with a tragedy of character, 'meaning that the heroine has a fatal flaw, and because of this fatal flaw she dies'.[9]

One element which undermined Hare's reading of *King Lear* was that you did not fear for Anthony Hopkins' Lear when you saw him, but the casting was not responsible for the directorial errors of a dragging pace in the early scenes, a lack of human contact or sexuality, unrealistic ceremony and overriding gentility. Hare's Shakespearian debut as a director was an eastern-influenced ritual of reverence. As Lear divided up his kingdom, the court was deliberately static and unresponsive, unmoved and unmoving in a rigid embroidery. When his daughters berated Lear's 'disordered rabble' (KL I.iv.262) his followers sat as passive spectators to the scene. When the soldiers were sent to fetch Gloucester for blinding, one apparently ignored the order and stood centre stage, preserving the balance of the stage picture. Lear was deliberately 'confin'd to exhibition' (KL I.ii.25). Like many of the performance art groups of the eighties, Hare had – following on from *The Bay at Nice* – raised the white ritual of the stage itself to the level of an aesthetic.

If unity of being – full self-knowledge – comes only in the confrontation with death, then – as for Yeats – it can be gained by the living only in the salvation of art itself. When David Hare went into the theatre, 'I'd no idea what I wanted from it but I think, in the event, it was the salvation of me ... It's only when I tried to write a play that I discovered I was who I thought I was.'[10] 'I only ever thought I was political in the sense of trying to drag adult concerns into the theatre.'[11] With *King Lear* Hare took on the responsibility of those adult concerns, and looked not like an angry young man but a maturing potentially major dramatist who no longer needed the gloss of politics to justify his vision; when Edgar rejoins the map as the final image of Hare's *Lear*, it solves nothing, for innocence has still been destroyed and, as Janetta was told in *Heading Home*, innocence is, in itself, a form of cowardice.

What made *The Secret Rapture* in Hare's view 'a political play' was simply that 'it challenges the common orthodoxy that there are simple solutions to human problems; there aren't and I think it's a terrible cruelty to pretend there are'.[12] It is for this reason that Hare was still angry after all these years. It is for this reason, this 'sense of intellectual outrage' rather than for any positive belief in its programmes, that, as he explained in the *Spectator* in 1987, Hare would still vote Labour. As John Bull wrote of Hammett in *The Great Exhibition*, so might one have written of Hare:

He is neither an old socialist, with his origins in traditional trade-union and working-class activity, nor a member of the New Left. He had become a socialist 'like other people go into the law', as a profession 'half out of eloquence, half out of guilt', and had subsequently realised his complete failure to relate to the historical period through which he is crawling toward death.[13]

'I sat down at the age of twenty-one and I thought I'm going to need some enthusiasms to get me to the grave. And I chose three. Food, sex and socialism', declared Hammett (*Great Exhibition*, p. 64). Hare apparently chose two – socialism and sex (in the sense of love). As talk of the class war has declined, so talk, and indeed re-presentation, of sex increased. 'As the eloquence got greater, so did the guilt' (*Great Exhibition*, p. 68). But when he was invited to be marooned on *Desert Island Discs* in 1989, David Hare wanted – along with the complete works of Shakespeare and the Bible – a copy of the encyclopaedia of French cookery, *Larousse Gastronomique*.

The parallel is, of course, over-simplistic. In the tracing of the irresistible rise of Lambert Le Roux in *Pravda,* Hare (and Brenton) began to confront the scattering not only of the Left but of the Liberal centre ground. 'It was', says Hare, 'the failure of the opposition to organise in those years that seems to me almost more culpable than the behaviour of people who at least were behaving in a way they believed in.'[14] Hare then picked up from Goneril and Regan the idea of women who claim their inheritance with severe consequences for the nation and put the successful Tory women – respectively Euro and Westminster MPs – at the heart of *Paris By Night* and *The Secret Rapture*.

Throughout his writing, Hare has been 'strongly influenced by the women I have known'.[15] In 1970, Hare had dedicated *Slag* to Margaret (Matheson); in 1978, *Plenty* was dedicated to Kate (Nelligan) and *The Secret Rapture* was for actress Blair Brown. In this context Hare compares with Evelyn Waugh, whose novel *A Handful of Dust* is deeply informed by a nostalgia not only for marriage and fidelity but for the passing of a way of life. Like Waugh's hero, Tony Last, Hare left England after his own separation in 1980. In *Saigon: Year of the Cat* (1983) Hare's colonialism was but faintly disguised by the problematic voice-over of Barbara Dean, who stood as the moral critic of American blundering in Vietnam. In *A Map of the World*, too, the instinct to put things right was deeply colonial, but it has become clear and became explicit in *Heading Home* that British class differences are much less significant than nationality, than the idea of Englishness. Hare's earlier 'political' anger can be interpreted at least in part as a form of revenge for his own class alienation and the disillusionment of the post-war, post-colonial, post-Vietnam generation, while the plays of the eighties were increasingly informed by the concerns of middle age.

The mystery is no longer merely political, it is eternally human; the surprise is no longer that a political playwright is so successful, but that David Hare had so long been subject to one-dimensional analysis. The war on two fronts was not just the world war and the class war, but the tragic and the epic, the individual and history, in which 'The catharsis itself is grounded in the power of the aesthetic form to call fate by its name, to demystify its force, to give the word to the victims – the power of recognition which gives the individual a modicum of freedom and fulfilment in the realm of unfreedom.'[16] For David Hare, then, art will ever be a dissenting force,[17] a way of expressing what cannot be said, and his theatre is, as it was for Erwin Piscator, a *Bekenntnistheater,* making a statement of faith.

As the 1990s dawned, Hare stood on the brink of something fresh. He remarried, to designer Nicole Farhi, and he turned his attention back to the stage with his most ambitious of theatrical projects – a trilogy on British institutions. In *Racing Demon*, Hare's most successful play for a decade, it was not his own religious convictions which were addressed, nor even the theological divisions of the Church of England, but the value of belief in a grim inner-city landscape. By minimising the satirical content and making use of the confessional capacity of prayer, Hare worked to achieve the 'democratic laughter' which eluded him in *Pravda*.

In 1973 Hare's first play for television, *Man Above Men*, which is unpublished and which was wiped long ago, had at its centre a High Court Judge; in 1992 he was announcing his intention to commit the offence of *Murmuring Judges* by turning his attention to the law. 'The wheel is come full circle' (KL v.iii.176) with public themes in large-scale plays directed by Richard Eyre. If theatre was literally a court, however, it was not so much concepts of socialist judgement which were on trial but questions of ethical choice.

In *Strapless* and *Heading Home* Hare's women were self-support-ing, creating their strength by their own decisions and commit-ment, but ultimately change is not achieved by individuals. Frances might have been on a plane at the end of *Racing Demon*, heading into the sun in search of a country with values, but Irina and Sandra remained inside the establishment in *Murmuring Judges*. Although the individuals in dissent retain their sanity and their livelihood, it is in *The Absence of War* that Hare reaffirmed that, despite its recent failures, the Labour Party is the only *institution* that can deliver social change. Against the background of the inheritance of 1945, Hare drew his analysis as the personal tragedy of the leader tying together the two overlapping strands of his work since 1973. Hare had faced the existentialist dilemma and reclaimed tragedy only to realise that tragedy may be part of the ideology of stasis which leads to inaction and lack of change.

David Hare had once said that writing was to discover what you believe; in *Heading Home*, it became clear that the 'you' involved is not the writer but the audience, and it is in the trilogy that he finds a new expression for that belief in a theatre of juxtaposition. There is no clear right and wrong in history or anywhere else, just shades of grey in contemporary issues, conflicting demands which are equally balanced and simultaneous action which is unresolved. We, the audience, must choose our own destiny and our own society. It is in these choices that change is possible and in juxtaposing conflicting positions without the comfort of a dictated outcome, Hare's trilogy points a way forward for his third decade of writing: 'To give up seems cowardly. Finally that is always the choice' (*Bay*, pp. 39-40).

NOTES

Introduction: a statement of departure

1 Peter Ansorge, *Disrupting the Spectacle: Five Years of Experimental and Fringe Theatre in Britain* (Pitman Publishing, London, 1975).
2 John Bull, *New British Political Dramatists* (Macmillan, London and Basingstoke, 1984).
3 David Hare, 'Time of Unease', *At the Royal Court, 25 Years of the English Stage Company*, ed. Richard Findlater (Amber Lane Press, Derbyshire, 1981) p. 142.
4 Angus Calder, *The People's War: Britain 1939–45* (Granada, London, 1982 edition).
5 Catherine Itzin, *Stages in the Revolution. Political Theatre in Britain since 1968* (Eyre Methuen, London, 1980).

1: The sixties revolution

1 David Hare, quoted by Ann McFerran, 'End of the Acid Era', *Time Out*, 29 Aug.–4 Sept. 1975.
2 David Hare, quoted by Catherine Itzin and Simon Trussler, 'From Portable Theatre to Joint Stock… via Shaftesbury Avenue', *Theatre Quarterly*, vol. 5, no. 19, Sept.–Nov. 1975, pp. 108–15, p. 112.
3 Howard Brenton quoted by Itzin, *Stages in the Revolution*, p. 189.
4 David Hare, 'End of the Acid Era'.
5 David Hare, 'From Portable Theatre', p. 111.
6 David Hare in interview with the writer, 15 June 1988, published in part as 'A Dramatist of Surprise', *Plays and Players*, no.

420, Sept. 1988, pp. 5–7 (known hereafter as Second Interview with the writer).

7 David Hare, quoted by Hugh Hebert, 'Putting the Knuckle In', *The Guardian*, 4 March 1974.

8 David Hare, 'A Lecture', King's College, Cambridge, 5 March 1978. Published with *Licking Hitler* (Faber & Faber, London, 1978), p. 68 and as 'The Playwright as Historian', *Sunday Times*, 26 Nov. 1978, and as 'The Play is in the Air: On Political Theatre', *Writing Left Handed* (Faber & Faber, London, 1991) (known hereafter as Hare, Lecture).

9 Harold Pinter, 'Writing for the Theatre', speech to National Student Drama Festival 1962, published as 'Introduction', *Plays: One* (Methuen, London, 1976), p. 11.

10 Sylvia Plath, 'Daddy' in *Ariel, Poems by Sylvia Plath* (Faber, London, 1965: 1976 edition).

2 Stepping into the past

1 Hare, Lecture, p. 66.

2 David Hare, quoted by Peter Ansorge, 'Current Concerns', *Plays and Players*, vol. 21, no. 10, July 1974, pp. 18–22, p. 20 (known hereafter as Hare, 'Current Concerns').

3 Arnold Wesker, *Chicken Soup with Barley, The Wesker Trilogy* (Harmondsworth, Penguin, 1982 edition), p. 71.

4 Richard Eyre speaking on the *South Bank Show* on David Hare and *A Map of the World*, ed. and presented by Melvyn Bragg, London Weekend Television, 30 Jan. 1983 (known hereafter as First *South Bank Show*).

5 Gregory Mason, 'Documentary Drama from Revue to Tribunal', *Modern Drama*, vol. 20, no. 3, Sept. 1977, pp. 263–77, p. 263.

6 Hebert quoting Hare, 'Putting the Knuckle In'.

7 Howard Brenton, David Hare, Tony Bicât, Brian Clark, David Edgar, Francis Fuchs and Snoo Wilson, *England's Ireland* (unpublished).

8 Hare, Lecture, p. 61.

9 Ibid., p. 64.

10 Ibid., p. 66.

11 Ibid.

12 Ted Hughes, *Crow* (Faber & Faber, London, 1972, 1974 edition), p. 20.

13 Howard Brenton quoted by Peter Ansorge, 'Humanity and Compassion Don't Count' in 'Underground Explorations No. 1: Portable Playwrights', *Plays and Players,* vol. 19, no. 5, Feb.1972, pp. 14–23, p. 18.

14 Howard Brenton quoted by Catherine Itzin and Simon Trussler, 'Petrol Bombs Through the Proscenium Arch', *Theatre Quarterly*, vol. 5, no. 17, Spring 1975, pp. 4–20, p. 19.

15 Hare quoted by Ronald Hayman, 'David Hare: Coming out of a Different Trap', *The Times*, 30 Aug. 1975.

16 Hare, 'From Portable Theatre', p. 111.

17 Hare, 'Current Concerns'.

18 Howard Brenton and Trevor Griffiths with Ken Campbell and David Hare, *Deeds, Plays and Players*, vol. 25, nos. 8 (pp. 41–50) and 9 (pp. 43–50), May and June 1978.

19 Hare, 'Time of Unease', p. 139.

20 Hare, Lecture, p. 62.

21 Hare, 'From Portable Theatre', p. 114.

3 A turning over

1 David Hare, 'After *Fanshen*: a Discussion with the Joint Stock Theatre Company, David Hare, Trevor Griffiths and Steve Gooch', *Performance and Politics in Popular Drama,* eds. David Bradby, Louis James and Bernard Sharratt (Cambridge University Press, 1980), p. 298.

2 Bill Gaskill, quoted by Michael Coveney, 'Turning Over a New Life', *Plays and Players,* vol. 22, no. 9, June 1975, pp. 10–13, p. 12.

3 Ibid.

4 Brecht, *Small Organum for the Theatre,* quoted by Martin Esslin, *Brecht, a Choice of Evils* (Heinemann Educational Books, London, 1973 edition), p. 112.

5 Hare, 'After *Fanshen*', p. 297.

6 *Damage*, dir Louis Malle, 1993.

7 David Hare's version (unpublished) of Bertolt Brecht's *The Life of Galileo*, directed by Jonathan Kent, opened at the Almeida Theatre, 11 February 1994.

8 Rob Ritchie, ed. and introduction, *The Joint Stock Book, The Making of a Theatre Collective* (Methuen, London, 1987), p. 19.

9 Hare, 'From Portable Theatre', p. 113.

10 Hare, *The Joint Stock Book*, p. 108.

11 Hare, Lecture, p. 63.

12 Hare, 'Underground Explorations', p. 18.

13 Esslin, *Brecht: a Choice of Evils*, p. 128.

14 Hare, Lecture, p. 63.

15 David Hare, Platform Performance on *Fanshen* at the National Theatre, 5 April 1988 (unpublished).

16 Bertolt Brecht, 'Alienation Effects in Chinese Acting' (1936) in *Brecht on Theatre: The Development of an Aesthetic*, ed. & trans. John Willett (Methuen, London, 1978 edition), p. 97.

17 Hare, Platform Performance on *Fanshen*.

18 Brenton, 'Petrol Bombs', p. 8.

19 Hare, Lecture, p. 63.

20 Ibid. pp. 57–8.

21 Brenton, 'Petrol Bombs', pp. 13–14.

22 Ibid. p. 10.

23 Hare, quoted by Oleg Kerensky, *The New British Drama, 14 Playwrights since Osborne and Pinter* (Hamish Hamilton, London, 1977), p. 185.

24 Hare, Platform Performance on *Fanshen*.

25 Brecht, 'Formal Problems Arising from the Theatre's New Content, a Dialogue with Friedrich Wolf in Dresden, 1952' in Willett, *Brecht on Theatre*, p. 226.

26 Peter Brook, *The Empty Space* (Penguin, Harmondsworth, 1972 edition), p. 96.

27 Hare, Platform Performance on *Fanshen*.

28 Ibid.

29 Hare, Lecture, p. 64.

4 The people's war and peace

1 Hare, Lecture, p. 69.

2 Hare, 'Underground Explorations', p. 18.

3 David Hare in interview with the writer, 15 October 1983, published in part as 'Interview: David Hare', *Cover, What's On in*

Norwich, no. 74, 21 Oct.–3 Nov. 1983, pp. 14–15 (known hereafter as First Interview with the author).

4 Hare, *History Plays.*

5 Hare, Lecture, p. 66.

6 Christopher Hampton, *George Steiner's The Portage to San
Christobal of A.H.* (Faber & Faber, London, 1983), p. 45.

7 First Interview with the writer.

8 Hare, *History Plays,* p. 14.

9 Hare, quoted in 'Honourable Guess', *New Yorker,* 24 Jan. 1983.

10 Hare, quoted by Anne Busby, 'David Hare', an interview in the
programme for the National Theatre production of *The Secret
Rapture,* Oct. 1988 (known hereafter as Busby, SR).

11 Hare, Lecture, pp. 57–8.

12 Hare, quoted by Steve Grant, 'Peace and Plenty', *Time Out,* 7
April 1978.

13 Hare, quoted by George Perry, 'Friends in Peace and Plenty', *The
Sunday Times Magazine,* 9 April 1978.

14 Hare, quoted by Ann McFerran, 'End of the Acid Era', *Time Out.*

15 Hare, Lecture, p. 67.

16 Ibid. p. 69.

17 Mason, 'Documentary Drama', p. 264.

18 First Interview with the writer.

5 Sense of an ending

1 First Interview with the writer.

2 Ibid.

3 George Perry, 'Love in a Political Climate', *The Sunday
Times Magazine,* 27 Nov. 1983.

4 Hare, Platform Performance on *Fanshen.*

5 Voice-over addition not in printed script.

6 First Interview with the writer.

7 Hare, *The Asian Plays* (Faber & Faber, London, 1986) p .vii.

6 The foundry of lies

1 Harold Evans, *Good Times, Bad Times* (Weidenfeld & Nicolson,
London, 1983).

2 Hare, quoted by Michael Billington, interview with David Hare, 'Weekend Arts', *The Guardian*, 2 March 1985.

3 Hare, *History Plays*, p. 10.

4 Howard Brenton, quoted by Anne Busby, 'Interview with David Hare and Howard Brenton', programme to the National Theatre production of *Pravda*, May 1985.

5 Hare, Lecture, p. 59.

6 The back cover of the second edition of *Pravda* declares as much in quoting Frank Rich from the *New York Times*.

7 Henry Porter, *Lies, Damned Lies and Some Exclusives, Fleet Street Exposed* (Chatto and Windus, The Hogarth Press, London 1984).

8 Hare, quoted by Hugh Hebert, 'Putting the Knuckle In'.

9 Howard Brenton, quoted by Tony Mitchell, 'The Red Theatre Under the Bed', *New Theatre Quarterly*, vol. 3, no. 11, Aug. 1987, pp. 195–201, p. 196.

10 Howard Brenton, 'Writing for Democratic Laughter', *Drama*, 1985/3, no. 157, pp. 9–11, p. 11.

11 Hare, quoted by Busby, SR.

12 Hare, quoted by Jim Hiley, 'The Wetherby Report', *Observer Magazine*, 10 March 1985.

13 Hare, First *South Bank Show*.

14 Hare, Lecture, p. 64.

15 Hugh Hebert, 'Still Slogging the Road to Utopia', *The Guardian*, 9 Sept. 1983.

16 Hare, quoted by Hiley, 'The Wetherby Report'.

17 Second Interview with the writer.

18 Hare, Platform Performance on *Fanshen*.

7 Dreams of leaving

1 John Caughie, 'Rhetoric, Pleasure and "Art Television" – Dreams of Leaving', *Screen*, vol. 22, no. 4, 1981, pp. 9–31.

2 First Interview with the writer.

3 Ibid.

4 Interview with Michael Billington, 'Broken Rules', *Radio Times*, 12–18 Jan. 1980.

5 Richard Wollheim, *Freud*, Fontana Modern Masters series, ed. Frank Kermode (Fontana, London, 1971), p. 67, quoting

Sigmund Freud, vol. xv, p. 129 (from the Standard Edition of *The Complete Works of Sigmund Freud*, ed. James Strachey, London, 1953).

6 Hare, 'From Portable Theatre', p. 111.

7 Wollheim, *Freud,* p. 66, quoting Freud, vol. iv, p. 160.

8 Hare, Lecture, pp. 65–6.

9 First Interview with the writer.

10 Hare, quoted by Paul Kerr, 'David Hare and Saigon: Leaping out of the Cage', *Stills,* vol. 1, no. 9, Nov.–Dec. 1983, pp. 64–7, p. 66.

11 Ian McEwan, 'Getting Out and Copping Out', *Times Literary Supplement,* 25 Jan. 1980.

8 Drawing a map of the world

1 Hare, First *South Bank Show.*

2 Ibid.

3 Hare, 'Arts Guardian', *The Guardian,* 3 Feb. 1983.

4 Hare, First *South Bank Show.*

5 Hare, Lecture, p. 65.

6 Hare, First *South Bank Show.*

7 Hare, *Asian Plays,* p. xiv.

8 Tom Stoppard, *Professional Foul,* published with *Every Good Boy Deserves Favour* (Faber & Faber, London, 1978), p. 56.

9 Hare, First *South Bank Show.*

10 C. W. E. Bigsby, assoc. ed. *Contemporary English Drama,* Stratford-upon-Avon Studies 19, gen. eds. Malcolm Bradbury and David Palmer (Edward Arnold, London, 1981), p. 43.

11 Hare, *Asian Plays,* pp. xiii–xiv.

12 David Hare, National Theatre Platform Performance on *A Map of the World,* 26 April 1983 (known hereafter as Platform Performance, *Map*).

13 Hare, First *South Bank Show.*

9 All our escapes

1 Line as spoken and not as printed in the text p. 47.

2 Hare, 'Hare's Breadth', *Stills,* no. 16, Feb. 1985, pp. 14–15.

3 David Bradby *et al.,* 'After *Fanshen*', p. 298.

4 Hare, *Asian Plays*, p. 10.
5 Michael Billington, 'Weekend Arts'.
6 Hare, quoted by Julian Petley, 'The Upright Houses and the Romantic Englishwoman', *Monthly Film Bulletin*, vol. 52, no. 614, March 1985, pp. 71–2.
7 Pinter, 'Writing for the Theatre', p. 15.
8 Second Interview with the writer.
9 Hare, quoted by Petley, 'The Upright Houses'.
10 Hare, quoted by Kevin Jackson, 'The Common Pursuit', *The Independent*, 13 Feb. 1988.
11 Hare, quoted in Billington, 'Weekend Arts'.
12 Howard Brenton, *Bloody Poetry* (Methuen, London, 1988 edn.), pp. 67–8.
13 Hare, quoted in Billington, 'Weekend Arts'.
14 Hare quotes Freud in 'Looking Foolish', *Writing Left Handed*, p. 58.
15 Iris Murdoch, *Sartre: Romantic Rationalist* (Fontana, London, 1967), p. 32.

10 Painting pictures

1 'Sarah Stein's Notes, 1908' in Jack D. Flam, *Matisse on Art* (Phaidon, Oxford, second edn 1978), pp. 42–3
2 Second Interview with the writer .
3 Ibid.
4 Hare, 'From Portable Theatre', p. 112.
5 Simon Trussler, ed., 'Tom Stoppard, Ambushes for the Audience', in *New Theatre Voices of the Seventies, Interviews from Theatre Quarterly 1970–1980* (Eyre Methuen, London, 1981), p. 66.
6 Henri Matisse, 'Notes of a Painter' in Flam, *Matisse on Art*, pp. 35–40, p. 35.
7 Hare, quoted by Vera Lustig, 'Soul Searching', *Drama*, vol. 4, 1988, pp. 15–18.
8 Herbert Marcuse, *The Aesthetic Dimension, Towards a Critique of Marxist Aesthetics*, transl. and rev. Herbert Marcuse and Erica Sherover (Macmillan, London & Basingstoke, 1979), p. 8.
9 Hare, quoted by Lustig, 'Soul Searching'.
10 John Russell , *The World of Matisse* (Time–Life, Nederland, 1979 edn) p. 59.

11   The moment of unification

1   David Hare, introduction to *Paris By Night* (Faber & Faber, London, 1988), p. ix.
2   Ibid.
3   Hare, interviewed by Carol Lawson, 'At the Movies', *New York Times,* 11 Oct. 1985.
4   Hare in interview with Anne Busby in the programme to *The Secret Rapture.*
5   Vera Lustig, 'Parisian Nights', interview with David Hare, *Films and Filming,* June 1989, pp. 24–6.
6   Second Interview with the writer .
7   David Hare in conversation with Rosemary Harthill, 'Writers Revealed', BBC Radio 4, May 1991.
8   Hare, 'Oh Goodness', *Writing Left Handed,* p. 159.
9   Hare,'Looking Foolish', *Writing Left Handed,* p. 56.
10 Hare, 'Writers Revealed'.
11 Hare, 'Oh Goodness!', p. 158.
12 Ibid., p. 46.

13   Heading home?

1   Hare, *Writing Left Handed,* p. 159.
2   Hare, 'Writers Revealed'.

14   Stepping into the future

1   David Hare, *Writing Left Handed,* p. 55.
2   Ibid., pp. 52–3.
3   Ibid., p. 39.
4   *Twelve Angry Men*, dir. Sidney Lumet, 1957.
5   Hare, 'Writers Revealed'.
6   Hare, quoted by Mark Lawson, 'Making Mischief', *The Independent Magazine,* 16 Oct. 1993, pp. 48–54, p. 52.
7   Hare speaking on *The Late Show,* a discussion with Michael Billington, Hugo Young and Polly Toynbee chaired by Michael Ignatieff, BBC2, 4 Oct. 1993 (known hereafter as Hare, *The Late Show*).

8 Hare, 'Making Mischief'.

9 Ibid.

10 Hare, *The Late Show*.

11 Hare, 'Don't They Know What a Play Is?', *Fabian Review*, vol. 106, no. 1, Jan.–Feb. 1994, pp. 18–20.

12 Michael Billington, in Hare, *The Late Show*.

13 Hare, ibid.

Conclusion: A statement of arrival

1 Hare, quoted by Anne Busby, in the programme for the National Theatre production of *King Lear,* December 1986 (known hereafter as Busby, KL).

2 Peter Brook, *The Empty Space* (Penguin, Harmondsworth, 1972).

3 Peter Brook quoted on the *South Bank Show* on *King Lear*, edited and presented by Melvyn Bragg, London Weekend Television, 11 Jan. 1987 (known hereafter as Second *South Bank Show*).

4 Hare, quoted by Busby, KL.

5 Hare, ibid.

6 Hare, Second *South Bank Show*.

7 Jan Kott, '"King Lear" or "Endgame"', *Shakespeare Our Contemporary,* transl. Boleslaw Taborski (Methuen University Paperback Series, London, 1967), p. 116.

8 Hare in Busby, KL.

9 Second Interview with the writer.

10 Peter Lewis, '"The Lone Wolf of the Radical Pack", Profile: David Hare, Playwright of Conviction', *The Independent,* 8 Oct. 1988 (known hereafter as Profile).

11 Second Interview with the writer.

12 Hare, quoted by Mick Brown, 'Still Angry After All These Years', *Elle,* Dec. 1988, pp. 40–5, p. 45.

13 Bull, *New British Political Dramatists,* pp. 65–6.

14 Hare, 'Writers Revealed'.

15 Hare, Profile.

16 Marcuse, *The Aesthetic Dimension,* p. 10.

17 Ibid., pp. 5–7.

SELECT BIBLIOGRAPHY

David Hare

PUBLISHED PLAYS AND FILMS

The Absence of War. London: Faber & Faber, 1993

The Asian Plays. London: Faber & Faber, 1986

The Bay at Nice and Wrecked Eggs. London: Faber & Faber, 1986

Brassneck. Written with Howard Brenton. London: Eyre Methuen, 1974 and in *Plays and Players*, vol. 21, no. 1, Oct. 1973, pp. i–xvi, 43–5

Deeds. Howard Brenton and Trevor Griffiths with Ken Campbell and David Hare. *Plays and Players*, vol. 21, no. 8, May 1978, pp. 41–50 and June 1978, pp. 43–50

Dreams of Leaving. London: Faber & Faber, 1980

The Early Plays. London: Faber & Faber, 1992

Fanshen. London: Faber & Faber, 1976

The Great Exhibition. London: Faber & Faber, 1972 and in *Plays and Players*, vol. 19, no. 8, May 1972, pp. 63–81

Heading Home (with *Wetherby* and *Dreams of Leaving*), London: Faber & Faber, 1991

The History Plays. London: Faber & Faber, 1984

How Brophy Made Good. Gambit, 17, 1971, pp. 84–125

Knuckle. London: Faber & Faber, 1974

Lay By. Written with Howard Brenton, Brian Clark, Trevor Griffiths, Stephen Poliakoff, Hugh Stoddart, and Snoo Wilson. London: Calder & Boyars, 1972 and in *Plays and Players*, vol. 19, no. 2, Nov. 1971, pp. 65–75

Licking Hitler. London: Faber & Faber, 1978

A Map of the World. London: Faber & Faber, 1983

Murmuring Judges. London: Faber & Faber, 1992
Paris By Night. London: Faber & Faber, 1988
Plenty. London: Faber & Faber, 1978
Pravda. Written with Howard Brenton. London: Methuen, 1985 and
    rev. edn 1986
Racing Demon. London: Faber & Faber, 1990
Saigon: Year of the Cat. London: Faber & Faber, 1983
The Secret Rapture. London: Faber & Faber, 1988
Slag. London: Faber & Faber, 1971
Strapless. London: Faber & Faber, 1989
Teeth 'n' Smiles. London: Faber & Faber, 1976
Wetherby. London: Faber & Faber, 1985

ARTICLES, LECTURES, REVIEWS AND BOOKS

'Arts Guardian'. *The Guardian*, 3 Feb. 1983
Asking Around. London: Faber & Faber, 1993
'Author's Preface'. *Fanshen*. London: Faber & Faber, 1976
'Diary'. *Spectator,* 27 Feb., 5 March, 12 March, 1988
'Don't They Know What a Play Is?', *Fabian Review*, vol. 106, no. 1,
    Jan.–Feb. 1994, pp. 18–20
'Enter a Free Man'. *Gambit*, vol. 3, no. 12, pp. 108–9
'The espion age'. *Spectator*, 12 Dec. 1970
'Green Room'. *Plays and Players*, no. 337, Oct. 1981, pp. 49–50
'Hare-raising Story of Paris By Night'. *New Woman*, Sept. 1988, pp. 55–7
'How to Spend a Million'. *Sunday Times*, 3 March 1985
'Introduction', *The Asian Plays*. London: Faber & Faber, 1986
'Introduction', *The History Plays*. London: Faber & Faber, 1984
'A Lecture'. King's College, Cambridge, 5 March 1978. Published with
    Licking Hitler, London: Faber & Faber, 1978
'Polemic'. *The Guardian*, 30 Jan. 1981
'Why I Shall Vote Labour'. *Spectator*, 23 May 1987
Writing Left Handed (collection). London: Faber & Faber, 1991

INTERVIEWS AND DISCUSSIONS

Ansorge, Peter. 'Current Concerns'. *Plays and Players*, vol. 21, no. 10,
    July 1974, pp. 18–22

'David Hare: a War on Two Fronts'. Plays and Players, vol. 25, no. 7, April 1978, pp. 12–16

'Disrupting the Spectacle'. *Plays and Players*, vol. 20, no. 10, July 1973, pp. 22–3

'Humanity and Compassion Don't Count' in "Underground Explorations No. 1: Portable Playwrights". *Plays and Players*, vol. 19, no. 5, Feb. 1972, pp. 14–23

Banks-Smith, Nancy. 'Licking Hitler'. *The Guardian*, 11 Jan. 1978

Billington, Michael. 'Broken Rules'. *Radio Times*, 12–18 Jan. 1980

'Weekend Arts'. *The Guardian*, 2 March 1985

Bradby, David, Louis James, Bernard Sharratt, eds. 'After Fanshen: a Discussion, with the Joint Stock Theatre Company, David Hare, Trevor Griffiths and Steve Gooch'. *Performance and Politics in Popular Drama*. Cambridge University Press, 1980

Bragg, Melvyn, ed. *South Bank Show* on *King Lear*. 11 Jan. 1987

South Bank Show on *A Map of the World*. 30 Jan. 1983

Brenton, Howard. 'Writing for Democratic Laughter'. *Drama*, 1985/3, no. 157, pp. 9–11

Brown, Mick. 'Still Angry After all these Years'. *Elle*, Dec. 1988, pp. 40–5

Busby, Anne. Interview with David Hare in the programme for the National Theatre production of *King Lear*, Dec. 1986

Interview with David Hare and Howard Brenton in the programme for the National Theatre production of *Pravda*, May 1985

'David Hare'. Programme to the National Theatre production of *The Secret Rapture*, Oct. 1988

Canham, Kingsley and Jayne Pilling. 'David Hare: Dreams of Plenty'. *The Screen on the Tube: Filmed TV Drama,* Dossier Number 1, Norwich: Cinema City, 1983

Coveney, Michael. 'Turning Over a New Life'. *Plays and Players*, vol. 22, no. 9, June 1975, pp. 10–13

'Worlds Apart'. *Time Out*, 21–27 Jan. 1983

Desert Island Discs. David Hare talks to Sue Lawley. BBC Radio 4, 26 Feb. 1989

Dugdale, John. 'Love, Death and Edwina'. *The Listener*, 15 Sept 1988, pp. 38–9

Ford, John. 'Getting the Carp out of the Mud'. *Plays and Players*, vol. 19, no. 2, Nov. 1971, pp. 20/83

Garnham, Nicholas. 'TV Documentary and Ideology'. *Screen*, vol. 13, no.

2, Summer 1972, pp. 109–15

Goodman, Joan. 'New World'. *The Observer*, 23 Jan. 1983

Grant, Steve. 'Act All About It'. *The Observer*, 28 April 1985
  'Peace and "Plenty"'. *Time Out*, 7 April 1978

'Hare's Breadth'. *Stills*, no. 16, Feb. 1985, pp. 14–15

Hayman, Ronald. 'David Hare'. *The Times*, 22 May 1971
  'David Hare: Coming Out of a Different Trap'. *The Times*,
    30 Aug. 1975

Hebert, Hugh. 'Putting the Knuckle In'. *The Guardian*, 4 March 1974
  'Still Slogging the Road to Utopia'. *The Guardian*, 9 Sept. 1983

Hiley, Jim. 'The Wetherby Report'. *Observer Magazine*, 10 March 1985

Homden, Carol. 'The Best Lack All Conviction', *The Times Literary Supplement*, no. 4724, 15 Oct. 1993, p. 16
  'A Dramatist of Surprise'. *Plays and Players*, no. 420, Sept. 1988,
    pp. 5–7
  'Interview: David Hare'. *Cover, What's On in Norwich*, no. 74, 21 Oct.–
    3 Nov. 1983, pp. 14–15

'Honourable Guess'. *New Yorker*, 24 Jan. 1983

Hudson, Roger, Catherine Itzin and Simon Trussler. 'Ambushes for the Audience: Towards a High Comedy of Ideas'. *Theatre Quarterly*, vol. IV, no. 14, May–July 1974, pp. 3–17

Itzin, Catherine and Simon Trussler. 'From Portable Theatre to Joint Stock... via Shaftesbury Avenue'. *Theatre Quarterly*, vol. V, no. 19, Sept.–Nov. 1975, pp. 108–15
  'Petrol Bombs Through the Proscenium Arch'. *Theatre Quarterly*, vol. V, no. 17, Spring 1975, pp. 4–20

Jackson, Kevin. 'The Common Pursuit'. *The Independent*, 13 Feb. 1988

Kerr, Paul. 'David Hare and Saigon: Leaping out of the Cage'. *Stills*, vol. I, no. 9, Nov.–Dec. 1983, pp. 64–7

The Late Show. Discussion chaired by Michael Ignatieff, BBC2,
    4 Oct. 1993

Lawson, Carol. 'At the Movies'. *New York Times*, 11 Oct. 1985

Lawson, Mark. 'Making Mischief'. *The Independent Magazine*, 16 Oct.
    1993, pp. 48–54

Lewis, Peter. 'Time and Place'. Programme for the National Theatre production of *A Map of the World*, Jan. 1983
  '"The Lone Wolf of the Radical Pack"', Profile: David Hare, Playwright of Conviction'. *The Independent*, 8 Oct. 1988

Lustig, Vera. 'Soul Searching'. *Drama*, vol. 4, 1988, pp. 15–18
   'Parisian Nights'. *Films and Filming*, June 1989, pp. 24–6
McEwan, Ian. 'Getting Out and Copping Out'. *The Times Literary*
   Supplement, 25 Jan. 1980
McFerran, Ann. 'End of the Acid Era'. *Time Out*, 29 Aug.–4 Sept. 1975
Mansfield, Paul. 'More Mr Nice Guy'. *The Guardian*, 8 Dec. 1988
Mason, Gregory. 'Documentary Drama from Revue to the Tribunal'.
   Modern Drama, vol. 20, no. 3, Sept. 1977, pp. 263–77
Mitchell, Tony. 'The Red Theatre under the Bed'. *New Theatre Quarterly*,
   vol. 3, no. 11, Aug. 1987, pp. 195–201
Myerson, Jonathan. 'David Hare: Fringe Graduate'. *Drama*, no. 149,
   autumn 1983, pp. 26–8
Perry, George. 'Love in a Political Climate'. *The Sunday Times Magazine*,
   27 Nov. 1983
Petley, Julian. 'The Upright Houses and the Romantic Englishwoman'.
   Monthly Film Bulletin, vol. 52, no. 614, March 1985, pp. 71–2
Taylor, John Russell. 'In and Out of Court'. *Plays and Players*, no. 340,
   Jan.1982, pp. 12–14
Whiting, John. 'At Ease in a Bright Red Tie'. *The Observer*, 12 July 1959
Williams, Raymond. 'English Brecht'. *London Review of Books*, 16 July–
   5 Aug. 1981
'A Time for Loving, a Time for Leaving', *Studio*, autumn 1983, pp. 18–19
Wilkes, Angela. 'Making Fun of Fleet Street'. *The Sunday Times*,
   16 Dec. 1984
'Writers Revealed', David Hare interviewed by Rosemary Harthill, BBC
   Radio 4, May 1991

Works of criticism, history and philosophy

Ansorge, Peter. *Disrupting the Spectacle, Five Years of Experimental and*
   Fringe Theatre in Britain. London: Pitman Publishing, 1975
Aristotle. *The Poetics. Aristotle's Theory of Poetry and Fine Art.* Ed. S. H.
   Butcher, London: Macmillan, 1895
Bigsby, C.W.E., assoc. ed. *Contemporary English Drama.* Stratford-upon-
   Avon Studies 19, gen. eds. Malcolm Bradbury and David Palmer.
   London: Edward Arnold, 1981
Brook, Peter. *The Empty Space.* Harmondsworth: Penguin, 1972

Bull, John. *New British Political Dramatists*. London and Basingstoke:
    Macmillan, 1984

Calder, Angus. *The People's War: Britain 1939–45*. London: Granada 1982
    edition

Canham, Kingsley and Jayne Pilling, eds. *The Screen on the Tube: Filmed
    TV Drama*, Dossier Number 1, Norwich: Cinema City, 1983

Craig, Sandy. *Dreams and Deconstructions: Alternative Theatre in Britain*.
    Derbyshire: Amber Lane Press, 1980

Danto, Arthur C. *Sartre*. Fontana Modern Masters. Series ed. Frank
    Kermode, London: Fontana, 1975

Esslin, Martin. *Brecht: a Choice of Evils*. London: Heinemann Educational
    Books, 1973 edition
    The Theatre of the Absurd. Middlesex: Pelican, 1968

Evans, Harold. *Good Times, Bad Times*. London: Weidenfeld & Nicolson,
    1983

Findlater, Richard, ed. *At the Royal Court, 25 Years of the English Stage
    Company*. Derbyshire: Amber Lane Press, 1981

Fitzwalter, Raymond and David Taylor. *Web of Corruption, The Story of
    J.G.L. Poulson and T. Dan Smith*. London: Granada, 1981

Flam, Jack D. *Matisse on Art*. Oxford: Phaidon, 1978 edition

Habermas, Jürgen. *Legitimation Crisis*. Trans. Thomas McCarthy,
    London: Heinemann Educational Books, 1976

Hinton, William. *Fanshen: A Documentary of Revolution in a Chinese
    Village*. New York & London: Monthly Review Press, 1966

Itzin, Catherine. *Stages in the Revolution. Political Theatre in Britain since
    1968*. London: Eyre Methuen, 1980

Kerensky, Oleg. *The New British Drama, 14 Playwrights since Osborne and
    Pinter*. London: Hamish Hamilton, 1977

Kott, Jan. *Shakespeare Our Contemporary*. Transl. Boleslaw Taborski,
    London: Methuen University Paperbacks Series, 1967

McArthur, Colin. *Television and History*. Television Monograph No. 8,
    London: BFI, 1978

McLuhan, Marshall. *The Medium is the Message*. Middlesex: Allen Lane,
    The Penguin Press, 1967

Marcuse, Herbert. *The Aesthetic Dimension, Towards a Critique of Marxist
    Aesthetics*. Transl. and rev. Herbert Marcuse and Erica Sherover,
    London & Basingstoke: Macmillan, 1979

Murdoch, Iris. *Sartre: Romantic Rationalist*. London: Fontana, 1967

Nietzsche, Wilhelm Friedrich. *The Birth of Tragedy from the Spirit of Music.* Trans. Francis Golffing, New York: Doubleday Anchor Books, 1956

Nuttall, Jeff. *Bomb Culture.* London: Paladin, 1970

Page, Malcolm and Julian Ria. 'Theatre Checklist No.8: David Hare', *Theatrefacts*, vol. 2, no. 4, 1975

Pike, Frank, ed. *Ah! Mischief: The Writer and Television.* London: Faber & Faber, 1982

Pinter, Harold. 'Writing for the Theatre'. Speech to National Student Drama Festival, 1962. Introduction to *Plays: One*, London: Methuen, 1976

Piscator, Erwin. *The Political Theatre*, transl. Hugh Rorrison, London: Eyre Methuen, 1980

Porter, Henry. *Lies, Damned Lies and Some Exclusives, Fleet Street Exposed.* London: Chatto & Windus, The Hogarth Press, 1984

Rabey, David Ian. *British and Irish Political Drama in the Twentieth Century.* London: Macmillan, 1986

Ritchie, Rob, ed. and intro. *The Joint Stock Book The Making of a Theatre Collective.* London: Methuen, 1987

Russell, John. *The World of Matisse.* Nederland: Time–Life, 1979 edition

Trussler, Simon, ed. *New Theatre Voices of the Seventies: Sixteen Interviews from Theatre Quarterly 1970–1980.* London: Eyre Methuen, 1981

Tynan, Kenneth. 'Withdrawing with Style from the Chaos'. *Show People.* London: Virgin Books, 1981

Wandor, Michelene. *Look Back in Gender, Sexuality and the Family in Post-war British Drama.* London: Methuen, 1987

Wilde, Oscar. 'The Soul of Man Under Socialism'. *Plays, Prose Writings and Poems.* Everyman's Library no. 858 reprinted 1966 (first included 1930)

Willett, John, ed. and trans. *Brecht on Theatre: The Development of an Aesthetic.* London: Methuen, 1978

Willett, John. *The Theatre of Erwin Piscator.* London: Eyre Methuen, 1978

Wittgenstein, Ludwig. *On Certainty.* Trans. Denis Paul & G.E.M. Anscombe, Oxford: Basil Blackwell, 1979

Philosophical Investigations. Trans. G.E.M. Anscombe, Oxford: Basil Blackwell, 1974

Tractatus Logico-Philosophicus. Trans. D.F. Pears & B.F. McGuinness, London: Routledge & Kegan Paul, 1977

Wolfe, Tom. *The Painted Word.* London: Bantam, 1976

Wollen, Peter. *Signs and Meaning in the Cinema*. Cinema One Series
    No.9. London: Secker & Warburg in association with the BFI, 1972
    edition
Wollheim, Richard. *Freud*. Fontana Modern Masters series. Ed. Frank
    Kermode, London: Fontana, 1971

Creative works cited

Apocalypse Now. Dir. Francis Ford Coppola, USA, 1979
Arden, John. *Plays: One*. London: Methuen, 1977
Beckett, Samuel. *Waiting for Godot*. London: Faber & Faber, 1956
Bleasdale, Alan. *The Boys from the Blackstuff*. Dir. Philip Saville, BBC2,
    Sept. and Oct. 1982. Published London: Granada, 1983
Bolt, Robert. *A Man for All Seasons*. London: Heinemann Educational, 1960
Brecht, Bertolt. *Mother Courage and her Children*. Trans. Eric Bentley,
    London: Methuen, 1962
    The Resistible Rise of Arturo Ui. Trans. Stefan S. Brecht, London: Eyre
    Methuen, 1976
Brenton, Howard. *The Churchill Play*. London: Eyre Methuen, 1974
    Bloody Poetry. Royal Court Writers Series, London: Methuen, 1988 edn.
    Dead Head. London: Methuen, 1987
    The Genius. Royal Court Writers Series, London: Methuen, 1983
    Greenland. Royal Court Writers Series, London: Methuen, 1988
    Magnificence. London: Eyre Methuen, 1980 edn
    Revenge. London: Methuen, 1970
    The Romans in Britain. London: Eyre Methuen, 1980
    Weapons of Happiness. London: Eyre Methuen, 1976
Brideshead Revisited. Dir. Charles Sturridge, adapted by John Mortimer
    from Evelyn Waugh's novel, Granada Television, Oct.–Dec. 1981
Casablanca. Dir. Michael Curtiz, USA, 1942
Churchill, Caryl. *Top Girls* . The Royal Court Writers Series, London:
    Methuen, 1982
    Serious Money. The Royal Court Writers Series, London: Methuen,
    1987
A Family at War. Created by John Finch, Granada Television, ITV, April
    1970–Feb. 1972
The Godfather. Dir. Francis Ford Coppola, USA, 1971

Griffiths, Trevor. *Country – A Tory Story*. London: Faber & Faber, 1981

Hampton, Christopher. *George Steiner's The Portage to San Christobal of A.H.* London: Faber & Faber, 1983

Handke, Peter. *Offending the Audience*. Trans. Michael Roloff, London: Methuen 1971.

Havel, Václav. *The Memorandum*. Trans. Vera Blackwell, London: Eyre Methuen, 1981.

Highsmith, Patricia. *The Tremor of Forgery*. London: William Heinemann, 1969

Hughes, Ted. *Crow*. London: Faber & Faber, 1974 edition

The Jewel in the Crown. Dir. Chris Morahan and Jim O'Brien, adapted by Ken Taylor from Paul Scott's Raj Quartet, Granada Television, screened ITV Jan.–April 1984

Littlewood, Joan, Charles Chilton and Theatre Workshop. *Oh What a Lovely War*. London: Methuen, 1965

Lowe, Stephen. *Touched*. London: Methuen, 1981

McEwan, Ian. *The Imitation Game*. London: Picador, 1982

Mitchell, Julian. *Another Country*. Oxford: Amber Lane Press, 1982

Osborne, John. *The Entertainer*. London: Faber & Faber, 1957
  Look Back in Anger. London: Faber & Faber, 1957

Osmond, Andrew. *Plenty* (based on the original screenplay by David Hare). London: Futura, 1985

Paradise Postponed. Dir. Alvin Rakoff, Thames Television, ITV, 25 Sept.–24 Nov. 1986, from the novel by John Mortimer (London: Viking, 1985)

Patrick, Robert. 'Kennedy's Children'. *Plays and Players,* vol. 22, no. 5, Feb. 1975, pp. 44–50 and vol. 22, no. 6, March 1975, pp. 43–49

Pinter, Harold. *Betrayal*. London: Methuen, 1978
  The Caretaker. London, Eyre Methuen, 1960
  Monologue. London: Covent Garden Press, 1973
  Plays: Three, London: Methuen, 1968

Pirandello, Luigi. *The Rules of the Game*. Trans. Robert Rietty, with *The Life I Gave You* and *Lazarus*, Harmondsworth: Penguin, 1959

Plath, Sylvia. *Ariel, Poems by Sylvia Plath*. London: Faber, 1976 edition

The Ploughman's Lunch. Dir. Richard Eyre, screenplay Ian McEwan, GB, 1982

Poliakoff, Stephen. *Bloody Kids*. Dir. Stephen Frears, Black Lion Films, ITV 23 March 1980

Priestley, J.B. *An Inspector Calls*. London: Samuel French, 1948

Sartre, Jean-Paul. *Nausea*. Trans. Robert Baldick, Middlesex: Penguin, 1965

Shakespeare, William. *The Tragedy of King Lear*. Ed. Russell Fraser, The Signet Classic Shakespeare Series, gen. ed. Sylvan Barnet, London: New English Library, 1963

    The Tragedy of King Richard the Second. Ed. Kenneth Muir, The Signet Classic Shakespeare Series, gen. ed. Sylvan Barnet, London: New English Library, 1963

Smith, Dodie. *Dear Octopus*. London: Samuel French, 1938

Stoppard, Tom. *Night and Day*. London: Faber & Faber 1979 edn

    Professional Foul. London: Faber & Faber, 1978

    The Real Thing. London: Faber & Faber, 1982

The Third Man. Dir. Carol Reed, screenplay by Graham Greene, GB 1949

Under Fire. Dir. Roger Spottiswode, USA, 1983

Waugh, Evelyn. *Decline and Fall*. Harmondsworth: Penguin 1937

    A Handful of Dust. Harmondsworth: Penguin, 1951

Wesker, Arnold. *The Wesker Trilogy*. Harmondsworth: Penguin, 1982 edn

    The Journalists. Harmondsworth: Penguin, 1980

The World at War. Exec. prod. Jeremy Isaacs, Thames Television, 26 episodes on ITV from Oct. 1973

The Year of Living Dangerously. Dir. Peter Weir, USA, 1983

Twelve Angry Men. Dir. Sidney Lumet. USA 1957

Yeats, W.B. *W.B. Yeats Selected Poetry*. Ed. A. Norman Jeffares, London: Pan Books Ltd, 1974

INDEX